To Darena,

[signature]

La Jolla
A Celebration
of Its Past

La Jolla

A Celebration of Its Past

Patricia Daly-Lipe

Barbara Dawson

Steele Lipe, Editor

Sunbelt Publications
San Diego, California

iv

La Jolla: A Celebration of Its Past
Sunbelt Publications, Inc.
Copyright © 2002 by the author
All rights reserved. First edition 2002. Second printing 2003.

Edited by Steele Lipe
Cover design by Leah Cooper
Composition by Steele Lipe
Project management by Jennifer Redmond
Printed in the United States of America

Sunbelt Publications, Inc.
P.O. Box 19112
San Diego, CA 92159-1126
(619) 258-4911
(619) 258-4916 fax
www.sunbeltbooks.com
mail@sunbeltpub.com

07 06 05 04 03   5 4 3 2

Library of Congress Cataloging-in-Publications Data

La Jolla : a celebration of its past / [compiled] by Patricia Daly-Lipe
and Barbara Dawson ; Steele Lipe, Editor.-- 1st ed.
        p. cm.
Includes index.
   ISBN 0-932653-55-3
  1. La Jolla (San Diego, Calif.)--History. 2. La Jolla (San Diego, Calif.)--Biography. 3. Historic sites--California--San
Diego. 4. San Diego (Calif.)--History. 5. San Diego (Calif.)--Biography. I. Daly-Lipe, Patricia, 1942- II. Dawson, Barbara,
1916- III. Lipe, Steele, 1938-
   F869.S22 L3 2002
   979.4'985--dc21
                                                                                                    2002003627

Cover photo: Courtesy of Barbara Dawson
Back Cover photos: Courtesy of La Jolla Historical Society and San Diego Historical Society Photograph Collection
        Text page from *The Joyous Child* by H. Hubbard, courtesy of Mrs. Helen Reynolds

Table of Contents

Biographies

Patricia Daly-Lipe   Co-Author

Born and raised in La Jolla, Patricia left after graduating from The Bishop's School and completed her undergraduate studies at Vassar College. After several years in Europe, she returned to the United States, was married and raised three children.

Later, with a Ph.D. in Philosophy, Patricia spent her post-child-rearing years pursuing two creative endeavors: writing and painting. Many of her articles have appeared in magazines and newspapers. In the early 1990s, after several years teaching college English, Dr. Daly began a writing class at the Maryland Hall for the Creative Arts in Annapolis and at the Writing Center, Anne Arundel Community College. As a result of this experience, in December, 1999, she published *Myth, Magic & Metaphor*: *A Journey into the Heart of Creativity.* (One of her paintings appears on the cover.)

In 1997, Patricia returned to La Jolla after marrying Steele Lipe, her first boyfriend (1960). In 1999, she began, in association with Barbara Dawson, compiling weekly articles on 'Old La Jolla' for *La Jolla Village News* at the behest of its editor, Anne Terhune. Patricia is the 2002-2004 President of the National League of American Pen Women, La Jolla Branch.

In 2003 The San Diego Book Awards Association presented to Patricia and Barbara Dawson the "Certificate of Excellence" as the 2002 winner of published books, San Diego County category for *La Jolla: A Celebration of Its Past,* (first printing).

Barbara Dawson   Co-Author

Born in London during World War I, Barbara Gaines immigrated to La Jolla with her parents when she was three and a half years old. She attended La Jolla Elementary School and La Jolla Jr.-Sr. High School and then San Diego State College (now University) where she earned both B.A. and M.A. degrees. Receiving a fellowship from Claremont Graduate School, she continued her education.

For thirty years, Barbara served both as a teacher and a school principal. In 1974, Barbara Gaines Dawson retired from the San Diego Unified School District. In 1963, Barbara was chosen to accept the gavel and work with a group of old-timers to organize a historical society in La Jolla. She became its first president. Barbara has served on the Education Committee of the San Diego Zoo, has traveled to sixty foreign countries and is an avid (and talented) tennis player (rated fifth in the nation in her age group in doubles).

Contributing Authors

Grace Brophy   Darlington House (Contributor)

The Chapter on the Social Service League of La Jolla and the Darlington House was written with the assistance of Grace Brophy. Much of the information was gathered from research left to the League by Peg Breder, President from 1967-70. It was Mrs. Breder who indoctrinated all new members about its history.

Gary Fogel   Silent Wings over La Jolla (Author)

Gary Fogel, a native La Jollan, published the book *Wind and Wings: the History of Soaring in San Diego*. He is an honorary member and historian of the local Associated Glider Clubs of Southern California, the current chairman of the Torrey Pines Gliderport Historical Society, and holds several records in radio controlled model aviation including the US altitude record, three distance records, and a world record for goal and return.

Marnie Hutchinson
Powell Blankenship   Nothing but the Best (Contributors)

Marnie Hutchinson and Powell Blankenship have been assisting John Best with his autobiography. Both are native La Jollans.

Powell Blankenship was a teacher in the San Diego City School District. Currently a tennis instructor, in 1999 Powell was named teaching pro of the year by the San Diego District Tennis Association. He has written about tennis in *Spearlearning II* in part because of his being the coach to such notables as Brian Teacher.

Marnie Hutchinson was an advertising executive in New York City and an editor for *Vogue Magazine*. She and her husband Bernie Gurevitz, an accomplished artist, live on an island off the coast of New York, but come back to La Jolla every year.

Steele Lipe   La Jolla's Bicycle Pioneer (Author)
One Thousand Made Homeless by Naval Ammunition Explosion (Contributor)

The son of one of La Jolla's earliest doctors, J T Lipe, and La Jolla's leading watercolorist, Georgeanna Lipe, Steele left La Jolla after graduating from San Diego State College to attend Vanderbilt University, School of Medicine, in Nashville, Tennessee. He did his internship and residency in Anesthesiology at UC San Francisco and practiced for nearly 30 years in the Sacramento, California area where he specialized in cardiac, cardiac transplant and neonatal surgery. He is a Fellow of the American College of Anesthesiology and a Diplomate of the American Board of Anesthesiology. Having flown aircraft and gliders since 1972 he has written articles as well as lectured for the Soaring Society of America on the use of oxygen at high altitude. After retiring he married Patricia Daly and moved back to La Jolla and is busier than he ever was.

Susanna Lipe   Las Patronas (Author)

Susanna Lipe is a native La Jollan and the youngest daughter of Dr. J T and Georgeanna Lipe. After graduating from the University of Southern California, she worked for Sea World, San Diego before moving to Washington, D. C. There she worked for the 1976 Bicentennial Committee and Anheuser Busch's theme park in Williamsburg, Virginia. She returned to La Jolla to become an active volunteer for The Bishop's School, San Diego Museum of Art, Sharp Hospital Foundation and was the 2001-2002, President of Las Patronas. She is the mother of Troy and Adam Smith.

Joan Ogelsby   The Pacific Ocean, a Prized Part of La Jolla's Past (Contributor)

Joan Kapsala Ogelsby grew up in La Mesa, California. In 1978, she married La Jollan Bill Ogelsby. She has always loved writing—from personal letters to editing her high school yearbook, which received a National Scholastic Press award. Her contribution to the second section of this article is titled "More on our Local Surf Culture."

Cliff Robertson   Childhood Memories (Author)

Clifford Parker Robertson III was born in La Jolla in 1925. By age 13, he was a "dedicated hangar rat," riding his bicycle 13 miles from La Jolla to Speer Airport near the present site of Lindbergh field. His passion for flying and for airplanes continues including several flights in films. In *J. W. Coop* a film he wrote, directed and starred in, he flew a Tiger Moth (biplane). In *The Pilot* another film he directed and had a leading roll, Mr. Robertson flew a DC-8.

Cliff Robertson began his career in journalism but soon found his niche on stage. In the '50s, he began a career in films and TV episodes. After playing the part in a TV production, Cliff fought for seven years to bring *Charly* to the screen and, in 1968, received an Oscar for his performance in this film. In the early '60s, President John F. Kennedy selected Mr. Robertson to play his younger self in *PT 109* (1963). In 1965, he won an Emmy for his performance in "Bob Hope Presents the Chrysler Theater: The Game." Although he has starred in over fifty-eight feature films, Cliff Robertson has never lost his bent for writing. Like flying, writing is his passion.

George Silvani   **Transportation in Old La Jolla** (Contributor)
Cornelious "Neil" Bohannon (Author)
One Thousand Made Homeless by Naval Ammunition Explosion (Contributor)
Guns at Bird Rock (Author)

George Silvani is a native Californian from the central part of the state. His Naval career of 26 years included service on destroyers and carriers and a destroyer command. George and his wife, Helen, made La Jolla their home before retiring here in 1973 while serving as a civilian consultant for naval architecture and marine engineering firms. George is a longtime photo archive volunteer for the San Diego Historical Society.

Mary Ellen Stratthaus   **Flaw in the Jewel, Housing Discrimination against Jews In La Jolla** (Author)

Based on an article by Mary Ellen Stratthaus in *American Jewish History* (American Jewish Historical Society Quarterly Publication, September 1996). A resident of La Jolla since 1991 and a staff member, student and faculty wife at UCSD, Mary Ellen Stratthaus wrote "Flaw in the Jewel" in her first year of graduate school in the History Department at UCSD. Prior to coming to La Jolla, Mary Ellen worked in Hollywood for several years in television production and at one time was assistant to the producer of the Red Skelton Show. She received a BA in History from UCSD in 1995 and completed one year in the graduate program there but withdrew to concentrate on nonacademic writing. Special interests include racism and anti-semitism in the United States.

Robert Thiele   **Dramatic Cave Creates History and Commerce** (Contributor)

Thanks to Robert Thiele, author of *Cave Curio History*, for information help in writing this article. Robert was born and raised in La Jolla. He is the grandson of Ross Thiele who established Ross Thiele Interiors in 1932 and son of John Thiele whose business is now called Ross Thiele & Son. All three generations are proud to be La Jollans. Robert Thiele, who is an Architect (A.I.A.), earned his undergraduate degree in archeological studies from Arizona State University, class of '71. Robert developed philosophies in architecture working with local sculptor James Hubble for 10 years, apprenticing with Paula Soler in the Arizona desert, and working with environmental artist Christo on the "Umbrellas Project." Robert also apprenticed with local architect S. M. Bruce Richards. Ongoing projects include the Sea Cliff Cave Store property, a fascinating undertaking that involves multiple disciplines including geology, paleontology, archeology, as well as cultural preservation.

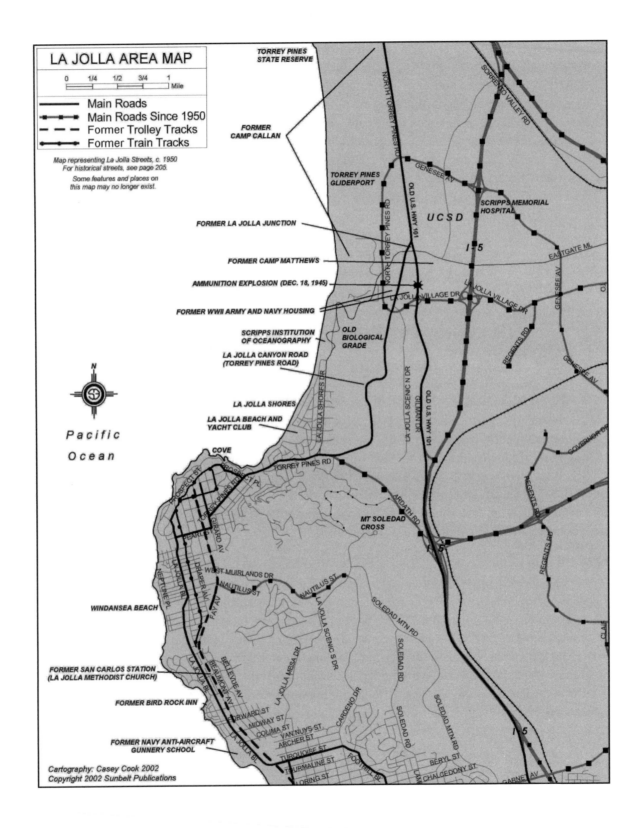

LA JOLLA AREA MAP

0   1/4   1/2   3/4   1
Mile

— Main Roads
▪—▪ Main Roads Since 1950
– – – Former Trolley Tracks
•—•— Former Train Tracks

Map representing La Jolla Streets, c. 1950
For historical streets, see page 205.

Some features and places on
this map may no longer exist.

TORREY PINES
STATE RESERVE

FORMER
CAMP CALLAN

TORREY PINES
GLIDERPORT

FORMER LA JOLLA JUNCTION

FORMER CAMP MATTHEWS

AMMUNITION EXPLOSION (DEC. 18, 1945)

FORMER WWII ARMY AND NAVY HOUSING

SCRIPPS INSTITUTION
OF OCEANOGRAPHY

LA JOLLA CANYON ROAD
(TORREY PINES ROAD)

LA JOLLA SHORES

LA JOLLA BEACH AND
YACHT CLUB

COVE

WINDANSEA BEACH

FORMER SAN CARLOS STATION
(LA JOLLA METHODIST CHURCH)

FORMER BIRD ROCK INN

FORMER NAVY ANTI-AIRCRAFT
GUNNERY SCHOOL

Pacific

Ocean

N

UCSD

SCRIPPS MEMORIAL
HOSPITAL

I-5

EASTGATE ML.

GENESEE AV.

LA JOLLA VILLAGE DR.

REGENTS RD.

OLD
BIOLOGICAL
GRADE

MT SOLEDAD
CROSS

NORTH TORREY PINES RD.

SORRENTO VALLEY RD.

GENESEE AV.

OLD U.S. HWY 101

LA JOLLA SCENIC N DR.

GILMAN DR.

OLD U.S. HWY 101

ARDATH RD.

GOVERNOR DR.

REGENTS RD.

TORREY PINES RD.

PROSPECT ST.

PROSPECT PL.

TORREY PINES RD.

GIRARD AV.

PEARL ST.

LA JOLLA BL.

DRAPER AV.

NEPTUNE PL.

NAUTILUS ST.

FAY AV.

WEST MUIRLANDS DR.

NAUTILUS ST.

LA JOLLA SCENIC S DR.

SOLEDAD MTN RD.

SOLEDAD RD.

BELLEVUE AV.

BEAUMONT AV.

LA JOLLA BL.

FORWARD ST.

MIDWAY ST.

COLIMA ST.

VAN NUYS ST.

ARCHER ST.

TURQUOISE ST.

THURMALINE ST.

LORING ST.

LA JOLLA MESA DR.

CARDENO DR.

SOLEDAD RD.

SOLEDAD MTN RD.

FOOTHILL BL.

BERYL ST.

CHALCEDONY ST.

GARNET AV.

I-5

Cartography: Casey Cook 2002
Copyright 2002 Sunbelt Publications

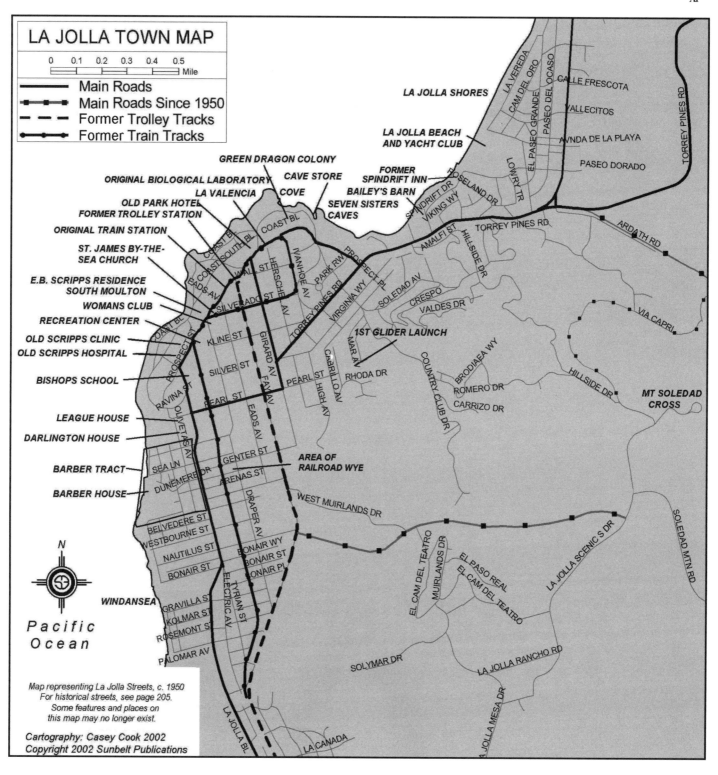

LA JOLLA TOWN MAP

0   0.1   0.2   0.3   0.4   0.5 Mile

——— Main Roads
—■— Main Roads Since 1950
— — — Former Trolley Tracks
—●— Former Train Tracks

GREEN DRAGON COLONY
ORIGINAL BIOLOGICAL LABORATORY
CAVE STORE
LA VALENCIA
COVE
OLD PARK HOTEL
FORMER TROLLEY STATION
ORIGINAL TRAIN STATION
ST. JAMES BY-THE-SEA CHURCH
E.B. SCRIPPS RESIDENCE
SOUTH MOULTON
WOMANS CLUB
RECREATION CENTER
OLD SCRIPPS CLINIC
OLD SCRIPPS HOSPITAL
BISHOPS SCHOOL
LEAGUE HOUSE
DARLINGTON HOUSE
BARBER TRACT
BARBER HOUSE

FORMER SPINDRIFT INN
BAILEY'S BARN
SEVEN SISTERS
CAVES

LA JOLLA SHORES
LA JOLLA BEACH
AND YACHT CLUB

1ST GLIDER LAUNCH
MT SOLEDAD CROSS
AREA OF RAILROAD WYE

WINDANSEA

N

Pacific
Ocean

Map representing La Jolla Streets, c. 1950
For historical streets, see page 205.
Some features and places on
this map may no longer exist.

Cartography: Casey Cook 2002
Copyright 2002 Sunbelt Publications

Searching for the Spirit of La Jolla

People will not look forward to posterity who never look backward to their ancestors.   **Edmund Burke (1729-1797)**

La Jolla is more than a town, more than just a pretty seaside place in the sun. There is a spirit about this place. The essence of La Jolla comes not only from the sea, the surf, the sun, the cliffs, and the caves, but also from its unique and bountiful history which includes some very special citizens, people who contributed to and were responsible for its evolution. La Jolla is called home by Nobel Laureates, politicians, gurus of the internet, as well as actors, authors, and artists of every genre.

What is it about this place? To find out, at the behest of Anne Terhune, editor of *La Jolla Village News*, we compiled a two year series of weekly articles exploring La Jolla's rich past. We read letters, visited libraries, searched through old books and manuscripts, listened to stories, walked around and through historical sites, and discovered, by exploring the past, the many facets and facts that make this little town so special. This book is the result of that quest and, although it does not contain all of the many characters and characteristics, hopefully it will stimulate the reader to come explore and learn about "the town with the funny name."

The existence of human beings on this planet goes back some two million years. Anthropologists believe that Homo sapiens came to North America about 40,000 years ago. About 10,000 years ago, these early nomadic hunters entered the eastern edge of what is now San Diego County. In the 1970s, a skull was found in the cliffs of Del Mar, California; according to the Scripps Institution of Oceanography, this skull may be older than 10,000 years. The cliffs themselves have sediments and ancient marine deposits that are over seventy million years old. La Jolla, on the other hand, is built on a marine terrace that was cut out not so long ago. (Terraces are formed when there is an uplift from deep within the earth.) Although La Jolla's early history is a mystery, most archeologists agree that there was a band of Indians living in this area around A.D. 500, based on the many Indian artifacts found buried in the sand off the coast of La Jolla Shores. However, our story does not begin with this indigenous group, but in 1869 with the purchase of Pueblo lot 1261, consisting of eighty acres for the sum of $100 ($1.25 an acre).

Patricia Daly-Lipe and Barbara Dawson, La Jolla, 2002

The authors wish to express their appreciation for the perseverance, diligence, and exactitude of Steele Lipe without whom this book would not be possible.

Introduction

History is Someone Else's Point of View.

In 1887, La Jolla could just barely be defined as a colony and she wasn't alone — all of California was under-developed and, to easterners, too remote and uncivilized to consider. All that changed when transportation and technology opened up the West. In 1903, the first cross-country trip was made by car, and a direct railroad link from Los Angeles to Salt Lake City was established. 1911 was the year of the first transcontinental flight and, in 1914 the Panama Canal was opened. By 1920, California was transformed into a full-fledged part of the United States, and La Jolla had grown from a small colony to the status of a village. With America's entrance in the Great War, military camps were set up in the vicinity of La Jolla. Many of the soldiers fell in love with the area and, after the war, stayed and settled. Soon La Jolla developed into a veritable town. Following World War II, her boundaries expanded as her population increased to the point that today, La Jolla has become a mini-city within a city.

However, despite the many changes, may we never forget the La Jolla that once was: a sunset land of bright solace and simple, anonymous living alongside brown mountain slopes and a serene blue sea.

La Jolla's Early History

In 1886, Frank T. Botsford, a thirty-five year old New York City stock broker of substantial means, came to La Jolla with his wife. Fully aware of the land boom in San Diego, he began surveying the virgin territory above the Cove and the caves. On the 26th of January, he wrote in his diary: "Bought La Jolla!" Although he really wasn't the first to buy La Jolla, he was the first to truly develop the area. The land he bought initially included what we now refer to as "the village." A quarter interest was sold to George W. Heald.

For his own home, Mr. Botsford selected a lot at the southwest corner of what is now Prospect and Ivanhoe. Many early settlers followed his lead, building their shingled houses on the hillside that sloped down to the clear blue waters. Below were the cliffs and caves and the gentle bluffs with a protected beach wrapped in the arms of the rock formation known as Alligator Head

Mr. Frank Botsford surveying at the site where he built his home—SW corner of Ivanhoe and Prospect, 1887.
Courtesy of Barbara Dawson

Botsford House, 1889
Courtesy of Barbara Dawson

(most of which has succumbed to the surf in recent years). What a view these early residents had — the coastline stretching to the north totally barren, unpopulated and un-polluted. These early La Jollans could smell the fresh sea air, hear the barking seals, and watch the pelicans, cormorants, and sea gulls as they floated overhead on their way to and from the cliffs and caves below. Grey-green sagebrush and the darker chaparral covered the land in all directions. Behind, the eight hundred-foot high mountain named Soledad guarded this private little Para-dise. Every Spring, Mt. Soledad was covered with patches of brilliant wild flowers like shooting stars, Indian Paint-brush, lilies and California Poppies. In the canyons were Sycamores, Cottonwoods, Willows and Live Oak trees. Necessity caused these early settlers to learn how to use many of the native trees and shrubs for cooking and fuel. The ocean also was a source of food with abundant aba-lone, halibut, lobster, bass, cod, grouper and whitefish. The underwater park of waving sea grass and kelp that pro-vided homes to the sea life fascinated the early settlers and continues to make poets and artists of its residents.

Depicting this small area of enchanting seaside topography as barren as bone where La Jolla's history began is a poem written by John R. E. Sumner in 1913.

Great is La Jolla, Great Little Place

Great is La Jolla, great little place—
  Where your house is one of a nest of shacks
And you look from your front on your neighbor's backs,
  Dive under their washing to reach the street…
Where the houses are built in curious tangles,
  And the windows jut out as such various angles,
And one which for days and months was dark
  Gleams bright some night with electric spark…
Quaint La Jolla, quaint little place—
  Where you can't deny the chance is fine
To study the human form divine,

(Not always built on the classic line)
  Where a Boston lady got such a jar
  That she actually used the vernacular…
She had not guessed how far could reach
  The liberties of the bathing beach,
And a bathing suit may excuse a scare
  If worn on a principal thoroughfare.
But why this is thus and these things those,
  Nobody cares and nobody knows,
For it's only La Jolla and everything goes
  But you don't get too hot and you never get friz–
Great little city La Jolla is.

At first, La Jolla was hard to reach from San Diego because of a chain of low mountains. In 1894, the railroad came to the sea resort with its steam and gas trains. La Jolla was launched! Within four years, there were one hundred homes, plus several stores, in the colony.

Mr. Heald, who had bought a quarter interest in Mr. Botsford's initial land purchase, built a two-story building on the corner of Herschel Avenue and Wall Street. It is thought that this may have been the first general store in La Jolla. We do know, however, that in 1896 the second floor was used as a school room. (The store was subsequently moved to the corner of Girard and Prospect as the Chase and Ludington store.)

Mr. Botsford and his family left La Jolla and returned to San Diego. However, he asked Nellie McGilvery Mills to manage his La Jolla property. Unlike most women of her day Nellie was the bread winner in her family. Her husband, Anson P. Mills was more than happy to play second fiddle and act as general handy man to his ambitious wife. Besides managing Botsford's properties, Nellie bought her own cottages to rent out. Quite the promoter, Nellie met trains coming from San Diego and handed out cards advertising rentals. Thus the first true real estate mogul of La Jolla was a lady. The Mills' daughter, Ellen Morrill Mills, became not only a published poet but co-owner of the *La Jolla Journal* (1926-1941).

Houses and stores sprang up at random along the streets of Prospect, Girard, Wall, Herschel, Ivanhoe, and Coast. For water, Mr. Botsford had purchased property in Rose Canyon. Huge whisky barrels were filled with the water from the canyon and hauled up the hill (the present Torrey Pines Rd.) by George and Fred, two horses owned by John Kennedy, to the little settlement of homes. From time to time, for unknown reasons, the water supply was unavailable. It is difficult to imagine living without fresh water, but the early settlers were tough and somehow managed. Later, water came to La Jolla through pipes, but the pipes were very small so the pressure was low and the amount of water was small and unpredictable.

Chase and Ludington Store on the corner of Girard Avenue and Prospect Street, 1903.
Courtesy of Barbara Dawson

Myron C. Close, a Civil War pensioner from the Battle of Gettysburg had a curio shop across from the Cove where he sold trinkets and whatnots and was supposed to have a mummified mermaid.
Courtesy of San Diego Historical Society Photograph Collection

An amusing account tells of one industrious group who felt that the climate and soil in La Jolla was perfect for the harvesting of grapes. They imported plants from Italy and attempted a vineyard with the intent of making wine. Unfortunately, the climatic needs were not complete as a primary source of water just wasn't there.

When Walter Lieber took the train to this coastal resort, instead of stopping for a brief visit, he decided to stay. He said the one hundred or so cottages were "inhabited by old maids and widows, with men very scarce." What incentive for a bachelor. (Some early inhabitants were more cynical. According to one, "La Jolla was all old maids and damned red geraniums.")

Mr. Lieber rented a cottage, paying all of nine dollars a month. "Scripps Park was then a place of tents…piles of manure, tins, and bottles. La Jolla had cow paths in lieu of streets, deep to the ankle in summer with dust, in winter as deep in mud," Lieber writes. "…water only fed into the village by a two-inch pipe, and none in that pipe during the day, so we had to stay up at nights to get enough water for the next day's needs." To make life even more difficult, "there were (only) three bath tubs in the village, fed by cold water… ."

Despite these odd circumstances, La Jolla continued to expand with buildings and churches being literally picked up and moved from one location to another as a permanent population increased.

The Lure

I am La Jolla, still I call my own
And still they come, though why they do not know
From the grey fringes where the desert ends.
From the tropic splendors, and from heights of snow.

Hear! I am calling in the waves that reach
And murmur, eager-lipped, against the sand!
Look! I am waving from brown cliff and beach,
Where argosies of dreams might come to land.

See! When the sullen red of sunset dyes
The leaden-blue of sea, at after glow,
When the spent sea birds seek the rocky lee,
I call to you, although you may not know.

For though you roam, and farther yet, maybe
From days when all my potent spell was new
By sunset waters, windows from off the sea,
I am La Jolla, and I call to you.

Ellen Morrill Mills

The Colony Becomes A Village

La Jolla on the Move

From 1887 to 1920, the little colony of La Jolla developed into a village. Modest single-family cottages and bungalows grew in number and many were moved from one location in La Jolla to another.

Dr. Martin Lizerbraum, who came from Philadelphia in 1968, owns Redwood Hollow aka Prospect View where Walter Lieber (pronounced, "Lee-bear") "built three vacation cottages in approximately 1915-1919." (More cottages were added later.) Dr. Lizerbraum writes that Mr. Lieber "and his wife, Jennie Beaudine Lieber, purchased the lot in 1907, which was at the extreme edge of any development in the original La Jolla Park Subdivision." Born in Philadelphia in 1860, Mr. Lieber had been in Mexico doing mining exploration, became ill, and, in 1904, ended up in La Jolla. Over the years into the 1920s, Mr. Lieber built several cottage colonies for vacationers. Clearly, Lieber was one of La Jolla's very first real estate moguls.

Mr. Lieber was also a community philanthropist. "I have an early post card of Coast Boulevard around Scripps Park," Dr. Lizerbraum states, "where Mr. Lieber wrote, 'I planted all of these trees many years ago' referring to the still existing Washingtonia palms which line Coast Boulevard today." (Dr. Lizerbraum purchased this postcard, not in La Jolla, but in an antique shop in Jenkintown, PA, a borough of Philadelphia, the hometown of both gentlemen a century apart!) Several acres of land containing Eucalyptus trees in East County were also purchased by Mr. Lieber, which he then donated for a County Park. "It is of interest," Dr. Lizerbraum adds, that Mr. Lieber was "a practicing Jew before La Jolla had much of a social fabric in the early part of this century."

Burnwell Cottage, c. 1888, typical of many of the early board and batten cottages of La Jolla. The Patterson Family is in front.
Courtesy of San Diego Historical Society Photograph Collection

Early La Jolla dwellings were quite modest. Mainly board and batten, these cottages were approximately 850 square feet, and (generally) contained two bedrooms and one bathroom (sans tub). For many years, there was only one house in the village with a bath tub. Because it didn't quite fit the owner had a hole cut in her bathroom wall. That way, she could enjoy the view of the coastline and fresh air while bathing. Her house was located on the sloping land just west of Torrey Pines Road and north of Prospect. Her name was Anna Held.

At the turn of the 20th century, La Jolla was a small area "of enchanting seaside topography as barren as a bone." The last remnants of this time are the Brockton Villa, built in 1894 and preserved as a wonderful restaurant and the two cottages called the Red Rest, built by Mr. George Julian Leavy, and the Red Roost also known as Neptune, built by Eugene Fishburn in 1895. Designated as historical sites in 1975, these bungalows are "monuments of American Architecture" (according to Professor Eugene Ray, whose thesis included the historical importance of the two bungalows by the Cove and who helped obtain their historical designation). By 1910 the major American residential type of architecture, these bungalows (the word coming from Bengali, first built in the West Indies) represent "folk building," a style which grew in response to actual need. Known in Europe as "California Bungalows," this residential type of architecture, in particular the Red Roost and Red Rest, although they may be "very humble structures on the surface…represent the earliest most vital La Jolla spirit." Professor Ray points out, "La Jolla has an Arcadian spirit. It is a place where the sun, the sea, and the land have worked together in a magical way to produce a paradisal situation. The spirit of the bungalows in their relation to the cove are our earliest metaphor of this and indeed the standard bearers of this greatest residential dream of (the twentieth) century." Imagine owning a home by the sea for $200-$300!

There were other cottages and bungalows dotting the hillside. Most of these little houses were furnished and rented by Walter Lieber & Co. whose phone number was simply, Sunset 91. (The telephone came to La Jolla in 1899.)

Dr. Parker's house on the move.
Courtesy of R. E. Gaines

Some of the cottages had roofs over the front porches supported by concrete pillars embedded in cobblestones, which had been gathered below the cliffs at Bird Rock. Many of these houses also had low concrete walls containing the same round stones from the sea designating their property lines. Unfortunately, only a few of these little "stoned walls" remain. One such wall can be seen around St. James by-the-Sea Episcopal Church on Prospect and Silverado and another (though covered with cement) at John Cole's Book Store, originally the Wisteria Cottage at Prospect and Eads.

In the early years, it was not unusual to see business buildings, houses, or churches being towed down the street. When the Parker house was being moved, four ladies were inside playing Bridge. Every so often, they would stop playing, go to the window, and wave to the pedestrians who were watching the house as it was passing by!

In 1929, the original St. James Episcopal Church, designed by architect Irving Gill, was moved from the triangular property bordered by Prospect, Silverado, and Eads to its current location at Draper and Genter. Purchased by the Baptist Church, it was used as a sanctuary and meeting place until the late 1950s. Presently, it is the Baptist Fellowship Hall and a polling place during elections.

The first library, known as the Reading Room, was built on the northeast corner of Wall and Girard in 1898. It was later moved to Draper where Silver Street dead ends. The old Heald Store, at the corner of Wall and Herschel, was moved in October, 1899, to the southeast corner of Girard and Prospect and was renamed the Chase and Ludington Building.

The first building of St. James by-the-Sea Episcopal Church in the early 1910s. It was moved six blocks south along Draper Street to Genter Street. The Railroad tracks can bee seen both on Prospect and Silverado Streets. *Courtesy of St James by-the-Sea Episcopal Church*

In the 1920s, there was a group of six small bungalows referred to as the Plaza Court at the corner of Wall and Ivanhoe. They were removed when the United States Post Office was built in 1931. One of these cottages was relocated to the rear of a lot in the 7400 block of Fay Avenue and retains its "air cooled" pantry.

Many of the early houses had names like Honeysuckle Lodge (on Fay Avenue) and Wisteria. Some names were more humorous like Red Rest and Neptune mentioned above as well as Aksarben, which is Nebraska spelled backward. Aksarben had originally been the stable behind the Botsford house on the corner of Ivanhoe and Prospect. The Botsfords moved into their home in 1887, but lived there only three years before moving to San Diego. Although the Botsford house was torn down in 1938, the remodeled stable remained until 1954. The Wilsons (Spencer Wilson's family) came from Arklow, Ireland. Their home was named Arklow.

The Geranium Cottage at 830 Kline has a special history. Originally built in 1904, it is an architecturally significant building. With many characteristics of a "bungalow cottage," it is reportedly only one of two similar one and a half story side-gable bungalow cottages built in La Jolla. It is zoned commercial and, according to Alex Bevel, this cottage "is one of a rapidly diminishing number of modest single-family cottages and bungalows that once identified La Jolla nation-wide as a beachfront 'cottage community.'" The original owners were La Jolla's second doctor, Dr. Edward Howard, and his wife Eliza B. Howard. The cottage was used both as their home and as the doctor's medical office. Dr. Howard was not only a General Practitioner for the La Jolla community, he was also appointed one of the area's first county health officers. His wife served as President of the La Jolla Woman's Club from 1911-12. It was also Mrs. Howard who was responsible for initiating ornamental plantings along the shoreline. In 1914, when their house was relocated to Kline Street to make way for Miss Scripps' gift to the community of the Children's Playground, the Howards moved into what is now the Cottage Restaurant on Fay and Kline and rented their former home, now on Kline Street, just behind their cottage. In 1998, thanks to the efforts of Kay Abbott and her daughter Kerry Wade, this cottage at 830 Kline Street was designated as a San Diego County Historical Site.

Another historical site is the result of a strong woman's community in La Jolla. Established as an organization in 1894, the La Jolla Woman's Club grew so rapidly that, by 1912, it was apparent that a Club House was needed. Miss Ellen Browning Scripps came to the rescue underwriting the design and construction of what would become one of Irving J. Gill's best maintained and most celebrated buildings. It could be called one of the first "pre-fab" structures. The innovative technology was Gill's adaptation of the Aiken system of "tilt-slab" concrete construction. Each wall was completed separately, brought to the construction site and placed horizontally on the ground. With all four sides in place, one at a time the sides were raised and attached at the corners. At the dedication ceremony, in 1913, Miss Scripps was asked to "draw a pen picture of the future of La Jolla." Although her words are buried in the walls, a copy of her speech was saved. The words are poignant and prophetic and well worth reading if only to remind us of the values that were held by the founders and benefactors of La Jolla. In part, she said:

> "Wealth, subordinate to art and culture, may create a suburb of stately homes envisioned by beautiful parks and avenues of tropical luxuriousness; may produce a fitting jewel to the setting that nature has provided in her picturesque coast line backed by the illimitable eternal sea, with its every varying wondrous colors and moods and aspects; the radiant sky above and the mountain tops afar off.

> "…In this practical, prosy, every day world of ours it is only labor that wins success; the labor no less of thought and education and brain culture than of brawn and muscle.

> "…There can be no evolution without involution; no bringing forth, without first putting in. It is through the travail of the artistic soul that beauty is born. Patience and labor are the essentials, not the mere incidents of success; not the labor that is sordid, but that, that is loving and intelligent; not the patience that means idle waiting, but that, that imitates the Divine Creator in His construction of the universe. The fruition of our hopes and aspirations can be attained only by our own determination and acts."

By 1920, the population of La Jolla was approximately 2,500. (This was double the population of 1910.) Despite the growth, by today's standards La Jolla, was a very small community. As an early example, there is a photograph of the La Jolla Woman's Club taken in 1916. In front of the Club House, a cow was staked out happily gnawing on the wild grasses. Syd Gaines and his wife, Daisy (who came to La Jolla in 1912), were the caretakers both of the club and of the cow. Once a day, Mr. Gaines would milk the cow and take some of his collection to Miss Scripps who lived directly across the street. Rich and not-so-rich lived side by side in harmony. Life was simple.

La Jolla was a "magic land." It was a place where "People in the old age of their youth and people in the youth of their old age come…and wonder why they remain so young." In a seaside setting with almost constant sunshine, a place with neither Fall nor Winter, just continuous Spring, the lifestyle of the early citizens reflected quiet simplicity. And yet, despite being easygoing and informal, the town had a disproportionately large number of authors, scientists, musicians, painters, sculptors, world travelers and famous people. "May La Jolla as her sophistication increases not lose her charm." (John Sumner)

Roslyn Lane Ramblings, 1909-1930

by Franklin D. Smith

My grandfather, Frank Cicero Robertson, while on a visit to California from Mississippi in about 1909, was persuaded by my mother and father, Marguerite Robertson and Corrie Dow Smith, to join them in buying a lot and building a house in La Jolla. Marguerite and Corrie were then living with their two young daughters, Margaret Lyle and Jessica, on Third Street in San Diego. Carrie was working for a bank in downtown San Diego, I believe the First National Bank. The site selected was 1221 Waverly Lane, later renamed Roslyn Lane. The house was a redwood two-story bungalow which they named the Chalet. On completion of construction in 1909 or 1910, Frank Cicero returned to Mississippi and the house was rented to Miss Lucile Jeardeau (later La Jolla's first and only policewoma), and her sister and their mother, while their house, the Winnebago, was being built on the corner of Ocean Lane and South Coast Boulevard. In 1911, Marguerite and Carrie sold the Third Street house and permanently moved to the Chalet, after adding a sun room (third bedroom). Carrie commuted daily to work on the San Diego, Pacific Beach, and La Jolla Railroad trains. Corrie died unexpectedly in January 1915. I was born in the Chalet in July, assisted by Dr. Martha Corey.

Marguerite moved her young family in 1917, first for a few months to the Sea Breeze cottage on South Coast Boulevard between Jenner and Eads Streets, and then to La Mesa, until about 1920, when the family returned to the Chalet. Marguerite soon discovered that she could rent the Chalet to others for more than she would have to pay for quarters for her family elsewhere. My uncle, Walter G. Robertson, also living in La Jolla, moved us in his four-door Essex touring car. I have vivid recollections of loading into and out of this automobile at the Chalet.

Roslyn Lane, the entire one block of it from Ivanhoe Avenue to Prospect Street, was an exciting place to me. Most of the lots on the north side of the Lane were vacant. This was fun for kids for whatever it is that kids do for fun in vacant lots. Several of the houses on the south side of the Lane were enclosed by low fences or stone walls and were well stocked with plants and trees, many of them native. There were California quail in abundance and in residence all year, and there were mourning doves, rabbits, ground squirrels, skunks, and gophers in considerable number, and an occasional coyote and fox. The houses all had names. Starting at the Ivanhoe end there was the Waverly, built by Walter S. Lieber, and occupied by the Burdick family. Of the children, Marston was the youngest, several years older than I. Next came the Michiquita, also built by Walter S. Lieber, lived in first by a pleasant older couple and later by my aunt, Emma G. Robertson. East of the Chalet were two cottages, names not remembered; one was occupied by Miss Kate Neal and Miss Blodgett, very proper Victorian ladies always formally and severely dressed from neck to wrist and toe in white, gray, and black shades, with much lace and high laced black shoes. Boys and girls were seldom invited into their home. Miss Neal operated a kindergarten in the Playhouse cottage facing Cave Street. In the other Cottage lived Miss Rosa Harrison, a working lady, who cared for several cats. They were her babies, outrageously pampered with fresh fish and liver, as well as milk, at every meal. A fish bone became lodged in Rosa's throat one night, causing quite a stir in the neighborhood until the doctor arrived to help retrieve the bone. Then came the Rauceby, a two story house built by the Tomlinson family, and occupied by the Aller's, good friends of my parents. Tim Aller, ten or so years older than I, was the youngest. Next came Barbara Gardner's two story house, surrounded by a three foot high wall of beach stones, the yard profuse in shrubs and trees. I believe this was the house rented and lived in by Katherine Cutler and her son John, my age, during the period 1925 to the spring of 1928. Katherine worked for Mrs. Siegfried, who operated The Jack-O-Lantern, a gift shop and private lending library on Girard Avenue a few doors down the hill from the H & R Grocery Store. The dark wooden sign denoting the shop was distinctive, for it had an orange colored pumpkin painted on it…. Behind this house, on the same property, was a small one story cottage named the Arborvitae, occupied by Captain Coleson, and behind it, facing Cave Street, was the Bohemia cottage, occupied by a Navy chaplain, Clinton A. Neyman, and his family. The three Neyman children were important friends of mine for years. Bob Neyman and I spent many hours in the large mulberry tree in the back yard devouring fruit and looking into the adjoining back yards. Then came the small white cottage lived in by Mr. and Mrs. Jesse Steckler and their son Kenneth. The Stecklers operated the H & B. Grocery Store at the north end of Girard Street. Next came the two-story house at the corner of Prospect Street, occupied by Mr. and Mrs. Lang and their daughter. Mr. Lang collected stamps; he bargained me out of a mint set of the often eagerly sought after Graf Zeppelin stamps issued in 1930. This event has become one of the great regrets of my life, as the face value of the sets of three stamps is $4.55, what I paid for them at the post office, valued today at over $ 3,000. Opposite the Lang house was a vacant lot along Prospect Street, on which several kids my age, with the help of the grown ups, put on a circus, animals, tent, and all. This was in 1925. Participants included Harle (Garth Montgomery) and Bill Garth, Bill Eastman, Finlay and Donald Drummond, Ken Steckler, John Cutler, Dick Cromwell, and me. There were several others, possibly including John and Dick Bancroft. Our animals included garage man Bill Zader's goat, John Cutler's Boston bull terrier Bambino, and a police dog. Then came a clay tennis court extending from Prospect to the Lane, which later became the site of Mira Monte Apartments, built and owned by the Drummond family. Further west on the Lane were several single wooden garages or vacant lots behind houses fronting on Prospect, including the Vine and Fig Tree Restaurant, formerly the Brown Bear Restaurant, operated by Phil Acker's parents. Later on, this restaurant became Smiths' Bungalow Inn, having moved there from Pacific Beach. The Smiths served a remarkably delicious dinner, including entree, vegetables, soup, salad, and dessert for the sum of seventy-five cents or one dollar. Further west on Roslyn Lane, opposite the Michiquita, was the Humpty-Dumpty cottage, with its large pepper tree eminently suitable for climbing, owned by Martha Ingersoll Robinson, and occupied by May L. Arthur, a maiden lady and dear person who was a friend for years, and who made delicious white fudge. An earlier occupant was Mr. Dickson, a tennis player who was friendly to children and who looked just like Vincent Van Gogh. Next to the Humpty-Dumpty, on the corner of Ivanhoe Avenue, was the Blarney Castle, also owned by Mrs. Robinson, with a huge century plant and a large star pine in the yard suitable for more than one tree house. Across Ivanhoe at the head of Roslyn Lane in a white cottage lived Dinty Moore, a local policeman and his wife. Dinty was our scoutmaster, interested in all the kids, but he had a hard time performing due to an extreme excess of weight; he was quite a sight in uniform.

I recall three horse-drawn wagon operations in Roslyn Lane. First, there was Charley, the Chinese vegetable man who regularly made his rounds selling an assortment of fresh fruits and vegetables. Charley wore his left shoe on his right foot and his right shoe on his left foot, so that the shoe toe points faced outwards instead of inwards as is normally the case; and he and the horse both wore straw hats. Often, Charley would lift me up into the seat next to him for a ride down the Lane, speaking to me the entire time in Chinese. Several years later Marguerite claimed that my first spoken words were in Chinese, obviously picked up from Charley. Next, there was the horse and wagon belonging to my uncle, Walter G. Robertson, who owned and operated the village's Fuel and Feed Store, and driven by Arthur Burke. Arthur would deliver large burlap sacks filled with kindling, eucalyptus wood, or lumps of soft coal for use in our fireplace in the living room. Arthur was very adept at backing up the wagon into just the right spots for loading or unloading. I often rode with him on his rounds, and he and I became lifelong friends. He influenced me in many ways. I recall two of his humorous stories about the irascible and determined Miss Virginia Scripps. He died in La Jolla in about 1980. Lastly, there was the wagon driven by Dan, the Gardner, a taciturn, unfriendly person with a high pitched voice, who often drove through the Lane. Dan's large, barking, snarling Airedale dog chained in the back of the open wagon was a source of periodic apprehension. Dan's horse, too, sported a straw hat….

Particular friends about my age living along Roslyn Lane were Phil Acker, John Cutler, and Kenneth Steckler. Phil and I fashioned several hiding dens in the salt bush hedges between houses, and we built and slept in an Indian tepee in the Chalet's back yard. Steckler and I often rode the H & R Grocery Store delivery truck. Trips to Sorrento Valley to pick up huge crates of eggs were great fun, particularly going down the twisting dirt road through brush-covered canyons from the Marine Corps Rifle Range (Camp Matthews) to Sorrento. Ken and I remained good friends for years, except for one brief period when Harry Weber and I "had it in for him." One Sunday morning on our way home from Sunday School we "beat him up" behind Barbara Gardner's stone wall because he was "spoiled," sending him home in tears. Fifteen minutes later Mr. and Mrs. Steckler caught up with us in their open touring car and straightened us out. Finlay Drummond was a demon. He enticed me into assisting him in setting off a loud firecracker in the Congregational Church on the corner of Cave and Ivanhoe one Sunday evening during services. Church personnel pursued us over fence and under hedge for half an hour, but we successfully evaded them. I had other favorite contemporaries living elsewhere in La Jolla, but of them all I only recall Sam Roberts as a frequent visitor to Roslyn Lane, coming up from his home on Prospect Street or, later, down from his home on Torrey Pines Road. He usually wore corduroy knickers, a sloppy sweater, and long socks down around his ankles. We had great times together in the Chalet's playroom, and we owned a sailboat. Often at dinner time Mrs. Roberts would telephone for Sam, speaking in a sweet, slow drawl. "Is Sammy there? Please send him home right away." Eldred (Gregory) Peck, who lived nearby on Exchange Place, and I used the wood shed behind the Chalet for "secret meetings" — for what purpose I don't recall — and to avoid the grownups. Eldred had one of friendliest mongrel dogs I've ever known, always smiling and wagging his tail, even after we repeatedly abused him one way or another. Entering the Exchange Place house through an unlocked window in search of food was another of our pastimes.

The Chalet, as the family homestead of my early years, evokes many memories. Marguerite was the central personality around whom my entire existence evolved. She was mother and father, all in one, to me, always loving, guiding, and caring, and she was always understanding and trusting. I do not recall that she ever expressed anger, disgust, or even disappointment in me — though she had many opportunities to do so. She was always available to brush away tears, and to proffer hugs and kisses. She was all business, too, and early on encouraged me to find my own path in the world, and to make my own decisions. I recall that once or twice, when my activities were apparently pretty bad, requiring correction, she, with great reluctance and in tears, sent me to the hedge between the Chalet and Michiquita to break off a suitable switch so she could discipline me. This activity was performed with great hesitation, and I'm sure it hurt her more than it did me. She never asked her brother, Walter G. Robertson, to take me in tow or discipline me in any way — that was entirely her job.

About 1925, my grandfather returned to La Jolla to stay. I remember him as a very formal, serious man, always dressed in coat, vest, tie and hat whenever he left the house to walk to the Fuel and Feed Store to sit, smoke his pipe, and talk to Walter or customers, and watch the world go by. He died in 1928, and I recall the wicker casket bearing his body being carried from the house. Both my grandfather and uncle accepted me with familial affection and tolerance, but neither of them became a father image to me. At no time did they or Marguerite counsel me about the facts of life — that finally came without any accurate or objective advice from any source.

We always had at least one pet, the favorite being Toby, a black cat with white paws and nose. He joined the Navy as a kitten in Brooklyn, New York, in the early 1920's, and traveled to many places including a trip through the Panama Canal to Australia on board the destroyer tender *Altair* in 1925 then on to San Diego where he came to us by way of the Neyman family. He was a pretty smart cat. He could open the front door of the Chalet, if not locked, by reaching up to the loose doorknob with his out-stretched paw and turning or jiggling the doorknob until it became unlatched; then he would push against the door until it opened. He also could enter the house through a small screened window opening onto the roof; if the window and screen were left unlocked, which was usually the case, all he had to do was to push the screen with his nose and paw and jump down to the floor of the second story bathroom…. He would sit on the front stoop in the late afternoon waiting for Marguerite to return from her real estate activities. She, being the provider, was Toby's principal object of affection. Sadly, he disappeared for several weeks one fall, returning home late one night via the upstairs bathroom window. He was all skin and bones, shaggy and unkempt, and his paws were tough and scarred. With care, he quickly recovered, and lived for several more years before being buried under a rose bush in the backyard….

In the early 1920's, a cottage was added behind the Chalet. One winter about 1930 it was occupied by Mrs. Whittaker, whose husband operated several general stores and gas stations in Yellowstone National Park. Through her I was able to get summer jobs in Yellowstone for two years running, my first working experience away from home. The woodshed next to this cottage was covered with gorgeous morning glory vines; I see them now, fresh in the morning sun. From there, when there was a mild Santa Ana weather pattern, we could hear the "pings' of rifle shots, sometimes slow and sometimes rapid fire, from the Marine Corps Rifle Range located above Scripps Institute.

John Forward, head of the Union Title Insurance Company and later mayor of San Diego, had been a business associate and friend of my father's when he was County Treasurer. For several years following Corrie's death John stayed in touch with Marguerite. Each time he appeared at the house on his brief visits he would take me aside, put his arm around my shoulder and silently put into my hand a beautiful shiny silver dollar coin. That was always an exciting treat. Esther Roth, who worked for the Yellowstone Park Hotel Company in its winter quarters in La Jolla at the head of Exchange Place, lived with us one year. She remained a family friend until her death in the early 1980's. Marguerite and Jessica frequently baked angel food cakes (hand beaten eggs, too) for sale to the Women's Exchange on Wall Street, owned and operated by Mr. and Mrs. Hunter.

Events and activities in Roslyn Lane, particularly around the Chalet, never seemed to end. For most of these years Marguerite was active full time in the real estate business, first working for Nellie Mills, and then later on her own. She was also involved in the Women's Club, the Christian Science Church, and other activities as well as caring for her three children. She also had acquired a new black two door Ford sedan which was a joy to all of us. Jessica and Lyle assisted in the housework — cooking and cleaning. I had a paper route from age six on, and I "worked in the yard" pulling weeds for Walter S. Lieber at ten cents an hour. Neither my sisters nor I seemed to have any major problems in school, and we progressed along year by year. Once in awhile we became involved in readying houses for rent, by being given jobs inventorying linens, keys, silver, and utensils, or watering plants. I recall being quite familiar with the two cottages Brownie I and Brownie II, across from the Cove, for I could combine swimming with chores. Our household laundry at the Chalet was done by Wo Lee's Chinese Hand Laundry on Fay Street. Wo Lee, the owner, was a happy, smiling, smelly, cheerful person with horrible breath and worse teeth, but he produced clean laundry. He drove a Model T Ford touring car with great abandon; all people and animals stayed out of his way when he appeared. He invariably drove up to the Chalet at high speed, and, having no brakes, would press the middle (reverse) pedal down until the rear wheels spun in reverse, stopping the car with a shudder. At the time of Chinese New Year he would appear at the front door laden with mounds of Chinese goodies wrapped in red such as ginger, rice cakes, kumquats, tea, leechinuts, and sugar coated coconut slices. He could not be outdone. Our household groceries, other than raw milk which was delivered by Rannell's Dairy, fruits and vegetables obtained from Charley, the Chinaman, and breads and cakes from Fay's Bakery, came from the Barnes and Calloway Grocery Store on Girard Street. The Calloways lived not far from us, and Mr. Galloway, slim, quick, well dressed in shirt and tie, cheerful and sociable walked to work in the morning, pencil and receipt book in hand, stopping at most of his customers' back doors on the way to take orders for delivery later in the day. It was a happy day when my paper boy and weed pulling activities produced enough money for me to buy, with Marguerite's help, a second hand bicycle.

Rannell's Dairy for years delivered only rich raw milk. Normally the cream at the top of the bottles was skimmed off before being placed in the screened "cooler," built on the outside of the Chalet's kitchen wall, but entered by a door from inside the kitchen. On cold January mornings if the bottles had not been "skimmed," the rich cream would expand and freeze, pushing out through the tops of the bottles. Our small ice box was really a supplement to the cooler.

On Thanksgiving and Christmas, our turkeys were taken early in the morning to Fay's Bakery for roasting in his mammoth bread oven. Mr. Fay made the best cinnamon rolls I've ever eaten; the trick was that he made them with bread dough — there were no egg yolks used.

An occasional tramp would knock at the back door for a handout, which was invariably given. Gypsies, in horse drawn wagons, passed along Prospect Street once or twice. Aviation had its place in Roslyn Lane, too. At the time of Charles A. Lindbergh's flight in the Spirit of St. Louis in 1927, the Chalet was quarantined, as I had the measles. The afternoon after the flight I sat on the front steps waiting for the paper boy, Ramon Molina, to appear so I could learn the latest about that great event. When Ramon appeared, we read all there was about the flight, and then talked for a good half hour speculating on the future of airplanes and their influence on ships and automobiles. It was about this time that, each evening at about eight o'clock to the east of town, one could hear the Ford trimotor airmail plane on its daily flight from San Diego to Los Angeles. Also, Major Dexter Rumsey, "The Major," was an object of aviation interest, as it was said that he had been in the U.S. Army Air Corps and that an airplane accident had brought about his medical discharge from the Air Corps.

The Major was truly one of La Jolla's unique characters. He lived with his mother and sister in the Tyrolean Colony on Prospect Street, and frequently used the Lane as a thoroughfare to downtown La Jolla and the public tennis courts on Draper Street, rackets and a string bag of tennis balls in hand. Often he was accompanied by his mother and sister, or a cousin, always dressed in all cream-colored long sleeved costumes, almost to the ground, and white tennis shoes. The Major was an excellent horse back rider, tennis player and swimmer, and I believe those activities consumed most of his daily life. He was a well built man, well proportioned, muscular, blond with a nice friendly smile, and sun tanned over most of his hairy body. His tennis garb usually consisted of a white, short sleeved knit shirt, dozens of silver bracelets on each arm, white billowing girls' gym bloomers pulled above his knees, and white, low smart looking tennis shoes arid half-length white socks. His dress, combined with his beautiful athlete's physique, and a high pitched voice, marked him as a person one would not soon forget. He was always friendly to me, but never offered to bring me into his world of tennis or swimming. Now and then he rode his horse down the Lane, always dressed properly in correct riding garb. He was a strong swimmer and could often be seen standing on or diving from "the Major's rock," a small one person water-level rock just off alligator head. I did not know at the time, but learned later that he had been married to Rhoda Worth from La Mesa, and that she and her husband had had two children, a boy and a girl. Years later, in 1951, the Major's son, Dexter Rumsey, Junior, and I, both Captains in the Navy, were shipmates in the cruiser USS *Des Moines* on the staff of the Commander U.S. Sixth Fleet in the Mediterranean. Dexter, Junior, and I, not knowing, talked at some length about our pasts late one afternoon at a lonely, desolate Greek Air Force airfield somewhere on Peloponnesus, Greece, while waiting for a plane from one of our aircraft carriers to come pick us up. We quickly discovered that we had several unusual things in common, i.e. that we both came from the San Diego area, that neither one of us had known his own father, and that we both knew of the Major. At the time of their parents' divorce the children went to live with their mother at her parents' home, and apparently never were given the opportunity to continue to know their father....

Roslyn Lane Ramblings must end as I've written enough for now about what it was like growing up in La Jolla. (recorded for Barbara Dawson, December 10, 1988)

La Jolla Develops and Expands
Before and After The Great War

We retain in mind as permanent possessions the memory of many physical and material things that have passed away from sight. Our memories are also spiritual possessions to be brought up at will for our enjoyment, encouragement and inspiration.
Written in 1917

Early life in La Jolla was pleasant despite the living conditions being what we today would consider primitive. All of the people knew one another. Doors were never locked. Notices were put on the Post Office wall inviting everyone to join the party or dance on a Saturday night at the Pavilion. The little colony was also becoming quite a cultural center. Clubs were organized and the library was established. La Jolla's innate beauty, lovely climate, and its developing charm attracted many visitors any of whom could rent a cottage near the Cove. When our country became involved in World War I, soldiers were stationed at Camp Kearney just east of La Jolla on the mesa. The soldiers brought their families and La Jolla grew. In turn, a few years later, land developers subdivided more of the area into La Jolla Hermosa, the Muirlands, and La Jolla Shores.

In the early 1920s, R. C. Rose, a gentleman who had come to La Jolla from Germantown, Pennsylvania with his young family, started a spectacular real estate development. Standing at the northern base of Mt. Soledad, Mr. Rose gazed north toward the George G. Scripps Memorial

Jackie Coogan (in sailor suit) on the auctioneer's stand during the La Jolla Shores land sale. Barbara Gaines (Dawson), between Jackie Coogan and the cameraman, was caught climbing on the auctioneer's stand.
Courtesy of Barbara Dawson

La Jolla Shores from Mt. Soledad before any development,
about the time of Mr. R. C. Rose, 1925.
Courtesy of San Diego Historical Society Photograph Collection

Building (the only building of Scripps Institution of Oceanography at the time) and surveyed the virgin flatlands. In the spring and summer the land was covered with tall, wild mustard (a good screen for bootleggers who once landed on this La Jolla beach). The so-called flatlands was bordered on the west by the Pacific Ocean and to the north by the Torrey Pines Grade that rose up to the village of La Jolla. To the east was the coastal range. Mr. Rose was a man of vision. He contacted his grandmother, Mrs. Lowry (in Germantown), requesting a financial loan in order to purchase 550 acres of this land. With his grandmother's funds, he bought the land, had it surveyed, and then planned a big, colorful land sale.

Notices were posted. A bandstand was erected in the middle of the acreage and the famous child star from Hollywood, Jackie Coogan, was the stellar attraction. Crowds came. Many lots were auctioned off to eager buyers. However, it was ten years before much building occurred on the La Jolla Shores. One couple bought two lots but, after a decade of paying taxes, traded their La Jolla Shores property for two lots in Pacific Beach. Bad timing! It was soon after this transaction that the La Jolla lots escalated in value far surpassing those of Pacific Beach.

In the proper town of La Jolla, up the hill from La Jolla Shores, lots averaged $500. All lots (and cars) were paid for in cash in those days. There were many empty lots and the houses were just scattered around. Aside from a few roads (and they were dirt), there were no alleys in La Jolla, just lanes like Drury Lane, Bishops Lane, and Roslyn Lane. The early citizens walked everywhere and the children spent entire summer days at the Cove. There were wooden steps down to the sand and in the beginning, there was no bath house above the Cove. No need, explained one "old timer" because there were very few tourists. Everyone knew each other and summer people were made welcome by natives. Instead of spending the summer day at the Cove, sometimes the children hiked or picnicked on the slopes of Mount Soledad. "We would save (sticky buns) to eat when we sat very high up (or so I thought) with a perfect view of 'my' ocean. And not a house in sight," said one "old timer." Mount Soledad was barren except for dry sagebrush and the indigenous population of bobcats, skunks, and trap-door spiders.

Harle Garth Montgomery recalls, "In 1928 or so, there was the beginning of a real estate boom. A developer had put in a network of roads and bridges between Hillside Drive and Country Club Drive. Then the bust came and no one bought any property leaving the construction site to us. We pushed our bicycles to the top and then, whooping and whistling, we coasted madly down hill in a frenzy only to turn around and push up again! Under the bridges, we built forts of mud and stones and stocked them with mud balls in case an enemy appeared. The concrete railings of the bridges challenged us too. A good 10 to 12 inches wide, we had to walk across at least one to amount to anything. To-day, when I look at the one I crossed, my heart leaps. If our parents had known!"

Although the real estate boom of the twenties stopped suddenly with the crash of 1929, on the whole La Jolla breezed through the Depression years without much visible change. The 1930 Blue Book cover stated that la Jolla was "the new Riviera" with a "population of substantial people…reserved but not narrow." Max Miller, a La Jolla writer, observed, "Some of us here have been important once — elsewhere." But, he adds philosophically, "they outgrew it." As for the younger people, they "may hope some day to become important, whatever that means, but most likely they will have to leave to do so." (Or, as Georgeanna Lipe says, "La Jolla was a place where old people came to visit their parents. Most everybody had been

La Jolla Shores in 1929 was a surf-swimmers' paradise, a beautiful long beach, virtually uninhabited during the week. The few Spanish-style houses were erected just before the Depression, and the land was sparsely occupied until after the W.W.II. The Scripps Institution of Oceanography with its pier (top of the picture) became the nucleus, in the 1960s, around which the La Jolla campus of the University of California, San Diego, was built.
Courtesy of San Diego Historical Society Photograph Collection

somebody somewhere else.") Meanwhile, tourists continued to come to relax and enjoy the sea, the tide pools, the ambiance, and the serenity of this "little town with a funny name." By 1936, the population was 4000, but on the weekends and in the summer, it increased dramatically and the old poem was still apropos:

> *"You too don't care if nobody knows*
> *Why this is thus and these are those,*
> *For this is La Jolla where everything goes.*" John R. E. Sumner, 1913.

In the 1960s, Barbara Dawson recorded some of the then 'old timers.' Gene McCormack's recording describes so well life as it was growing up in La Jolla in the '20s and early '30s. Gene came to La Jolla with his family at the age of three in 1920. His father worked at the Evide Battery and Electric Station at Hershel and Prospect across from the Cabrillo Hotel. The block from Hershel to Girard had numerous small stores including Dr. Gillespie's office the police station and a radio shop. The family lived on Herschel next to a horse stable on Torrey Pines Rd. By the time Gene began Junior-Senior High School, the stable was gone.

Tape begins: *Gene McCormick 1917-1984*

"A new Presbyterian Church was being built and the old wooden one was moved onto the property where the stable had been. It became the American Legion Hall…Mr. Talboy (at the Rec center) always had something going on for boys…we weren't quite old enough to notice girls yet, but we sure did play a lot of ball there.

"…that Children's Pool down by the Casa de Mañana was something! I helped build that and inspected it a lot. There's a sandy beach there but it's not supposed to be a beach because right close to where that concrete wall is connected to the mainland, there was a tunnel under there with sliding doors…and it's supposed to be so you could lift those doors and water would run through and wash all that sand out so you could have a pool where you don't get sandy before you went swimming. You went down the steps and jumped in. But this fellow who designed it was also the fellow who designed the first dam across the Nile River in Egypt but he probably never monkeyed around with the ocean . . . We could watch the water, but it didn't take too long for mother nature to just fill that up and I don't think they have opened those for generations.

"Before that Cove was the original one. You know, the one with the alligator head and all that. That's where I learned to swim…. You went down to the Cove with your bathing suit on. Mine was made of wool, had a shirt and had two buttons on the shoulder…(the Cove was the) place to swim…. And there were some row boats there that sometimes people would use them and they would be there for a long time. After awhile, they'd let us kids borrow them and I remember the time they let us borrow canoes with paddles and we went clear over to Spindrift Beach over by the La Jolla Beach and Yacht Club. Riding a surf in a canoe is impossible. You get in, pretty soon it turns broadside, and you roll. That's called 'broaching'. Oh boy, one moonlit night…no, I won't tell about the time I rode the girl around Scripps Pier in a canoe…. There is all kinds of things you can do . . .but surfing in a canoe isn't the thing to do."

Anna Held and the Green Dragon Colony

"for years the best known place in La Jolla"

"One hundred and sixty-five dollars. And it's a bargain! Fifty feet along the street, some 200 feet deep, and it widens like a fan so that it is 150 feet along the seashore. It's a bargain, I tell you!" said Dr. Rhodes. Anna Held made the deal giving the doctor a $50.00 deposit on the land, sight unseen. Three days later, Mr. and Mrs. Ulysses S. Grant, Jr. drove their nanny to see her "estate" by the sea. "The air was soft and balmy, a gentle breeze from the ocean caressed the blue expanse of False Bay (now Mission Bay), the hills wore the velvet of a springtime green." From San Diego, they drove two hours before reaching La Jolla. "The three left the carriage, and Anna led the way to her 'estate'. The view was breathtaking! From the level on which they stood the land fell sharply to the edge of the ocean. Across the narrow inlet bay, near by, rose a kindred height, with a rough, rocky point jutting out into the sea. Then began a magnificent sweep of yellow shore — a rim of golden cliffs, curving far to the westward clasped the ocean's cobalt blue like a jewel. The sight was wonderful… ." Anna stayed for several minutes transfixed, staring out to sea, smelling the salt air, listening to the pounding surf as it attacked the cliffs and swelled in and out of the cave below. This was to be the first home of her very own.

Anna Held's first house on her "estate," c. 1894.
Courtesy of Barbara Dawson

Anna Held was born Nov. 3, 1849 in Berlin, Germany. She was the fifth child out of a total of ten. As a youngster, she loved playing the piano. She became a pupil at the Neue Akademie der Tonkunst (affectionately referred to as "Kullak's Academy") in Berlin. Theodor Kullak (1818-1882) was one of the greatest teachers of the nineteenth century with a list of pupils almost as comprehensive as that of Franz Liszt. It is clear that Miss Held was a fine musician, but at some point she decided to leave

Germany and come to the United States as a governess. Because of her training in Germany (which included working with Dr. Froebel's theory of educating a child as early as his third year), she was encouraged to start a "Kindergarten" in New York City. Opening in the 1870s, it was the first of its kind in the United States. In 1876, at the Centennial Exposition in Philadelphia, Anna conducted daily demonstrations of the "Froebel Kindergarten System of child training." Despite her success with schooling the youth, Anna preferred being with a family. When the Ulysses S. Grant, Jr. family decided to move west for health reasons, they asked Miss Held to join them and be the nanny for their three girls and one boy. She was happy to accept. Sometime in 1892, they arrived in San Diego.

Although San Diego was a beautiful place to live, the Grants and their nanny preferred relaxing in a quaint little village just up the coast. Located on a promontory jutting out to sea, La Jolla was different from any place Anna Held had ever seen. With its primitive simplicity and its exquisite natural beauty, stretching straight out into a sapphire blue ocean, La Jolla was for Anna and the Grants a jewel, the epitome of serenity. Besides the sea and surf and sky, there was the air, salty and dry and soothing. Upon their return to San Diego, Anna and the children couldn't wait until their next trip back up to La Jolla. They traveled there often. So when the land was offered to her, Anna jumped at the chance to own a small piece of the jewel.

The first structure she built on this land was a fireplace. It was constructed from rocks she had gathered on her own property. Methodically, she placed each one herself. For awhile, the fireplace stood alone. Later, with the help of a young architect friend she had met in San Diego, Anna had a house built around her beloved fireplace. The architect was Irving Gill "whose love for house designing," she wrote, "was coupled with ability." For this first commission, Irving Gill received $15, five percent of the total cost. "Inch thick boards, ten inches wide, battened with two inch strips formed the bungalow. Eight steps led to the front porch. A Dutch door 'broken in two in the middle' led into a room 16 x 16 feet, out of which extended a tiny kitchen, 4 x 6 feet, and the corner diagonally across the room was the staircase that led to the bedroom above. Leaded windows…lent a hint of age to the room." However, the main attraction was the fireplace, the "altar" of hospitality.

Compared to the prior photo, Anna Held's home Wahnfried was growing up, c. 1900. There are now early eucalyptus trees planted.
Courtesy of J. Wilson

The following Thanksgiving, Anna invited the Grant family, including the wife of the former President of the United States, Mrs. U. S. Grant, Sr., her children and grandchildren, to come and celebrate the holiday in her new home. The Grants arrived in four carriages, bringing along their entire household staff and family. Together they sat around a blazing fire while the feast cooked in its flames.

One day Anna took a new friend, Kate Sessions (whom she had met at the Grant's), out to her property. Kate had brought what looked like sticks with her. (Miss Sessions would one day be recognized as San Diego's "pioneer horticulturist." Mr. Marston called her "the Queen Mother of the Whole Floral Kingdom.") Together, the ladies planted the "sticks" which Kate said would become giant Eucalyptus trees to shade and beautify the property. She warned Anna that they would need plenty of water. Water at that time cost 40 cents per barrel in La

Jolla, so Anna tried to be economical. One day she noticed some white strings fluttering from the planted "sticks." Upon examination, she found in Kate Sessions' handwriting the terse message: "This tree needs water!" Anna was more careful after that, watering them plentifully. The heavens helped too when the rainy season came. Before long, the "sticks" grew into saplings and ultimately into magnificent trees. Soon scrubs and flowers were planted and winding steps were built leading down to the beach.

Knowing that she had purchased the property in La Jolla, many of Anna's friends wrote indicating their interest in coming to visit her. They urged Anna to build more little cottages or even set up tents. In 1902 she borrowed $2000 from General William J. Palmer, for whose family she had previously served as governess before joining the Grants to purchase additional lots above the Cove. Thus began the collection of tiny houses that would come to be known as the Green Dragon Colony, "for years the best known place in La Jolla." It was the author of the novel, *At the Sign of the Green Dragon*, Beatrice Haraden, who ultimately named the little "colony" of cottages. And it was here, on the point that extends into the sea just across the inlet from the "Colony," that Miss Haraden wrote *Ships that Pass in the Night*, considered her best work.

This magical spot would become a place of inspiration for many authors, poets, artists, and musicians through the years. La Jolla was that kind of place and Anna Held was that kind of lady. One day, Anna bought an upright piano in San Diego. Once it was delivered, however, there was no room big enough for it to fit in her little house. Like the fireplace before, the piano stood alone covered by a tarpaulin for protection against the elements. "Long time plans were not part of Anna's agenda but longtime dreams were," wrote Havrah Hubbard. When walls and a roof were built around and over the piano, the music room came into being.

Anna was a gifted pianist but she wanted to her share delight in music. One day, Anna and a young violinist she had met in San Diego got together and practiced for two days. Then they put up a notice at the Post Office (located in the Dance Pavilion in the park behind the Cove) inviting everyone to hear music at the Green Dragon. The grocery man and his wife, a German farmer from up the coast, the Misses Scripps who were about to build "a large house just a little farther down the coast," Portuguese fishermen from down the other end of the coast at Long Beach (now La Jolla Shores) with their young families, "wealth and culture sat side by side with poverty and the illiterate." The magic of music leveled them all. Anna and her "boy," Fred Baker, thus performed the first concert in La Jolla. The concerts became weekly affairs and were only the beginning of Anna Held's remarkable influence on the early history of La Jolla.

Anna started a kindergarten. She also knitted, darned, sowed, dressed dolls, and made

The Green Dragon Camp along Prospect Street.
Courtesy of Barbara Dawson

A later view of Anna Held's Green Dragon Colony house with modern day transportation and mature eucalyptus trees.
Courtesy of Barbara Dawson

decorative fish nets. This was a lady who never wasted time. She shared her talents with the locals and gave away most of the items she made.

The Green Dragon Colony in La Jolla Park, Southern California (the address in those days) was the veritable cultural center of La Jolla. Each cottage she had built was unique and its name only bore testimony to this: The Arc, Gables, The Wigwam, Kleiber Aber Mein, Open Door, Wahnfried, The Den, The Barn, The Outlook, Matterhorn, and The Studio were some of her cottages that covered the hillside above the sea.

Some of Anna Held's guests included Madame Helena Modjeska (Polish actress who lived in the United States after 1876, considered among the greatest tragic actresses of her time, especially in Shakespearian plays.), Ignace Jan Paderewski (Polish statesman, composer, and pianist making his American debut in 1891), Dame Ellen Terry (Shakespearean stage performer and Anna's best friend), and Beatrice Harradan. Miss Held, who had a genius for everything she undertook, also opened a tea room where "the weariness, the fever and the fret" of modern life would seem dim and distant. Her concept was, "If you prefer the picturesque to the conventional, atmosphere to style; if you care for individuality that is gracious, informality that is refined; if you know that art is a necessity, not a luxury in life, that beauty is a food and drink; if you are one of these, …the Green Dragon will cast its subtle spell upon you!"

One day while she was relaxing with a book, Anna heard some beautiful piano music and the voice of a talented soprano. Looking for the source of this lovely sound, she found two musicians. They were introduced as Max Heinrich, a well-known pianist and baritone, and his daughter, Julie. There must have been electricity in that first meeting for the very next day, Max proposed. Anna, who had never been married, was already past fifty. She asked Max to continue his musical tour of the United States and possibly reconsider, but after many letters, he returned from his tour on Oct. 7, 1904 to rekindle the relationship. Several weeks later, prodded by friends, Max asked Anna to marry him. The Grants arranged a wedding breakfast after the marriage ceremony. Madame Modjeska was a bridesmaid, Wheeler J. Bailey was the "congregation" and Count Bozenta was best man. Anna built a home for Max named Wahnfried (spirit-peace). "Anna and Max lived a life of music and pleasure at Wahnfried." Meanwhile, life went on at "The Green Dragon" with visitors and guests coming and going.

In a letter written February 28, 1905, Anna wrote: "Alice Dear, If you had settled the bill with me you would have had a reduction for good behavior but perhaps you would have scorned the idea of getting 'rates' at a hotel so all is well and thank you. Yes, the watch was found at once by the faithful Lena & she gave it to me & I carefully packed it in a little box (as the front had come off) took it to town & intended to telephone & ask you where to leave it but I didn't get to telephoning so I brought it back again & will leave it wherever you say. You are a Dear & I hope you will soon come again & I am always, Your loving, Tante." At the bottom of the letter she added, "My Max would send love but he is in Los Angeles hustling for our bread & butter." The letter, preserved over the years, lends some understanding of "Tante" Anna Held Heinrich's personality, a giving and caring individual. It is also interesting to note that she needed to go "to town" to use a telephone.

However, despite the constant turnover of guests, it wasn't long before the newlywed Max and Anna decided to travel to Europe. They wanted to be able to introduce each to the other's family and friends. Anna sold some of her property to provide funds for the trip which they needed since they preferred staying at the most expensive hotels and sailed on the most expensive ocean liners. One day, while they were in Germany, the police came to the door where Max and Anna were staying. Apparently, Max had not served in the military some thirty years earlier. He explained to the police that he had left Germany when he was young and had become an American citizen. The police explained that under those circumstances, his visit was limited by the timeframe of a visa: only three months. While her husband had to return to America, Anna was able to remain a little longer. She traveled about visiting family and friends, but finally, it was time to return to La Jolla. She needed to attend to her property, which had been sorely neglected in her absence. Max in the meantime was performing on the east coast. His plan was to return to La Jolla after two years, but he became ill and died soon after.

Eventually, Anna sold all of the Green Dragon Colony. The property that had originally cost $2165, sold for $30,000 with all its cottages. Anna continued to live in La Jolla on and off until shortly before her death. She wanted to take one last trip to Europe (she had been back forty-four times) and revisit places and people she had known earlier in her life. No longer having to take an ocean liner, Anna now enjoyed the freedom of flight. While in England, staying with Dorothy Palmer, the baby she had cared for so many years before, she died. It was December 14, 1941. Anna was ninety-three.

Anna had been happy all her life. She attracted the rich and famous like John Wakefield, Fritz Kreisler, Algernon (Charles) Swineburne, Robert Browning, Sarah Bernhardt, John Singer Sargent, and Walter Damrosche, as well as not-so-rich, everyday people. Everyone in La Jolla loved her.

Guests often inscribed notes to Anna carved into the beams of her cottage. One such beam has been preserved at the Athenaeum Library of the Arts and Music in La Jolla. The following are the inscriptions found inscribed on the two sides of the big beam.

"To Tante with love" followed by musical notes and "Charles Wakefield Cadman, 1918."

"Because I love you dearly, 10-24-18 M. E. N."

"Snug as a bug n a rug," H.-

"Wenig aber herzlich H. G. L. 1902"

"Music breathes what poet cannot write MA Sept 1900."

Ed note: Many of the quotations were taken from *The Joyous Child* a "personality sketch" by Havrah Hubbard, "1939, Jan. 26 Cozella" (another name for Anna Held).

A Dramatic Cave Creates
History and Commerce

Sand-strewn caverns, cool and deep, Where the winds are all asleep.
Matthew Arnold

Reportedly the oldest continuously operating business in La Jolla, the La Jolla Cave and Curio Shop evolved from the Cave Curio Store. Originally a cluster of one to two story board and batten shacks and cabins, the building was developed as a means for its owner — Professor Gustav Schulz, artist, photographer, professor, and engineer — to control access to the entrance of a man-made tunnel leading down to the nearby Sunny Jim Cave.

In 1902 Prof. Schulz bought the land above the cave from Miss Anna Held. One of the reasons he had chosen to live in San Diego was the existence of a colony of fellow German-Americans who had gravitated to the oceanfront village of La Jolla. The nucleus of this German-American enclave was focused in and around the "Green Dragon Colony." A ragtag collection of beach cottages hugging the hillside above La Jolla Cove, the Green Dragon Colony was organized by a native of Germany, Miss Anna Held, as a free-spirited artists' colony.

Although born in Germany, Prof. Schultz was raised in the Falkland Islands. As an adult, he traveled extensively, gathering works of art from every place that he visited. The art work was stored on the Falkland Islands. When he decided to remain in La Jolla, Prof. Schultz put up a building (which is the entrance to the cave) as a place to store all those works of art. When the

Professor Schultz with some of his extensive art collection.
Courtesy of La Jolla Historical Society

The small cabin (center) was the first building on the site where Professor Schultz sunk his tunnel.
Courtesy of La Jolla Historical Society

shipment arrived from the Falkland Islands, he immediately opened it. Inside were hundreds of empty beer bottles. Thieves had gone through, removing everything. This theft cost him about $50,000. He tried to collect insurance, but because he couldn't prove whether the theft had taken place on the ocean or on land, he was unable to recover any financial compensation.

It has been speculated that is was the loss of his life's possessions which forced Prof. Schulz to seek another means to sustain himself during his retirement years. Intrigued by the cave's unique geological features, he thought of a plan to profit by them. On one hand, he believed fellow scientists could use the interior of the cave to study the earth's strata. And, as a professor of geology, he also thought that the cave could be used to teach geological formations to the public. As a civil engineer, he would come up with a plan to make the interior of the cave more accessible to the general public and to his fellow scientists. On the other hand, near destitute, the professor also sought to find some means of income; therefore, he would charge admission.

Occupying a tiny studio cabin overlooking Goldfish Point, the land above the cave, Prof. Schulz began the work to sink a shaft down to the rear of the cave. November 1, 1903 two men began digging the tunnel. One man dug into the sandstone, piling earth into a wheelbarrow. Then the full barrow was hauled up the steep shaft by a rope to the other man who emptied it and returned it to the man below. By April 9th after months of digging through the soft sandstone, the tunnel was completed. Soon, it was opened to visitors who paid a small fee to climb down 125-feet. There were no stairs in those days so visitors had to use a rope anchored into the wall of the tunnel by eyebolts in order to keep from sliding. Because of its low ceiling, the descent into the cave and the ascent to the surface usually meant crawling on one's hands and knees using the rope for stability. 133 steps and a wooden platform at the foot of the tunnel were added in 1920.

Quite a dandy, the good professor was often seen swimming with a hat or floating while smoking a pipe. He was also quite popular with the ladies of La Jolla. Only after his death, on Dec. 19, 1912, did La Jollans find out that he had left a wife and seven children back in Germany. Or did he? According to Dr. Joshua L. Bailey, Jr., a member of the first Board of Counselors of the Torrey Pines Association and a La Jollan since 1902, the Professor's wife did not live in Germany. When Joshua Bailey was a child, he was an invalid and his mother found it difficult to watch him and do the housework and cooking as well. She hired a young woman named Dora Anderson to come to the house a few hours every day. At the end of the week, when it was time to pay Dora, Mrs. Bailey asked if she would accept a personal check. "Oh,

I couldn't do that," Dora replied. "If I did that I would have to endorse the check and everybody would know who I am. My name is not Dora Anderson; that's just what I call myself because I don't want my father to find out what I am doing here." Dora was from Wisconsin, but she didn't like it there. Her father would not approve of her living and working as a housekeeper in La Jolla. But that was not the whole story. Dora said she had a sister back in Wisconsin whose husband had deserted her and her children. "And he lives here in La Jolla. I know him, but he doesn't know me and I hate to think what he might do to me if he found out who I am." That man was Professor Schultz. When the Professor died, his estranged son came to La Jolla to settle the estate. So, Dr. Bailey says, "I guess Dora's story was quite correct the way she told it."

Meanwhile, of the Seven Sisters Caves at the base of the cliffs, Prof. Schulz' tunnel has made Sunny Jim the only one accessible by a means other than water. Over the years, visitors not envisioned by the professor have been attracted to the cave and tunnel. Smugglers have used it to bring in illegal Chinese and other immigrants. Contraband whiskey was also smuggled through the cave during Prohibition. More recently, on a positive note, the cave's accessibility has made it favorable for staging and filming pirate movies.

Approximately 10 to 15 feet north of the present cave curio shop along the northwestern entrance to the Coast Walk stood the Crescent Café. Photographic evidence indicates that the café was a classically inspired vernacular style commercial building built in a "D" shape to follow the contours of its site.

La Jolla Cliffs with the Seven Sisters Caves and Coast Walk.
Courtesy of La Jolla Historical Society

The Crescent Café
Courtesy of La Jolla Historical Society

Sunny Jim Cave
Courtesy of Steele Lipe

Photographs of the building have been dated approximately 1913-14 because the cafe burnt down sometime after that. While the Café no longer exists, its site should be recognized for its symbiotic relationship with the Cave Curio Store. Clearly, its business depended on refreshing visitors from Sunny Jim Cave after their vigorous trek up the tunnel shaft. In addition, it was one of several cafes and diners that catered to La Jolla's burgeoning tourist population during the early part of the 20th century. Unfortunately, because of its short life-span, there is a dearth of information about the Café.

In the new Millennium, the spirit of Anna Held's tea room has been revived with the opening of the new Cave Store in the building that replaced the Crescent Café. For twenty-two years, this had been the Shell Shop. Today, with photographs and paintings of early La Jolla hanging on the walls, the Cave Store and its unique garden is a place to relax and enjoy exotic teas and coffees. The garden was actually a discovery for the new owner of the property, Jim Allen. "When the Shell Shop owned the place," he said, "there was no way to get to the garden…it was all covered over on one whole rock wall. I found the door which led to the garden." So history comes back because the place where the garden is now was the site of the old Crescent Café. Mr. Allen, a thirty-five year resident of La Jolla says that he is proud and privileged to be able to preserve a little of La Jolla's heritage. In the year 2002, the cave store will celebrate 100 years of business making it the oldest business in La Jolla. "We've been here since 1902 and we'll be open for another 100 years," said Jim Allen speaking for the cave. "It's a historic site. It's also a lovely business."

From La Jolla's Sand Dunes
Come the Barber Tract Tales

Lives of great men all remind us
We can make our lives sublime,
And, departing, leave behind us
Footprints in the sands of time.
Henry Wadsworth Longfellow

Dr. James Mills Boal and his wife, Alma White, and their two daughters, Alma and Ione, moved to La Jolla in 1898. Originally from Ohio, James Mills Boal graduated from Hanneman College in New York with a degree of Doctor of Medicine; however, when he came to La Jolla with his family, it was not to practice medicine, but to retire. La Jolla was scarcely populated in those days and with so few residents, it was no secret that the doctor was there and that he still had his license. Many sought his help and he was gracious about assisting those in need. It could be said that, although he never had a medical office, in essence, Dr. Boal was La Jolla's first doctor.

The first house they lived in was called the Ford House, one of the first built in the center of town. Soon it became too crowded so they moved to a house "under the hill." According to Alma, the oldest daughter, "While we lived there Miss Ellen Scripps had a party for one of the Kellogg girls…. Mr. Chase, the grocer, brought his delivery wagon and took us all down to the Scripps place, which was considered out of town."

Alma and her sister attended the school which, Alma wrote, "was above the livery stable in a two story building. There was no fourth grade then. In fact, they had only eighty pupils the year before and were considering closing." The school was actually on the second floor

The Chase & Ludington store, c. 1900, located on the corner of Grand (Girard) and Prospect. The first school was located on the second floor before the building was moved from Wall Street to this location.
Courtesy of The Athenaeum Music and Arts Library

of the Heald store on Wall Street, but instead of closing the school, it was the store that was moved (to the corner of Girard and Prospect, becoming the Chase and Ludington store) and a new school was built. This school was partially donated by members of the community and was constructed on land that had belonged to Mr. Botsford on the west side of Herschel just south of Wall Street. It wasn't until 1906 that a more elaborate, two-story school was built approximately where the Stella Maris Academy is now. Both schools were painted red.

Soon the Boal family was ready to move again, this time "out west" to the sand dunes. The first summer, the family lived in a tent. When school started, the family must have built a home and a stable because Alma wrote that she walked or rode horseback to school.

Soon the good doctor took up a second vocation, developing land. He and his wife bought some of the railroad land held by the San Diego Land & Town Company. In 1899, the Boal's south La Jolla property, which they named Neptunia (after running a contest), went from the ocean front to the foothills in the east, and from the Scripps Property on the north to below the railroad station (now the Methodist Church) to the south. Some of the property sold; some went for taxes.

The property east of the railroad (where the La Jolla Elementary School is now) was sold to the Ben Genters. "The Maxwells also bought north of the sand dunes and built a two story house with an upstairs outside toilet which was a conversation piece to the travelers on the train," wrote Alma in her notebook.

At the advice of Miss Scripps, a portion of property was sold in order that Alma might attend Normal School (Teachers College). As a result, Alma became a teacher. In 1911, she married Louis Edward Stockton of Ramona. They had seven children. Somehow, motherhood did not prevent Alma from returning to the teaching profession. In 1929, after thirty-five years teaching first and second grades in the San Diego County schools, Alma Stockton was presented with a "life diploma" by the California State Board of Education.

In 1921, Philip P. Barber purchased the property between Marine Street to the north and Fern Glen to the south, the ocean to the west and La Jolla Boulevard to the east from Dr. Boal. Mr. Barber had retired and came to La Jolla from Englewood, New Jersey where he had been vice-president of the Barber & Company Steamship firm founded by his father. The land he purchased contained two large sand dunes. It was a beautiful, remote, and quiet place with a lovely beach enclosed at either end by rock formations full of tide pools and interesting crevices. In 1923, Mr. Barber finished construction of a Spanish Colonial oceanfront home on Dunemere Drive, in the midst of the dunes facing the beach and ocean, and moved in with his wife and four children (a fifth child was born later). A man with "a passion for woodworking and construction", his daughter Barbara believes her father was responsible for much of the design and construction of their home. In these early days, the property included a two-horse stable and a corral. The Barber children rode as far as Del Mar to the north and Mission Beach to the south. The three Barber boys were more interested in

The Barber House in the 1920s, the impetus for the Barber Tract.
Courtesy of Barbara Dawson

the surf. With his woodworking skills, their father helped his sons construct surfboards. Not a man to be idle, Mr. Barber soon came out of retirement inspired to develop the area, which became known as the "Barber Tract." Tar and gravel roads that were winding and narrow were built with street lights at the curbs in the intersections. All wiring was underground and there were no telephone poles. Nothing would impede the atmosphere and natural beauty. Architecturally, house styles were as diverse as they were charming. However, in the midst of all this developing, the Barber family left La Jolla. Then came the '30s and the Great Depression. It hit hard for many in La Jolla. Homes were not selling. Many were left vacant. Philip Barber was loosing money on his development and eventually was forced to relinquish his beloved

The often painted picturesque Johnson home on the corner of Fern Glen and Monte Vista. *Courtesy of Steele Lipe*

home to creditors. He remained in La Jolla until 1846, then moved to Julian. He died in 1963. The good news is that his home on Dunemere now belongs to the young man who once delivered newspapers to the home and who loved the beach (Marine Street Beach or Whispering Sands Beach) in front of the home as much as Mr. Barber and his boys did: Academy Award wining actor, director, producer, and writer, Cliff Robertson.

On one of the streets, originally called Surfton Place, now named Fern Glen, are three quaint little English cottage-style homes. One of the homes, shown at the right, was built for Florence P. Palmer, wife and business partner of architect Herbert C. Palmer, an Englishman said to be the "bastard" son of Edward VII. Constructed between 1928 and 1930 and locally known as "the little people's block," these homes are delightful with their whimsical rooflines, ivy-covered walls, and picturesque flower gardens.

In 1922, Ellen Clark Revelle's mother built a house overlooking the beach she and her children had enjoyed when coming to visit her relatives over the years. The name of the beach was "Whispering Sands" because of the "strange sounds made by walking on dry sand." The children loved collecting shells and playing in the protected coves sheltered in the rocks and bluffs at either end. Ellen recalls, "This beach was still a place where men could appear without tops to their bathing suits, which was not allowed at the Cove." This was the Barber Tract beach.

At the time Ellen's mother was having the house constructed, her cousin, Floy Kellogg, described it as being "dangerously far out from town." There were at that time very few houses nearby, just the empty, sandy land and the sand dunes. Because of the remote area, Ellen's mother had to buy her own telephone pole in order to have a telephone and electric service. The house also had its own septic tank. In 1940, Ellen and her husband, Roger Revelle, bought the house from her mother.

In 1956, long before the formation of the Coastal Commission, Ellen Revelle and her neighbor and friend Georgeanna Lipe, took a stand that would literally save Whispering Sands Beach.

Present day Whispering Sands Beach, at the foot of Marine Street, showing the condominium complex and the rocks on which they were to have been built at the lower left (north) corner of the photograph. The Barber House is about 1/4 of the distance north (below) the southerly point (top of the picture).
Courtesy of Steele Lipe

As was the custom after school vacations, the mothers in the Barber Tract met for a beach picnic at their favorite place, the north end of Whispering Sands Beach, to celebrate the great event called, "Back to School." This time, however, they noticed some unusual activity. The ladies were shocked. Large bulldozers were demolishing several small beach cottages, some of which had been above the beach, for as long as any of them could remember. The crushed cottages were being pushed down onto the rocks, the beach and into the lovely little cove between the rocks. The natural beauty of the coastline was being destroyed and their beloved beach was being desecrated.

Mr. Carpenter, a developer from Los Angeles, had purchased the property. His plan was to cover the debris with dirt and other material, and then gunite over it using this artificial foundation for the construction of large apartments on the site. Some of his project would extend forty feet out from the bluff line. He claimed ownership out to the mean high tide line.

The loss of the tiny cove was tragic enough, but then came the realization that once this project was completed as planned, all north-south access from Whispering Sands to the smaller beach to the north would disappear. This fact galvanized the formation of an informal "Save the Beach" committee consisting of J T and Georgeanna Lipe, Quintin and Betsy Stephen-Hassard, Polly Hudnall, Roger and Ellen Revelle and a sympathetic lawyer, longtime resident Sherwood Roberts.

Attorney Roberts obtained an "Order to Show Cause" causing all the work on the Carpenter project to be stopped until a court hearing could take place. During the intervening weeks, the "Save the Beach" committee had time to do research and prepare their case. The search of records on microfilm was tedious. Hours were spent at a machine at the San Diego Public Library scanning microfilm of old newspapers with the hope to locating and annotating every reference to public use of La Jolla beaches to combat Carpenter's claim of private ownership. Members of the group unearthed snapshots from family albums to show how widely used the beach was. Public interest in the case grew by word of mouth and the power of the local press. Petitions were also circulated to bring in support.

The committee's appeal for funds to pay the legal fees brought an unexpected response, including one from Miss Caroline Cummins, longtime Headmistress of The Bishop's School. Her only use of the beach was probably the new girls welcoming picnics traditionally held at the foot of Marine Street. When asked to join in the challenge, the City of San Diego said there were no funds for such a cause. However, the City later realized that an important precedent was being set and did join with City attorneys.

When the day came for the court hearing, sometime before June 22, the Revelle's 25th wedding anniversary, there was some concern that if they lost the anniversary would be celebrated in jail.

Roger Revelle was allowed to be among the first to testify as he had to catch a plane to Washington, D.C. Mr. Carpenter's Los Angeles lawyer asked him to state his credentials, which were impressive enough to embarrass the lawyer. Roger was at that time the Director of the Scripps Institution of Oceanography, part of the University of California, and had a Ph.D. in geology. He soon made it clear that his familiarity with beaches in general and the beach in question went way back. He left for Washington feeling downhearted however, worried about some of the evidence the opponents might be able to produce, including a picture of a large PRIVATE BEACH sign posted right in front of the Revelle house at the foot of Marine Street. This had obviously not been placed by the owners but by their tenants during the war years when the Revelles were in Washington. Still, it could be damaging.

One of the best witnesses was Douglas Inman, a geologist at Scripps Institution of Oceanography. Carpenter's lawyer tried to get Dr. Inman to agree that the property would be perfectly safe to build on once it was gunited. Doug, in his quiet low-keyed manner, soon dispelled that naive notion, mentioning various locations where gunite had failed completely.

Ellen Revelle's mother, Grace Scripps Clark Johanson (age 78 at the time) was called upon. The opposing lawyer told Mrs. Johanson that the plan of the proposed building would allow for some sort of passage under or through it to reach the next beach area. In answer to his suave, "So wouldn't that be perfectly satisfactory, Mrs. Johanson?" He was appalled when this frail and meek-looking little lady replied: "No! Not at all! The beaches have always been freely open to the public and should stay that way!"

"I have no more questions, your Honor," the lawyer stammered.

The original surveyor of the area who had been located by Sherwood Roberts was probably the most convincing. His recollection of surveying the coastal lots of La Jolla could not be shaken. No matter how he was questioned, he stayed firm. "The bluff line," he kept reiterating, "was the western boundary of all lots." His testimony may have been what led to a phone call to the Revelle house at around eleven the same evening. It was Sherwood Roberts reporting that Mr. Carpenter's lawyer had phoned him requesting a discussion that night with the principle members of the Beach group.

Carpenter claimed that he had had no idea of the strong feeling of the community regarding his project and would not like to come to town creating enemies and causing ill will. He proposed an out-of-court settlement agreement. This would include not only pulling his construction back to the bluff line, but also cleaning up the desecrated little cove in front of his property. The committee decided to settle.

On the big day of the beach clean up, the Save Our Beach group felt like celebrating with Champagne as they stood, at the very low tide, out on the reef and watched the extremely expensive equipment laboriously hauling out all the rubble and debris that had been pushed into the cove. The day after the court proceedings, the *San Diego Union* carried an account of the settlement agreement under the headline: "Never Underestimate the Power of Irate Women!"

During the huge storms of 1982-83, as the waves crashed against the windows of the Carpenter-built apartments, it was obvious that the battle to save the beach had also saved the adversary's investment. Had his buildings extended forty feet farther out from the bluff line, more rubble would have covered that section of the beach as well as the beach group's cherished little cove. The expense in this case would have been monetarily and emotionally prohibitive.

In 1989, the Barber Tract Association was formed. For several years the residents (who call themselves "Barberians") have received and contributed to their own newspaper called the Barber Tract Times, published by Gordon Johnson. Besides Ellen Revelle, John Best and Cliff Robertson (native La Jollan and actor) are among the Barberians.

"Childhood Memories"

by Cliff Robertson

In 1912, La Jolla was still a sleepy little town of about 1,000 people when Clifford Parker Robertson III's maternal grandmother moved to the village, not realizing at the time it was to be the perfect environment for the upbringing of her grandson.   Clifford was born in 1925. His father and mother divorced when he was still a baby and tragically, when he was 2½, his mother died. He was adopted by his grandmother who raised him with the help of his aunt and uncle. Cliff loved the beach, especially Marine Street beach. As fate would have it, one day he would own the Barber "estate", former residence of Philip Barber after whom the Barber Tract is named, a house that just happens to overlook his beloved beach. Constructed in 1923, the house is located in what were once the "remote" sand dunes, in those early days so far from "the village." Today, "it is my Walden Pond, my sanctuary," says Cliff Robertson.

Ever since he was five years old and saw an airplane perform acrobatics over La Jolla, Cliff has had a passion for airplanes. As a teenager, he would bicycle the twelve miles to Speer Airport, not far from the Naval Training Center in San Diego, and work at any job he could get just to be near the planes. He didn't get paid for the work, but when there wasn't much activity, the pilots would take him up and teach him how to fly. From ninth to eleventh grade, Cliff attended Brown Military Academy in Pacific Beach, but was allowed to return to La Jolla High for his senior year. Although he loved flying, he was equally interested in drama and was a member of the Drama Club at school. Again he didn't get paid, but when he was a senior, thanks to the recommendation of his drama teacher, Clifford earned a part, his first professional role, in the Old Globe production of A Place Elsewhere.

Cliff Robertson as a youth at Brown Military Academy.
Courtesy of Cliff Robertson

Cliff Robertson and Patricia Daly-Lipe (Co-Author) at the White Sands reception for Spence Wilson's 90th birthday.
Courtesy of Barbara Dawson

After graduating in 1941, Cliff joined the Merchant Marine. Dec. 7, 1941 was "a day in infamy" for America, but it was not only Pearl Harbor that was attacked. Stationed in the Philippines, Clifford's ship, the SS Admiral Cole, *was also attacked and sunk by the Japanese. News reached La Jolla that the ship was lost with no survivors. Had this been true, Clifford would have been La Jolla's first Gold Star casualty of war. His grandmother, however, refused to believe this was so. In the winter of 1942, she was proven right when Clifford returned home. No more ships, she said, it was time to attend college, so Cliff enrolled at Antioch College in Ohio as a liberal arts major. While there, he wrote part-time for the* Ohio Daily News. *Someone at the paper encouraged Cliff to write for the theater, but, they said, "To write for the theater, you need to learn about the theater."*

He started small, working in upstate New York touring with a small theater group, driving trucks, helping out in any way he could and, from time to time, acting in small roles.

Returning to New York City, Clifford applied to and was accepted by the prestigious Actors Studio. Only two or three actors were chosen a year out of 2000 applicants. The rest is history, beginning with the motion picture Picnic *in 1955 with William Holden and Kim Novak.*

In his home in La Jolla is a rocking chair. It is a replica of John F. Kennedy's famous White House rocker. It was in 1959 that he was chosen by President Kennedy to play his younger self in PT-109. *But it was a movie called* Charly *that stands out above the rest. It was Clifford's belief in the story that led him to purchase its screen rights. Produced initially for TV, the show won Cliff rave reviews for his performance as a mentally challenged man. The story is based on* Flowers for Algernon, *a novella written by Daniel Keyes in 1959. In 1968, Cliff won the Academy Award for Best Actor in his movie version of the story,* Charly.

Now that he had established himself as an actor, Cliff was ready to return to writing. In 1972, Columbia Pictures released his first film, J. W. Coop, *directed, produced and co-written by Cliff. The film is a "gritty character study" of an ex-con who returns home with hopes of becoming the number one rodeo star, the only way he knows to finally become a winner.*

Cliff fills his aeronautic appetite as well. He owns a biplane and a glider as well as a Beech Baron that he flies across the country from his New York home to his California "Sanctuary" in La Jolla. But, he says, it is when he is on commercial flights that he does his best writing. His poems are modern day Whitman and his prose disproves Thomas Wolfe. You can go home again. Now, in Cliff Robertson's own words:

Childhood memories are gauze-like. They seem soft and diaphanous. Rarely do they jar one's sensibilities. At least those are *my* early La Jolla remembrances. We were lucky in La Jolla. God had been generous with its proud, sentinel hills overlooking the sleepy little town, its white beaches and some 4000 contented souls. Some folk — in less idyllic environs — might have viewed us as smug or self satisfied. Understandable in the Depression-thirties. But there seemed little reason for *our* discontent, for La Jolla was our "jewel". It wasn't that everyone was rich, they were not, though it did attract some 400 moneyed summer visitors — "invaders" from our viewpoint. But they were tolerated easily for many brought pretty daughters. You could usually spot them and hear them. They didn't have "surf-smarts". Did not appear confident in the water. And the boys wore Brooks Brothers clothes. Hardly in-sync with our Hawaiian shirts and shorts. To us less was considerably more. La Jolla girls were active. They body surfed with the boys and did wonderful things with their sarongs — unselfconscious casual. They were tan and slim. The "eastern girls" spoke with regional accents — rarely surfed — seemed very self-conscious about their white soft bodies. Ordered hamburgers "rare" and sounded like over-indulged princesses with lockjaw. The boys also failed to fit our style. They would swim out of their depths — trying to impress their friends — and were the bane of our lifeguards. Our lifeguards were cool. From our own ranks. They would sit high — like rajahs — surveying the water. Our girls would position themselves at the back of the rajah "throne" — laughing, teasing — singing big band songs and Harry Owens' Hawaiian guitar chants. To us, Kipling had it right. The "East" and "West...never the twain shall meet." We could care less for we were a band of brothers bonded by the beach life, the young and vital "good life". But not spoiled princes.

Most of us had jobs in the summer as well as after school in the winter. I had a magazine route (*Liberty Magazine*) — a newspaper route (*San Diego Sun*) — and later a lobster route necessitating five a.m. departures in my two-man skiff through the surf below Nautilus Street. My rowing partner was a classmate, David Dunlop — a fine lad who was $\frac{1}{3}$ partner. My skiff was built by Philip Barber — an avuncular retired developer-builder who designed what is now known as the Barber Tract, before he kindly built my small skiff. Mr. Barber's youngest daughter was Tootle (Mary Ann), and she was the perfect La Jolla girl: gregarious, blond, tan and beautiful. Tootle was a great body surfer, had an artistic flair and delighted everyone — she wore her beauty naturally — and bewildered the eastern girls.

David Dunlop and I loved airplanes and boats. Together we fantasized joining the royal Canadian Air Force once we reached eighteen. We were fifteen and Pearl Harbor was four years away. But we were thrilled by the slight possibility that Canada might take us. Later they took David. He flew Spitfires in the Burma Theatre until he was killed Christmas Day 1944. By that time I was in officer training in the U .S. Maritime Service — Ft. Trumbull, Conn. The war removed the soft gauze of youth. We lost some of our bonded brothers and even though we returned home (and to beach) it wasn't the same. A few tried to luxuriate with help from the government ("the 52-20" club) but most of us began to realize that Thomas Wolfe was right.

I headed east to New York City — but kept an elastic cord to La Jolla. I could not and never would abandon my home town La Jolla. Years later I purchased Philip Barber's home. It is my anchor. An anchor that holds my life steady in this stormy life while all about is turbulence. This son has returned to the sunny shores of youth — older, perhaps wiser — but certain of one thing: La Jolla. Though she has her share of greed-seekers and she has lost much of her innocence, she is still my home.

Ellen Browning Scripps 1836-1932

…it seem to me that those who are trying to "do things" ought to know more of one another.   **(Ellen Browning Scripps)**

1976 was the year the United States celebrated the bicentennial of its founding. *Time* magazine acknowledged the celebration by printing 2810 paintings and photographs of American men, women, boys and girls who had gained notoriety and praise during the preceding one hundred years. Included was a picture of Ellen Browning Scripps on the February 22, 1926 cover of *Time*. She is shown sitting at her desk, a woman advanced in years (she was 90). What had this lady done to warrant this recognition and to be so honored? Who was Ellen Browning Scripps?

Ellen Browning Scripps was born October 18, 1836, at 13 South Moulton Street, London, England. Her father, James Mogg Scripps, was a book binder, her mother was the daughter of a customs clerk. Ellen was only four and a half when her mother died leaving six children behind. Ellen was the middle child with three younger siblings. Three years after her mother's death (Ellen had spent most of this time at boarding schools) Ellen and her family were taken on a great adventure. They set sail for America in a small barque landing in Boston six weeks later. From Boston, they traveled up to Albany and sailed to Buffalo by way of the Erie Canal, through the great lakes to Fort Dearborn (Chicago), overland, then down the Illinois River to the small frontier town of Rushville, Illinois. It was early July, 1844, when they arrived. There Ellen's bankrupt and twice widowed father settled on 160 acres of poor farmland bequeathed to him by his father.

James Mogg Scripps built a house and then sent for a beautiful lady he had met on the trip west. They were married and within the next ten years, five more little Scrippses joined the household.

This was a difficult time for James Mogg Scripps. He worked hard to provide a home and food for his family. His first daughter, aged thirteen, had a hearing problem, so it was Ellen Browning Scripps who assumed the household chores and care of the children. So very young for such responsibilities, Ellen proved, nonetheless, to be a loving and caring person even at the tender age of eight. By the time she

Ellen Scripps in her early years, age unknown.
Courtesy of The Bishop's School

was 14, Ellen had a younger sister and four brothers as well as her stepmother (who was constantly nursing a baby or expecting one) and her father to help care for. The house had no bathrooms. Mattresses were made of corn shucks. They ate beef, salt pork, and bread that Ellen baked daily. Vegetables were few and fruit was practically unknown. Her brother wrote, "Housekeeper she may have been but she was no disheveled drudge. I never saw any other woman but my sister Ellen who wore gloves in the house while she would be sweeping or making beds or handling laundry." Nevertheless, Ellen's desire for learning and her instinctive gentleness and sense of responsibility gave her the strength to endure those difficult years.

After completing her own education, Ellen taught school, saved money, and, after two years, was able to attend Knox College. In 1857, it was most unusual for a mid-western girl to attend college and those who did were taught in separate classes from the men. When she graduated, she received a certificate. Degrees were not given to women in those days. After graduation, Ellen returned to Rushville, was able to secure a permanent teaching position (for which she was paid nine dollars a month — the same job held by a man paid thirteen dollars) and resumed keeping house for her father until he died in 1873. She was 37 years old.

The same year Ellen began her college studies, her older brother, James, went to work for the *Detroit Tribune* and was soon joined by the youngest brother, E. W. (Edwin Willis). When a fire destroyed the company, the two brothers and Ellen started a paper of their own called the *Detroit News*. This afternoon edition paper sold for two cents. Later, their brother George joined them.

Ellen joined her brothers in Detroit after her father's death. She was a disciplined, hard worker. For the Detroit paper, she wrote a front page feature called "Matters and Things." To those who knew her well, this column was affectionately called "Miss Ellen's Miscellany." Her great niece feels that this may have made her the first newspaper "columnist." (This term itself dates from about 1920.) Her columns were written between December 16, 1881 and August 7, 1883, 99 altogether, each averaging ten typewritten pages long. They consisted of a variety of short subjects gathered from a myriad of resources. Here is one example:

"The lips and tongue of a lady in Indianapolis swell when she talks rapidly, to such an extent as to stop articulation. And all the husbands in that city are urging their wives to call on the lady, secretly hoping that the disease is contagious."

She also swept the floors and served as the leveling member at the business meetings with her three brothers. One brother made a profound statement when he said she had "the brains of a man."

Five years after the *Detroit News* was launched, Edward, who was then twenty-four, the Ellen's youngest half-brother, eighteen years her junior, became editor of the *Penny Press* in Cleveland. Independent in politics, it represented the views of 95% of the population. Ellen agreed to curtail sleep to write a "packet of miscellany" for her little brother's paper while continuing her immense tasks in Detroit. Edward recorded that Ellen's "packet" was often a life saver. This little newspaper became the immensely successful *Cleveland Press*.

Ellen Scripps was a quiet lady but very much aware of the problems facing the nation in the middle of the nineteenth century. She joined the Suffragette Association, was interested in labor unions, temperance societies, dress reform, and educational changes. She was also available to her relatives any time they were ill or having babies. Since she was always living with her numerous relatives, it was not until many years later that she would build her own home. That first home would be located in La Jolla.

In 1881, Edward, also known as E.W., became ill. He needed to live in a dry climate and decided to go to Algiers. He took Ellen with him. She was 45 years old, not young by 1880s standards and not easy in those before airplanes, travel agencies, and indoor plumbing days. It was also before women's suffrage; nevertheless, the trip proved to be a great success. While overseas, Ellen and E. W. also visited Palestine, Turkey, Egypt, and most of Europe. The newspaper had become so much a part of her life that as she traveled, Ellen continued to write sharing her experiences with readers back home in the form of letters. These were published in place of her usual column in the *Detroit News*. Some "letters" are amusing like the following:

"Now Macaroni is a very good thing in its way, if one hasn't seen the modus operandi of its manufacturer, but there is a respectable way of eating it , and --an Italian way. The Italian first heaps a small Vesuvius on the delicacy on his plate. Then he thrusts his fork down into the crater of the steaming, ropey mass and dexterously twirls it round and round till he has wound up some yards of the material. Then he opens wide the delicate mouth, which was never made for anything but smiles and kisses but which by long practice in the art of macaroni eating has acquired an incredible degree of flexibility and power of expansion, and partly by propulsion, partly by suction, he succeeds in getting the bulk of the coil into the dark abyss that closes upon it. But he is sure to masticate, and the long ends dangle from his classic chin, and wobble about in mid-air to the alarm of the nearest neighbors as he essays to draw them in."

Other letters are more serious, noting in particular the plight of women in some of the countries she visited. "The Mohammedan woman is a nonentity or a slave. When a boy is born to him the Arab says, 'it is a benediction.' When a girl is born he says, 'it is a malediction.'…. They get her out of the way by selling her to the highest bidder." And: "Civilization has advanced enough in southern Spain to permit the woman to appear on the street unveiled, but not enough to recognize her capacities for mental growth…." These letters from abroad make Ellen Browning Scripps the first female *foreign* correspondent (with the exception of Margaret Fuller, the first foreign correspondent of either sex who wrote for the *Tribune*). It was during this same period that the Scripps brothers succeeded in expanding their newspaper business.

Upon E. W.'s return to the United States, he married Nackey Holtsinger and visited San Diego County with his new bride. The climate agreed with him so much that he purchased acreage a few miles north of the City of San Diego on a dry mesa that he soon covered with Eucalyptus trees. He called his land Miramar since he could see the sea. The year was 1890. On another trip, he had visited the home of Maximilian (emperor of Mexico, 1864-1867). He was so impressed with the architecture that he had it duplicated on his own property in Miramar.

E. W. was by this time the head of the Scripps-McCrae newspaper chain (which later became the Scripps-Howard Newspapers). Ellen came to visit him in Miramar and, for awhile, had her own tower apartment there. E. W. recommended that it was time that she build herself a home. Ellen chose to build in the tiny seaside town of La Jolla. "What a daring, even courageous

The stable area of "Miramar" E. W. Scripps' San Diego home, today known as Scripps Ranch. All the Eucalyptus trees were planted by E. W. Scripps. Mt. Soledad and La Jolla are in the background.
Courtesy of Barbara Dawson

Pictures of the original South Moulton Villa (1897) which burned in 1915.
Courtesy of Barbara Dawson

move that was, to go so far away from the part of the country (mid-west) where she had lived ever since she was brought over from London as a young girl, and then to build her first house—at age 61!" exclaimed Ellen Revelle, (Miss Scripps' great niece).

In April 1896, Ellen Scripps bought two large lots on Prospect Street across from Draper Street on one side and sloping down to the ocean on the other. She had her house built of redwood and named it South Moulton Villa after the street in London where she was born. In 1897, the house was completed along with two cottages, one for a library, the other for visitors. The house was modest and unpretentious and she loved it. Throughout her life, Ellen continued the habits she had developed on the farm in Illinois. She woke at five AM, slept on an uncovered sleeping porch, and enjoyed walking through her gardens (which she shared with the people of La Jolla since "La Jolla had no park, and I have all the space here.") and along the beach collecting shells. From the beginning, Ellen was involved with the people, especially the children, and the activities of her adopted town. However, in 1915, disaster struck. According to La Jolla Historical Society docent, Sandy Spalding, "It was 8:30 p.m. when flames were discovered in the vestry of the St. James-by-the-Sea Episcopal church." The La Jolla Volunteer Fire Department was able to extinguish the fire before serious damage was done. "Scarcely an hour later," writes Ms. Spalding, "as Virginia Scripps left her sister Ellen's home, and headed to her own cottage, the Iris down the street, she was startled to see smoke coming from the cottage's bedroom window. Calling loudly for help, she rushed back to her sister's residence, where the elderly Miss Ellen had just retired. After the commotion created by the St. James fire, the tired firemen turned their attention to the new blaze while the hundreds of bystanders, who had just begun to settle down from the first fiery incident, were seized by new anxieties. It seemed evident that an arsonist was at work." Fearing for the safety of their own homes, many rushed away. "In the darkness, people stumbled over each other, adding to the chaotic scene." Then, while the firemen were trying to save the Iris cottage, a new eruption of fire was seen coming from Miss Ellen's home. "The firemen struggled to shift their equipment to the larger structure only to discover that the residence was 550 feet from the nearest hydrant and they had only 500 feet of hose." The La Jolla firefighters were overwhelmed. "Three times, the hose of the antiquated chemical engine used by the volunteers burst when the faucet was turned on. In addition, inadequate water pressure in the town contributed to the firefighters' inability to douse the flames." Fred Higgins, who was later to become Miss Scripps' chauffeur, told Barbara Dawson in an interview, "I remember the La Jolla fire (August 7, 1915) of Miss. E. B.

The second South Moulton Villa designed by Irving J. Gill from a postcard by L. L. Eno, San Diego, Calif.
Courtesy of Barbara Dawson

Scripps' which was almost a complete loss. The fire department had to come out from San Diego, but it was too late to save most of it." Miraculously, the library with all its treasured volumes was spared. The little guest cottage also escaped the fire, which pleased Ellen's great-niece. She was born in that house.

According to the *San Diego Union*, after the fire Miss Virginia was quoted as saying, "If only it had been an accident, it would have been much easier to bear. But my sister, whose life has been wrapped up in doing all she could to help mankind, cannot help but be stung by the thought of someone feeling malice toward her."

The La Jolla community was shocked by the fires. A meeting was called on the tennis courts at the playground Miss Scripps had recently donated to the children of La Jolla. "A committee was formed to meet with the city council to work on ideas to improve fire fighting capabilities in the village and pledges were taken for a $1000 reward for finding the villain responsible. Before adjourning, a resolution expressing the sympathy of the community for the Scripps and also its appreciation for all they had done for La Jolla was adopted."

Four months after the fire, the police located the arsonist. "Linked to the fire by an oil-soaked shirt found in the basement, William Peck, a 43-year-old Australian, who had been discharged as a gardener on the Scripps' grounds almost a year before the arson took place, was apprehended in Perris in Riverside County. After five days in jail, Peck was taken to the site of the burned Scripps' residence where he broke down and confessed to the crime, claiming to have been too drunk to know what he was doing. He denied harboring any ill will toward the Misses Scripps but did acknowledge a grudge against their housekeeper, who had fired him."

Ellen Scripps hired Irving J. Gill, the San Diego architect who had recently completed the Woman's Club, to design and build a new South Moulton. It was to be made of concrete and stucco, very modern for 1916; but more to the point, it was fireproof. Ellen Scripps was 79 and still enjoyed both a sense of adventure and the spirit of giving. Instead of building a house for herself, she had Mr. Gill design a house that could be left for some community use. This building now houses the Museum of Contemporary Art. Simple in its plainness of flat surfaces and straight lines, this house was built with the Pacific Ocean as its main attraction. From the front doors, down the hall way, you approached the living room on the farther side of the house. Here you faced an enormous plate glass window, covering almost the entire surface of the western side of the room. This immense window, undivided by any panes of glass, allowed an overwhelming view of the ocean. It is here Miss Scripps spent time, sitting on her comfortable divan, reading and looking out at the Pacific."

E. W., who still lived nearby in Miramar, advised Ellen that she needed to make plans for the utilization of her money. In 1900, her annual income was $750,000, an incomprehensible amount for that time. A great deal of thought and planning was necessary to maximize the use of her funds resulting in many projects that have helped and continue to help bring so much pleasure to so many people. "I'd…rather people take what I give them without expressing…any gratitude because it is annoying to feel that anyone is under obligation to me. But I do like to *see* and know any benefits that accrue from my giving."

Ellen always loved children and many of her plans included the little ones. One of the most popular projects was the Children's Pool. It was Ellen's desire that the children of La Jolla have a safe place to swim. In the little cove near the

The breakwater and Children's Pool, known to many locals as the "Casa Cove" was dedicated by Miss Scripps to all the children of San Diego. *Courtesy of Steele Lipe*

Casa de Mañana, Miss Scripps had a breakwater built using some of the rocks that washed up on the shore. The breakwater was completed in the spring of 1931. On May 31, in an elaborate ceremony, Mr. Jacob C. Harper, representing Miss Scripps, presented the pool to the City of San Diego in her name adding, "Adults must recognize that here at the Pool, the children have a primary claim."

The San Diego Zoo has also been a recipient of funds for projects that provide joy and educational experiences for children. Every October, the *ZOONOOZ* acknowledges the birthday of Miss Ellen Browning Scripps. Douglas G. Myers, Executive Director, wrote in the October, 1998 *ZOONOOZ*: "This wonderfully generous lady, and the Ellen Browning Scripps

Foundation that she left as her legacy, have provided the Zoological Society of San Diego over the years with more than $1 million in support for the San Diego Zoo, the San Diego Wild Animal Park, and the Center for Reproduction of Endangered Species (CRES). But it is not the dollar amount we pay tribute to each year; it is the history of consistent giving for which we celebrate Miss Scripps and her foundation." He goes on to list the many items that were donated or bought for the Zoo

The original statuette by James Tank Porter
Courtesy of Barbara Dawson

beginning with 12,500 linear feet of wire fencing for the zoo's 200 acres of grounds in 1922. Consequently, admission could be charged. The first admission charge took place on January 1, 1923: 10 cents for adults. Children were admitted free. The Scripps Flight Cage, the Zoo hospital (built in 1926, it now houses CRES), and, as the tradition continues, "almost every new exhibit built at the zoo in recent years" has come about thanks to the generosity of Ellen Browning Scripps and the Scripps family.

At her own home, Miss Scripps kept a shelf of toys, she always allowed the local children to ride their bikes on her walks and to play in her garden. Asked why she had ten gardeners and only one weekly cleaning woman, Miss Scripps is said to have replied, "Hundreds of people walk through my garden every week. It is always open to the public, and when I divide what it costs me by the number of people who enjoy it, I think it is one of the most economical civic duties I could perform."

Although she was given many awards by people and organizations, one that touched her deeply was the presentation of a stone bench and a bird bath with a statue of a little child scooping water into her hands for the birds to drink. All of the local school children contributed a penny toward this gift. In 1915, the same year as the fire, the statue was placed on the lawn in front of the Recreation Center Building (which she had donated). Tragically, in the mid-1990s, the little statue was stolen. Recognizing its debt to this grand lady, the community replaced the little figure with a new statue on June 28, 1997.

Behind the recreation center, the La Jolla Playground was a prototype for public playgrounds throughout the United States. It was opened to the public on July 3, 1915. There

La Jolla Playground, c. 1915
Courtesy of Barbara Dawson

were basketball courts (pictures of which are in the Basketball Hall of Fame in Springfield, Mass.), tennis courts, play equipment for youngsters, a sand box, and gym sets. One of the plaques on the building indicates how appreciative the children of La Jolla were for the consideration and generosity of Ellen Browning Scripps. It reads:

This Tablet Is Placed Here By
The Children of La Jolla
With Love And Gratitude
In Honor Of
Ellen Browning Scripps
The Donor Of This Playground
A.D. 1915

La Jolla Jr.-Sr. High School was the recipient of an athletic field. The Bishop's School received its share of gifts from Miss Scripps as well. "I am convinced that there is nothing so fundamental—and hence so vital—to the service of people as true education," she said in response to a request from President Blaisdell of Pomona College. Ellen Scripps had always been concerned with women and their education. President Blaisdell's dream had been to establish a group of small, associated colleges in Claremont. Miss Scripps was happy to help make this dream a reality but she was not pleased with his using her name for the new college for women. Not only did she detest personal recognition, she declared that Scripps was "a ridiculous name, without melody or charm, with its one futile vowel flanked by its six Nordic consonants." Since she could not make the trip to the college, the first graduating class and faculty came to her. She surprised them all when she was able to call each by name and make a pertinent comment. She had done her homework! As to her hopes for the new college, she said, "I like to picture a college whose motto is not 'Preparation for Life' but 'Life' itself."

Other local gifts include the La Jolla Woman's Club (the grounds, the building, and membership dues for anyone not able to afford it), the Torrey Pines State Park acreage and Lodge), the Public Library, Scripps Institution of Oceanography, Scripps Memorial Hospital, Scripps Metabolic Clinic, the Nurses' Home, Scripps Cottage at San Diego State College, the San Diego Natural History Society, the St. James by-the-Sea's chimes, and donations to every church in La Jolla.

During her last thirty years, Ellen Browning Scripps lived as many older women did in this little community. She joined the various local clubs, played cards, took part in plays, held open houses weekly, and traveled around California in her Rolls-Royce driven by her chauffeur, Fred Higgins. The car and driver were a gift from E. W. in 1916. E. W. had tested Fred Higgins first to be sure he was a good driver for the new car he had purchased for his half-sister. Fred was 19 at the time. Higgins' association with Miss Scripps was to continue for many years, first as a driver, later as a hospital maintenance engineer.

In an interview in 1965, Miss Scripps' chauffeur shared some insight about this special lady. Asked what time she usually got up in the morning, Mr. Higgins replied: "Oh, she'd get up anywhere after 4:30 (a.m.). Something like that. She would get up as soon as it got daylight you might say. She'd go right down to her office desk. Getting out of that old cot that she had. I had a hood made for her, you know, waterproof canvas. She'd get up in the rain and pull at that canvas out there...."

Ellen Browning Scripps, Mrs. S. T. Gillispie, Capt. Wesley Crandall, and Fred Higgins, 1929
Courtesy of Barbara Dawson

48

Miss Virginia and Miss Ellen Scripps in front of the new house (South Moulton Villa #2) now the Museum of Contemporary Art, San Diego, originally, the La Jolla Art Center, c. 1918.
Courtesy of Barbara Dawson

Of course, she had her bed she never slept in. I think it had to be an awful big rain to move her in. She loved the outdoors. She loved to sleep out on that porch." It seems that Miss Scripps slept out on that porch summer and winter. However, one morning, when she got up and attempted to make her bed, she fell. "You see she always made her own bed," Higgins continued. "That was when she stepped on the blanket. She was pulling the blanket up to get it straightened out and slipped." It was a couple of hours before someone found her. Fred Higgins and his brother carried her down the street to the little Gillispie Sanatorium (across from Bishop's School). Her stay there made her realize that La Jolla needed a bigger and more modern hospital. "The La Jolla Sanitarium," recalled Fred Higgins, "which Dr. and Mrs. Gillispie started in La Jolla…was started in the old Kline House which was later moved to Kline Street." On September 26, 1924, the Scripps Memorial Hospital was opened where the Sanatorium used to be, on Prospect.

The first cars came to La Jolla in 1912. Driving in those days could be precarious. "The streets were dirt," Higgins explained. "There used to be a watering trough at the foot of Girard right in the middle of the street across from…Hamilton's Grocery Store." If it rained, the cars would have a rough time negotiating the hills. "Yes, all the streets were dirt. I remember when we used to use a team of horses to pull a car up the Biological Grade during wet weather for the people who didn't have chains on their wheels." Cars would also slide down Kline Street toward what was then a ravine. Since the streets were dirt, the cars would land sideways against the brush and overgrowth along the ravine, only a block from Miss Scripps' house.

Miss Scripps' early attention to the community was reflected in a speech given in 1899.

"It lies with us residents and owners of La Jolla to make 'our jewel' what we will, only keeping it always in harmony with its glorious natural setting. To do this we must cultivate ourselves, in our hearts and lives, the spirit of all harmony and beauty and spirituality. From the upbuilding of our character comes the outbuilding of beauty…. It will matter little then if our homes are stately or unpretentious cottages. For here the poet will find his inspiration, the teacher his lessons. Here the artist shall realize his dream, the weary and suffering shall find rest and solace, and every soul shall be satisfied; for it shall awaken the likeness of its creator…."

Always inquiring, always learning, she said (when well over ninety), "Of course I know I may die any time. I do not fear death, but I should like to live a little longer to see (she mentions many issues of the day)…. Oh, life is just beginning to be so very interesting!" Nevertheless, the inevitable did happen. Just three months prior to her ninety-sixth birthday, Ellen Browning Scripps died. Her ashes were scattered off the coast, just within sight of her old vantage point, the porch of South Moulton.

From a Dream to the World Famous Scripps Institution of Oceanography

"So few people, but what they could do."

Ellen Browning Scripps and her half-sister, Virginia, moved to La Jolla in 1897. Both loved the ocean, its fish and animal life, as well as the fauna and flora of the ocean floor. They collected specimens and put them in jars on the mantel.

There were many others in San Diego, Coronado and La Jolla who were also interested in the sea. Some sought to establish a biological station. Numerous people and events made this possible.

First, Dr. Ritter met Miss E. B. Scripps. Second, George H. Scripps died at Miramar in 1900. Third, in 1903 Ellen's brother's estate of $750,000, a sizeable amount in those days, went to Ellen. Fourth, a Marine Biological Association was formed in 1909.

Starting an organization of this type is like starting any kind of club. The interested people have nothing but a dream—no members, no building, no money, no by-laws, no committees, not anything. Nevertheless, discussion and dreams begun the late 1800s, became a reality. Primarily under the direction of Dr. Ritter and the enthusiasm of Dr. Fred Baker who joined forces, the Marine Biological Association of San Diego was established.

William Emerson Ritter had grown up on a family farm in Wisconsin. He worked and paid his own way through State Normal College in Oshkosh. From there he entered Harvard University paying his way tutoring. From Harvard, he obtained both a masters and a doctorate. After graduation, Dr. Ritter came to California to head of the Zoology Department at the only University of California full time campus at the time, Berkeley.

A research study was being conducted in San Diego and Dr. Ritter was given permission by the President of the University

William Emerson Ritter, at work in his laboratory in the Marine Biological Association (Coronado Boat House), 1904.
Courtesy of SIO Archives/UCSD

to participate. A fish he needed for the project, the blind Goby, was found sheltered in the reefs off the Point Loma coast. Newly married to Mary E. Bennett (who had a M.A. in education), William and his bride first came down to San Diego in the summer of 1891. On Point Loma they met another couple, doctors Fred and Charlotte Baker. Dr. Fred Baker, a physician, had amassed a large collection of seashells and was convinced that San Diego was a perfect place for a permanent marine laboratory. Dr. Ritter joined enthusiastically in his quest. Dr. Baker was able to convince the Chamber of Commerce (it would be good for San Diego's economy and her educational community) who in turn set up a Marine Laboratory Committee. One of the first pledges for money came from a "wealthy rancher" named E. W. Scripps. After viewing Ritter's little marine laboratory in Coronado, E. W. was hooked. He told a friend that "there is little scientific concern in La Jolla (particularly) for investigating the living things of the ocean and the ocean itself. Hardly anybody knows or cares much about this. Yet," he stated prophetically, "it may make additions to knowledge that will be of great value to the world." E. W.'s sister, Ellen Browning Scripps, was also interested in the idea. She loved the sea and had specifically chosen a site by the side of the ocean in La Jolla to build her home. From her sun room she enjoyed looking and listening to the surf during the day. Her half-sister, Virginia, had already shown an avid interest in the marine life at the Cove. Another family member living locally, Fred Scripps, donated the most money toward the construction of the first laboratory in La Jolla

     In 1905, after initially starting in Coronado in 1903 on Glorietta Bay (where the Boat House of the Hotel del Coronado is now), a site in La Jolla was secured just above the Cove at Alligator Head not far from the Bath House (the City of San Diego provided the five-acre site free of charge). A 1440 square foot building was constructed containing three laboratories, a library, a reagent room and an aquarium-museum. It was known as the Little Green Laboratory. Visitors loved to visit the aquarium but the space was clearly inadequate for the research and equipment, much less the pollution factor. E. W. "had a brainstorm." There was a one hundred and seventy-acre parcel being sold at public auction (it is possible that E. W. "arranged" for the city to hold this public auction). Located above the cliffs north of "Long Beach" (now La Jolla Shores), this property was purchased for $1000. (Harry Titus, the attorney for John D. Spreckles, offered the sole bid on behalf of the Association for the property "worth thirty to fifty times as much even then.") In 1909-1910, the first buildings constructed were a water tower and the George H. Scripps Aquarium, also known as the "Old Scripps Building" designed by Irving J. Gill. Scripps Institution for Biological Research (as it was called after its association with the University of California in 1912) had found a home at last. Constructed by Perl Acton Company of La Jolla, the original cost was $15,816.09.

The original Biological Station called the "Little Green Laboratory" located at the cove, west and north of the Bath House. This view is from near Alligator Point.
Courtesy of SIO Archives/UCSD

     The Old Scripps Building is 26 feet high, 75 feet long and 50 feet wide. It was built of reinforced concrete using the "Trussed Bar system" developed by Julius Kahn about 1903. The steel reinforcing rods, which were included within the concrete walls, turned out to be earthquake resistant. Therefore, the building remarkably passes today's codes. San Francisco buildings that had similar systems designed by Kahn survived the 1906 earthquake.

All of the remaining Irving J. Gill plans (which his nephew was able to salvage) were given to the Art Department of the University of California, Santa Barbara. "We were able to get copies of the plans of this building," said Betty Shor, a docent of the "Old Scripps Building." Having the Gill blueprints was the impetus to restore this building, but, she said, it was mostly the "care and determined efforts" of Physics Professor Emeritus Fred and Sally Spiess that saved it. Several other professors and their spouses, gardeners, and other workers of Scripps Institution joined in the efforts contributing time, expertise, and money. In the end,

Northerly view of Scripps Institution of Oceanography, 1910.
Courtesy of SIO Archives/UCSD

$450,000 was used to put the building into its original shape along with hours of volunteer time and labor.

"Old Scripps" had been slated for demolition in 1976. This was "the oldest oceanographic laboratory building in the Western Hemisphere." Using this information, the SIO volunteers arranged for its listing as San Diego Historic Site Number 119. This assured them funding from the State Office of Historic Preservation and its listing on the National Register of Historic Places and as a National Landmark.

"We ripped out walls that didn't belong. We risked our lives and signed a document to that effect" (to indemnify the University), said Betty Shor, whose husband is Professor Emeritus George Shor.

John Henderson, A.I.A., did the design for the restoration. John Kariotis was the structural engineer. A consultant, Boris Bresler, was also hired. He was an expert on "rotten concrete." "Salt water and concrete do not mix." The offices on the ground floor in the early days were for biologists and each room had a saltwater tank on its south side. Some of the tanks had leaked into the columns and interior walls of the structure. Salt water weakens the limestone in the concrete and promotes rust on the reinforcing bars. There is no longer a salt water supply to this building.

All the interior windows had been covered with plywood. It was not unusual for students or professors to hammer a nail into the wood to hang a picture and hear a shattering of glass. On the floor upstairs, it was Professor of Biology Emeritus Martin W. Johnson who discovered "sidewalk lights" (glass prisms embedded in a sidewalk) as he chipped away the old flooring to expose the concrete of the original floor. These sidewalk lights let the natural sunlight from the roof skylight penetrate downstairs. This had been part of the original Irving Gill design.

The upstairs southwest area was Dr. and Mrs. William Ritter's "home" until the Director's house was built in 1913 and has also recently been restored. According to documentation, Mrs. Ritter said that this upstairs area was "the most difficult room to furnish and decorate." Mrs. Ritter devised a canvas awning to cover the skylight and cut down on the glare and heat. A canvas (not the original) awning remains today.

There used to be a balcony overlooking the ocean just outside the Ritter's home. This balcony has been replicated but was placed in front of the building (with the permission of the State Office of Historic Preservation). Originally, Gill had identical entrances at the front and the back of the then-isolated Scripps laboratory. In those early years, the main road passed on the ocean side of the building. Today there is a first floor addition to "Old Scripps" on the west and north sides. Once there was also a 24 X 48 foot wooden building to the north of "Old Scripps" which served as a public aquarium.

The northwest corner upstairs was once the office of Professor Hubbs and his "typewriter" (a job title in those days, it stood for a person not a machine). The southeast corner upstairs was Director Ritter's office. Used by several directors from 1910-1950, it has been restored to the way it appeared in a photograph taken in Director Ritter's time. Above the fireplace (which was used in the winter months and still functions) is a photograph of Charles Darwin obtained from England after extensive research by the docents. On the shelf of this office's library is a book, *Charles Darwin and the Golden Rule*. Written by William Ritter, it was published in 1954, a year after his death.

Let us return to the days when the Marine Biological Association was but an idea in the minds of people interested in this project and imagine what this part of La Jolla was like in the early 1900s. The property was two miles north of La Jolla. It was barren—no trees, no bushes, and no buildings. The large expanse of land between La Jolla and the dreamed of Institute was undeveloped mud flats with just car tracks, no road.

With a small staff, it was necessary to have housing, more buildings and roads. Miss Scripps gave "$10,000 to build a road connecting the laboratory to La Jolla on the south and Del Mar on the north." The houses were makeshift, "one-board" structures built and furnished for $1,000 each. Dr. Ritter must have felt like the little Dutch boy who put his finger in the dyke to stop the sea from flooding. The wind blew in the cracks and the roofs leaked. Mrs. Ritter described the cottages as "truly masculine in their planning and conveniences." The furnishings included $5 iron beds, $4 couches, and burlap curtains. There were no plants to help protect the homes from the weather or to make the landscape attractive. But the staff made due recognizing that the largest portion of E. W.'s funds were designated for research.

Despite the simplicity of structures, more money was needed. Ellen and her half-brother, E. W. Scripps, were cautious but supportive. For years the problems were enormous and costly. One of the first actions of the Marine Biological Board was to guarantee financial support for the Association for at least three years. Homer Peters, E. W. Scripps, and Ellen Scripps each agreed to provide $1500 a year for a three-year period so that the Biological Station would be assured a minimum annual budget of $4500.

1903-1915 were the pioneer years. Life was a struggle trying to establish the Scripps Institution of Oceanography, securing buildings, hiring scientists, and building houses. Mrs. Ritter committed herself to planting bushes and trees all over the surrounding acreage to help protect the flimsy residences from the bad weather as well as making the location more attractive.

There was no electricity and trips to the stores in La Jolla were taken over rough and often muddy roads. In 1915, E. W. Scripps in writ-

The Scripps Institution of Oceanography, c. 1914, showing several outbuildings and homes.
Courtesy of SIO Archives/UCSD

ing his thoughts, described the colony: "An Odd Place; A New Town Where High Thinking and Modest Living Is To Be the Rule."

In 1916, flooding rains caused three washouts on the road from Scripps Institution to La Jolla. Fortunately, workmen were there and, they had been building a pier for the Institution with timbers left from the work on the pier and with their horses were able to build three bridges along the "road" to La Jolla. One was near the Institution. The second was where La Jolla Canyon (now an extension of Torrey Pines Rd. going up to UCSD) meets (the uphill portion of) Torrey Pines Rd. The third bridge was placed where East Roseland Drive reached what they called "the boulevard."

The grouping of houses that formed the Biological Station was fondly called "The Bug House" by the children who lived there. In the early days, the Bug House consisted of twenty-five redwood board and batten cottages. There was no school at the station so the children had to ride the mail bus across the mud flat (now La Jolla Shores) and up Torrey Pines road to the little red school house near the corner of Torrey Pines and Girard (where the Stella Maris School is now). If the children missed the bus home, they had to walk the two miles back to the Bug House, careful not to sink down in the thick black mud. In the winter, the trip could be particularly perilous and when the rains came the trips were impossible. There was a big flood in 1927 and for a time the inhabitants of the Bug House were marooned. However, despite the isolation and the inconvenience of living "so far away from town," what a wonderful life for the children having beach and the tide pools as their "backyard."

"Way back when I was about eleven (1928)," said Gene McCormack in a taped interview, "Merle Krulish bought a yacht for five dollars. It was a row boat about twelve feet long with one side broken in…he was the carrier of the morning *Union* so he made more money than us guys who carried the *Sun* at night. So he bought this boat and I helped him fix it and we took it down and launched it at the Windansea Beach…and an older woman…sold Merle an outboard motor…(and) we could run that boat clear up to the caves and back and all of that, so finally, when we got up to the tenth grade, a boy named Herbert Sumner (who lived at the top of the biological grade with his dad, Francis B. Sumner) let us go up there and see where he was raising mice for studying evolution…(there's an aquarium at Scripps Institution named after Francis Sumner.) Herb asked me to design and build a yacht thirteen feet long. So we designed it, worked hard on it. We could go down to the beach down there. It wasn't Black's Beach in those days. A lot of people didn't get their clothes wet when they went swimming. We could pick up drift wood to help build the boat…(When) we had most of the work done on the boat, I said, 'Let's go down and see if we can lower ourselves to the beach. You drive a stake in the ground and loop a rope over it and slide down and then drive another stake.' I was looking for a place to drive the second stake and the darn cliff gave way and I bumped and knocked myself out and I fell 150 feet clear down to the beach near where somebody has (now) built an elevator that goes down the hill there. Herb was so scared and brave and strong, he climbed that cliff and called his dad and his dad was in a meeting of Scripps Institution of Oceanography, so the whole committee came out to try to get that kid back from the beach. The youngest fellow there (it was his first day at work at Scripps)…was the fastest runner and he came down and yelled at me and woke me up from my unconsciousness so I became the first thing that Roger Revelle ever removed from the beach of the Pacific Ocean! He and the police got me on a stretcher, took me back up, and I put in one night at the hospital but it was a whole week before I went sailing again. The boat that Herb and I built, I think it cost $42 including the chains we found of a Ford Model A block and anchor out of what was to be the La Jolla Beach and Yacht Club. Back of them (the Club) was a big puddle or a pond…so we launched the boat in there and I taught Herb to sail it." (Gene became a Model Yacht Regatta winner and was seen Canal boating in '77, '78, and '80 in Great Britain.

Up until 1960, progress and development came with great effort by all: scientists, their families, employees, and interested citizens. Many events, including W.W.I and W.W.II, took some of the leading scientists away. The research continued, however, including the discovery of the many uses of seaweed in developing food and fertilizer. It was under the direction of Dr. Roger Revelle that SIO saw its biggest expansion as well as its annexation to the UCSD campus of which he

Scripps Institution of Oceanography, aerial view in 1957.
Courtesy of SIO Archives/UCSD

was a prime proponent. Director from the early fifties until 1964, Dr. Revelle's influence went well beyond the Scripps campus. He was recognized as our nation's expert on global environmental studies and in 1961, was asked by Pres. Kennedy to become the United States first scientific advisor to Secretary of the Interior Stewart Udall. In 1964, Revelle accepted an endowed chair at Harvard and the directorship of its new Center for Population Studies. In 1993, he returned to UCSD as a professor of science and public policy. In 1990, Pres. George H. Bush presented Dr. Revelle with the National Medal of Science. In an interview at the time, Dr. Revelle said, "I'm not a very good scientist, but I've got a lot of imagination. The age of exploration of the sea was just right for me." Not only SIO but UCSD are forever indebted to this extraordinary man.

Year by year the facilities have expanded, modern equipment has been secured, boats have been acquired, and many scientists representing numerous disciplines extend the scope of research programs. To illustrate the growth, in the early 1900s, there was but a handful of staff. By 1999, the staff numbered some 1,273 people.

The Marine Biological Association was the title of the organization created July 1, 1912 for $10.00 and turned over to the Regents of the University of California. On October 14, 1925, it was renamed Scripps Institution of Oceanography and has since been referred to as SIO. From a small "Green Laboratory" above La Jolla Cove to the Scripps Institution of Oceanography on the cliffs of La Jolla Shores, this is a place where research is always on the cutting edge. From a time when scientists and students first came to study marine organisms up close to a century of accomplishments beyond the boundaries of the physical sciences to biological and social sciences. A veritable crisis faces today's marine ecosystems. Scientists need to devote attention to the interaction of humans with the ocean. Another threat is the global climate change taking place, first recognized by Charles D. Keeling at Scripps in the late '50s. The key to all of this is SIO's willingness to become more interdisciplinary in its approach to research. Beyond "blurring the boundaries between the disciplines, Scripps' researchers are increasingly working with economists, social scientists, and public policy makers to ensure that their scientific research benefits society as a whole."

In 2003, SIO celebrated its Centennial. From the Coronado boathouse laboratory to the ever expanding facility in La Jolla, Scripps Institution of Oceanography continues its "restless desire for discovery" knowing the journey ahead will not be easy. As Kevin Hardy, Scripps Centennial Director states: "Nothing worthwhile ever is."

Memories of Times Past

Wilma Harle Garth
Written in 1967

On the 14th floor of my "high rise" apartment I can look down and relive the last forty years of my life — and — I might add, the most interesting part. There were good years, bad years but never any really dull years — I hope this will continue.

When we moved to La Jolla, my husband had his degree to practice medicine from Stanford University and had completed a years internship at San Diego County Hospital. We came in the fall of 1925 — in time to put our two children Bill Jr. and Harle in grammar school — I well remember the first social function we attended, a Halloween party at the playground, with a wonderful bon-fire reaching to the sky. I was told people saved their trash for weeks in order to make the big "splash." We dressed Harle as a Witch riding her broom — incidentally, it was the fireplace broom from the house we were renting, and wouldn't we run into our landlady, who reminded us to be sure and return it! Bill Jr. made a magnificent pirate with his black eye patch, and we were indeed proud to be able to introduce our children to the Village that was to mean so much to us in the years to come.

In the ten years of our married life we had never really had a home — I moved to the Oklahoma oil fields as a bride, lived in lease houses and even one time a tent for a brief period. When the War came along I had become a mother, so we moved back to the family home in Beaumont, Texas where my husband worked in a war plant for the duration.

The end of the war found us jobless, with two babies to

Wilma Harle Garth, 1895-1988
Courtesy of Harle Montgomery

feed. We were faced with two decisions, whether to go back to the oil field (family owned) or go back to college and study medicine — hard decisions to make for people as young as we were, but we never regretted the harder of the two roads we took.

We sold our oil field tools, piled our worldly goods in a Model T Ford and headed for California — I think we were indeed the very first of the "Oakies" to migrate to California. Can you visualize these rash, bold young people starting out on such a journey? There were no paved roads, no filling stations — few restaurants and hotels, so nights we camped under the stars. Next morning there were diapers to be washed and hung on the car to "flap dry" — camp to unmake and off we went. If we made 150 miles per day it was good, but even so we made it across the desert in a record two weeks.

First we landed in Coachella and were tempted to buy a date ranch and forget medical school but when we asked the rancher what he expected to do, and when he replied "go to Medical School" LeRoy's mind was made up — "why send him to school when it's the only thing I really want to do myself."

The next day found us chugging along the plank road out of Imperial Desert to Pomona College where LeRoy's cousins were students. We both matriculated, but the first day I attended classes Bill got lost coming home from Nursery School and was found by a little old lady who admonished me in no uncertain words that I'd better stay at home and raise my family — oh well it was a good try!

After one year at Pomona, we again took to the road in our Model T — we first went to Berkeley but couldn't find a place to live — no houses were built during the war years, and let's face it, few if any students were married, certainly not with children — so down to Stanford we went, and we liked the climate so much that we bought a "ready cut" four room house, and with the help of Father Garth and LeRoy's two younger brothers we put it together on Bryant Street in Palo Alto and lived happily in it all through Medical School.

The next five years were frugal years but we were determined to make it on our own as the family thought we should have stayed on in the oil business, but we were idealistic and saw in it no future — only money! We owned our house, so we allocated ourselves to living and dressing on a hundred dollars a month — we had help there with birthday, Easter and Christmas checks but even so, it took some juggling to make the proverbial ends meet. I remember so well giving Bill a quarter with which to buy a round steak for dinner. When the butcher said "Son, it comes to 30 cents," and Bill replied in his best four year old business voice, "Well, Cain't you Cut the Round bone out?" With determination like that we had nothing to fear from the future.

Stanford being on the quarterly system, LeRoy was able to finish Medical school in 4 years by going to summer school each year — in between summer and fall sessions we usually went to Tahoe for a short camping trip — LeRoy was an avid mountain climber and there were few peaks in that region that we hadn't climbed by the time he finished college — I called myself his "half way house" because I neither had the love nor the lung capacity for mountain climbing, so the children and I would find an excuse to wait about "half way" until he made the top and returned for us.

Our social life during those years was almost nil — we did belong to a group who played bridge about once a month — then there were a few dances, but, on the whole, it was mostly work — LeRoy burned the midnight oil most every night, and I quizzed him before exams and kept the coffee pot hot. When Dr. Wilbur finally gave him his diploma, he remarked that "it seems there should be one for your wife, Doctor."

We sold the little house on Bryant Street when we moved to San Diego to intern at County Hospital — it was sad because it had been home for 4 years, the longest we had lived any one place since our marriage, but we sold it to Dr. Wilbur's son who was also a doctor and it made an ideal office as it was so well located.

The next year in San Diego was pleasant for all — good hospital — fine school for the children (Grant Elementary) and we managed to spend many week-ends exploring La Jolla with the intention of making it our home. While living in San Diego we were again confronted by a decision that would effect all our lives — LeRoy was offered the position as house physician to Hotel del Coronado — it was hard to turn down but we did — as we thought La Jolla, being smaller, and having a fine new Clinic as well a new 50 bed hospital would be better for us as a family in the long run. So here I am back in La Jolla with my life — I didn't mean to ramble so far back but it was necessary to tell how we decided to come here in the first place — even when the then practicing three physicians — Dr. Parker, Dr. LaZelle, Dr. Gillispie advised against it — just not enough work for four Doctors. We had been here six months and we had begun to think they were right, we had been too optimistic — then the "big three" began to take vacations and LeRoy was asked to look after their patients while they were away. Then too, for some reason La Jolla began to grow — the La Valencia was built, a new bank came to town (Bank of Italy), Girard had a face lift and so it went, slowly but permanently things began to change. The social life was centered around the Scripps children's playground where dances were held on the Tennis Courts and at the Casa de Mañana where the more formal entertaining was done.

Mrs. Isabel Morrison Hopkins was one of the most gracious hostesses La Jolla has ever known — her famous Sunday night parties were in great demand by the social elite — one was not really "in" until one had been invited. Then the Yacht and Tennis Club was built — of course the Yacht part was changed to Beach when it was found unfeasible to build a Yacht basin and settled for a duck pond instead.

My husband and I had a life membership to the Beach and Tennis Club and I gave the first party that was ever given there — and it was a "dud." The day arrived and the kitchen wasn't opened for business due to a strike in the kitchen help department. So, the last minute a caterer came out from San Diego and managed to serve something — what, I'll never know. However I learned a lesson — never again to try and be *first*.

Harle Garth Montgomery — What Her Parent's Never Knew.

Dr. Garth opened his La Jolla practice in a cottage where Prospect dips in a V, leading down to Scripps Park. "My father, being a proper Easterner, went to pay respects to the other three doctors in town (Parker, Gillespie, & LaZelle). They told him that another doctor was not needed. He put up his shingle anyway. So the three doctors sent all their dead-beat patients to him," said Harle Garth Montgomery.

Ellen Revelle remembers Dr. Garth. "I met him at a local dance. He asked if I had lived in La Jolla very long and I replied that I had been here almost every summer

Dr. William L. Garth, early La Jolla physician.
Courtesy of Harle Montgomery

The Bug House Kids. L to R: Corinne Copeland, Esther Allen, unidentified, and Margaret Allen. The boy fifth from the right is Paul McEwen.
Courtesy of SIO Archives/UCSD

and then had come back to live with my husband. He asked where we lived and I told him The Bug House. Well, you should have seen him. I was almost tossed off the dance floor. Literally pushed away. That's how we were treated in those days. Everyone thought anyone living at The Bug House was strange and contaminated." The Bug House was the name given by the children of the Scripps Institution of Oceanography scientists to the Institution where they lived.

Dr. Garth's daughter Harle, who was six at the time they arrived in La Jolla remembers: "We lived in the Top of the Cove (in the Frederick Brown house named after the Brown family) for four or five years. We all slept out on the sleeping porch." They could hear the surf and the salty air helped sooth them to sleep. There was no traffic in those days. Soon, her parents decided to build a house (which they would name, Castalanna), off Hillside Drive. While the house was being built, the family lived in the Matterhorn, a cottage on Prospect (near the present Crab Catcher), part of the Green Dragon Colony complex.

"When my father was a medical student, it was accepted to look into Indian graves and collect bones…the Stanford campus had previously been the site of an Indian settlement. My father dug up bones and studied them for anatomy. I remember my father arranging them on the floor of our Palo Alto home. When we came to San Diego they were put in a box. When we moved into the Hillside home my brother and I had a 'secret' attic. When we moved from that house, we kids decided to leave the box in the secret attic — They're still there! I have since realized how disrespectful it was."

Harle Garth in front of their home known as Top of the Cove.
Courtesy of Harle Montgomery

Mrs. Garth had always admired a home on Torrey Pines just below Coast Walk at the bluff edge with the caves directly across the water, belonging to Ivan Rice. One day she heard that Sidney Chaplin, the brother of Charlie Chaplin, was on his way down from Los Angeles to buy the property. Without wasting any time to consult her husband, she purchased the property, so when Sidney arrived the property had already been sold.

Harle recalls, "Growing up in La Jolla was like Tom Sawyer. We had the run of the hills, cliffs…. I jumped off the cliffs! No danger. No treats." In the summer, the children of La Jolla would go every Saturday morning to "Joy for a Penny." Located in a building across the street (Girard) from the Granada Theatre with

The Rice home on the bluff bought by Mrs. Garth.
Courtesy Harle Montgomery

a Lodge meeting room upstairs, "it was like a huge living room." The lady who ran it "must have been a dancer." Every child brought a penny. They danced and stretched and did "wonderful and relaxing exercises." At the end of the summer, "we put on a performance in the patio." They were also given a "shiny penny with a hole in it and a blue ribbon tied through it."

Harle recalls the independence they had as kids. Every Saturday, "we had house chores first thing in the morning. Then (when they did not attend 'Joy for a Penny'), we packed a lunch and took off for hikes." They hiked up Mt. Soledad, down Rose Canyon, through Sycamore Canyon (now State Rt. 52), then back up Mt. Soledad and back down and home. Other times, they hiked up Biological Grade to Box Canyon where there was a heavy wire "like a cable which you could go down to the bottom of another canyon, then to the beach (Black's Beach). It was easy for us to go down but very difficult to climb up, so when the tide was low, we would walk back along the beach. We had booklets that told the tides." Harle adds, "I had to do something to be able to go around with the boys. Once, I had to eat an eight inch slender jellyfish!" But "what a wonderful way to grow up. Such freedom!"

"When we went to school, we had singing lessons. We had a print shop. Theater, dancing, mechanical drawing…." She continues, "I feel so sorry for kids today. They have to be so protected. There are so many threats. They have to be picked up and delivered." She gives an example of the freedom from danger she

Harle and her mother playing on the beach.
Courtesy of Harle Montgomery

experienced as a child in the twenties and thirties. "I had my teeth straightened. I used to take the streetcar to the Medical Dental Building (in San Diego) and get my teeth tightened and come back home alone. Today, you wouldn't let a twelve year old girl go on a trip like that alone!"

"It was an interesting time to live in La Jolla. There were quite a lot of missionaries who lived here. They had been to places like China and came back here for 'r and r.' Many lived in the little cottages near the Green Dragon down the street toward La Jolla."

"We were staunch Democrats," says Mrs. Harle Montgomery of her family. "When FDR was elected in 1932, we had three cars parading through La Jolla. The Garths, Sheltons, and the Roberts. I think everyone else in La Jolla had their blinds drawn."

La Jolla was truly a small, quiet, and safe town in those days. What a wonderful time it must have been to be a child.

The Saga of Dr. Perkins

Abridged from an article written by J T Lipe, M. D., in 1983, for *Inside La Jolla*

Copyright © 1986 by La Jolla Historical Society

On October 15, 1936, I was asked to make a house call (doctors were making them in those days) upon Eugene C. Perkins, M.D., who lived at 1314 Virginia Way, La Jolla. Upon my arrival there, I was met at the door by an elderly Miss Emily Page, who was one of two maiden sisters who lived with and cared for Dr. Perkins. I immediately realized that Miss Emily Page's sister was senile. It was Miss Emily Page who escorted me to Dr. Perkins' bedroom and assisted me while I attended to Dr. Perkins.

Dr. Perkins told me he was a graduate of the University of Chicago, School of Medicine, and had practiced medicine in Chicago afterwards for many years. It was during those years that the two Page sisters had become patients of Dr. Perkins and they credited Dr. Perkins with saving their lives.

Years later, Dr. Perkins decided to retire and move to Florida with the two Page sisters and another woman named Margaret Curran. The four of them lived together in Florida for several years.

In 1926, they moved to La Jolla where they established residence at 1314 Virginia Way. That was ten years before I was called to visit the doctor. Miss Page told me that Dr. Perkins had married Margaret Curran in a Catholic Church secretly before they moved to La Jolla and that Margaret Curran had died about six months before I was called. Since Margaret died, the Doctor had been very depressed, would eat very little, was not interested in living, and had lost a great deal of weight.

Dr. Perkins never practiced medicine in La Jolla but was a familiar figure on the local streets and known by many, including Dr. Truman A. Parker, who described him as a "very nice, quiet, mousy little man."

Dr. Edward Elson was the minister of the La Jolla Presbyterian Church in 1936 and knew Dr. Perkins well. Dr. Elson was perhaps the only person who could describe Dr. Perkins accurately. He said Dr. Perkins was "a person of moderate

J T Lipe, M. D
Courtesy of Steele Lipe

height, perhaps 5' 7" or 8" tall, a well proportioned frame, fair complexioned and an up-to-date haircut…the Doctor spoke with a crisp high baritone voice and was skillful repartee."

Dr. Perkins had no specific complaints or symptoms. I found the patient in bed, mentally alert, cooperative, very weak, emaciated, and obviously near death. I did a complete physical examination in hopes of finding some physical cause for the moribund condition, but found none. I did, however, discover that Dr. Perkins was a female!

I was certain that Miss Page, who was standing at the foot of the bed, was aware that I had ascertained during the examination that Dr. Perkins was a female, but she did not let me know that she did. Had she done so and confided in me that she knew, the next 7-10 days would have been without event, but she did not. As a result, those days were anything but without event.

Since death was inevitable, I asked Miss Page to call me when the Doctor died—day or night. About 8:00 AM on October 22, 1936, Miss Page phoned to inform me that the doctor had died during the early hours. I asked why she had not notified me and she said she did not want to bother me. She told me she had dressed Dr. Perkins and had Bonham Brothers Mortuary in San Diego come and get the body.

I immediately went to the Perkins residence and consoled the Page sisters.

Since I had been told that there were no relatives, I asked them to sign an autopsy permit so I could properly fill out the death certificate as to the cause of death, and they did.

I immediately went to the Bonham Brothers Mortuary and performed the autopsy. One of the Bonham brothers told me that since the body was completely dressed in male attire, it was put in the men's morgue. Upon preparing the body to be embalmed, it was discovered that Perkins was a female! The body was quickly moved into the female morgue—as if it made any difference!

The autopsy revealed no definite cause of death and that the deceased was a female in every respect. I then had to decide how I should fill out the death certificate…. This caused a problem for me.

The Page sisters were so devoted and dedicated to Dr. Perkins that I did not wish to disillusion them by writing 'female' so I filled I filled it in with 'male.' Upon returning to my office, I told Dr. Parker (my associate) of my quandary regarding the sex on the death certificate, and he suggested that I call the coroner's office in San Diego. I did and when I explained my situation, someone in the Coroner's office…told me it must be signed 'female.' It really made sense…for the law stipulates the death certificate must be filled out accurately, and if Dr. Perkins had been a fugitive from justice and I had done the autopsy and still filled it out falsely, I would have been considered an accomplice. There upon I called the Coroner's office and had the certificate of Death corrected to 'female.'

The call to the Coroner's Office, however, opened a 'can of worms' for the newspaper hawks were just waiting for something to happen. With newspaper reporters hot on my tail, I went to visit Miss Page. I informed Miss Page that a newspaper reporter wanted to interview me about Dr. Perkins and she wanted to know why. I told her that Dr. Perkins was a female who had successfully been impersonating a man in La Jolla for 10 years and that was news! Miss Page replied that Dr. Perkins was a man. About that time, the reporter knocked on the door and Miss Page answered. When the reporter asked for a picture of Dr. Perkins, she slammed the door in his face.

That same afternoon on the bottom of the front page of the San Diego Evening Tribune there was an eight-column headline, "Woman Masquerades As A Man In La Jolla For Ten Years" and the subtitle, "Dr. Lipe misled!"

United Press and/or the Associated Press carried the story over their wires. Several of my medical classmates and friends across the USA wrote me asking if I had not yet discovered the difference between a woman and a man!

True story told by a man of wit, talent, and charm. We dedicate this article to the memory of JT Lipe, MD.

Transportation in Old La Jolla

We do not ride on the railroad; it rides upon us.
Henry David Thoreau, _Walden_, 1854

In the beginning, tourists and visitors would board the Horton House bus, a Concord coach drawn by four horses which carried eighteen passengers, to bring them out to the Cove for the day. It took two hours to get to the popular La Jolla picnic grounds from Fifth and Broadway, downtown San Diego. By 1893, the first railroad was planned to connect San Diego to La Jolla. The Articles of Incorporation were filed and directors were appointed. When built, it would be an extension of the San Diego, Old Town, and Pacific Beach Railroad. The railroad came up the east side of Mission Bay. A short section of the right of way can still be identified as Balboa Avenue, west of Interstate-5, to its intersection with Grand Avenue. The rail road continued north parallel to La Jolla Blvd. crossing Pearl St. at Cuvier and up Prospect St. to Virginia Scripps Cottage (Wisteria Cottage now John Cole's Book Store).

San Diegan's picknicing at what would be one day Scripp's Park in 1870. Note the baren landscape of undeveloped La Jolla.
Courtesy of The Library Assnociation of La Jolla

The first train of the San Diego, Old Town, Pacific Beach & La Jolla Railway arrived in La Jolla on Sunday, May 15, 1894. There was a big celebration including driving the final spike into the rail by a lady, "in honor of womankind generally." However, the citizens decided that the train track did not extend far enough. The end of the railroad was on Prospect Street, not far from the head of Draper Avenue, and just in front of Miss Scripps' residence. Many thought the La Jolla Park Hotel, just above the Cove, should be the ultimate destination. This required an extension of which not everyone was in favor. The Railroad Company learning that an injunction was being prepared to stop the extension had Mr. Boyd, the superintendent, put on an extra workforce. They worked covertly night and day over a weekend laying 1400 feet of track. By Monday morning the tracks extended to Fay Avenue and a small depot was hastily erected. After all, possession is 9/10ths of the law, isn't it? The opponents had been out-maneuvered! The extension ran along Prospect Street, almost to the front door of the La Jolla Park Hotel at Grand (now Girard).

The original depot was really nothing more than a shed. In January 1899, a windstorm blew it over but it was promptly

The end of the line with the hastily erected station shed near the present Fay & Prospect intersection.
Courtesy of Barbara Dawson

replaced with a structure not unlike its predecessor. This preliminary depot was located in the middle of Prospect Street near Fay Avenue. According to Fred Higgins, Miss Ellen B. Scripps' chauffeur, "most everyone remembers the little train that used to run from San Diego to La Jolla. It used to run down Prospect Street from the Shell Oil Station and then later down Silverado from the wooden depot on Silverado Street, then down around in front of E. B. Scripps' residence and past the Bishop's School on Cuvier Avenue. The conductor on the train was Daniel Mar; the brakeman was Smith. The road later would put on the gasoline motor car."

An amusing incident occurred after the first extension was added and the train tracks ended just in front of Miss Scripps' property. A friend who had been visiting Ellen and Virginia Scripps for a few days was preparing to leave. She packed her suitcases and walked a few feet down the street to board the train. However, when she reached the train, she realized that she had forgotten one suitcase. Informing the conductor, she asked if he could delay departure just a few minutes so she could run back to the house and get her bag. The conductor was not sympathetic. He had a train to run after all, and a schedule to maintain. Ellen Scripps' eccentric sister solved the problem. Virginia took one suitcase and placed it on the tracks. Then she sat down on it and refused to move until her friend returned with her forgotten bag. The conductor was not amused.

Bob Wilson, a long time early La Jollan, describes his first visit to La Jolla by rail in an essay published by the La Jolla Historical Society as follows:

"Bearing north we neared Mission Boulevard, through the farms and ranches of Bird Rock, into a sparsely settled south La Jolla, and there, great discoveries of all discoveries, the roundhouse and its wrecks of previous Abalone Limited rolling stock, including rusting boilers and decaying passenger coaches. What 13 year old boy could ask for anything more?"

Turntables and roundhouses usually go together. Bob must have ridden the train many times after his first trip. If the turntable was there, he probably would have mentioned it. Early writers place a train shed somewhere in south La Jolla, but until speaking with Isabel Baresch, it was not clear how trains were turned around.

As a teenager, Isabel Lessig (Baresch) commuted on the Abalone Limited to San Diego High, dubbed "The Old Gray Castle" (circa 1916). The trains, she said, did back down a few blocks on Silverado and what is now Cuvier Avenue to a point east of La Jolla Boulevard about where Genter Street is today. According to Miss Lessig, the train turned around on a wye switch, which is a track layout that looks like the letter Y. A train would back off the main line using one leg of the wye, then proceed on the tail of the wye. Switching to the other leg, the train emerged from the wye onto the mainline and proceeded down the line in a forward direction. Behind the wye there was a big shed where men repaired the trains. Frequent accidents plagued the La Jolla line and must have kept the repair crews busy. Isabel's statement on "train repairs" and Bob Wilson's "great discoveries of all discoveries" would seem to identify the only heavy industry ever conducted in La Jolla.

(Later the railroad wanted to push the tracks up Connecticut Avenue [Silverado Street] to a new station to be built at

Ivanhoe Avenue. This idea was opposed by two property owners who wanted $700.00 for the sixty feet they owned of the proposed right of way. Similar tactics to those of the Prospect Street extension were employed. The tracts were laid under cover of darkness before any protest could be made.)

Once the railroad was constructed, it was decided that San Diego visitors be encouraged to come to La Jolla (as if her beauty was not enough!). A month after the railroad's completion, a balloon ascension and parachute jump were staged featuring "Miss Hazel Keyes with her trained monkey, Yan-Yan, accompanied by Professor Romeo, the accomplished aeronaut." The railroad also did its share of construction in La Jolla building a harrowing flight of steps down the steep slope where abalones could be gathered at low tide. The descent was called "Devil's Slide." It should be noted that in the final years of the 19th century, *The San Diego Union* would publish the times of favorable low tides in La Jolla, the best time for visitors to explore the caves, collect shells and peek into the hidden world of the tide pools. According to Spencer Wilson, one of the highlights was viewing the "White Lady" at the bottom of the steps in the first cave to the left. At the wee hours of dawn, he said, if the tide was low and you entered the cave you would see perfectly outlined before you the image of a lady full of white light separating you from the Pacific.

A McKeen Motorcar known locally as the "Red Devil" parked in front of the Cabrillo Hotel in 1908. Anna Held is in front seat of the car. *Courtesy of San Diego Historical Society Photograph Collection*

During the summers of 1897-98, the railroad company hired "Professor" Horace Poole, a "flamboyant" stuntman, to dive from a springboard placed over the caves into the ocean below. It must have been quite a spectacle to be standing down near the Cove and watch a man dive off the cliff over one hundred feet and down into the pounding surf below. Fortunately, "Professor" Poole survived them all including one on July 4, 1898 when his body was covered with flammable oil and ignited just before the dive. For his prowess, the railway company paid him $25.00 per dive. Another tourist attraction provided by the railroad company was a dancing pavilion. Built in the Park, it had inside galleries, a dance floor and verandas overlooking the ocean. The Pavilion became the "social center" of La Jolla. Card games were held there and parties to which "every one in the village was invited, bar none." In 1907, the Pavilion was taken down and much of the wood was used for the construction of the Cabrillo Hotel. (On Prospect Street, the Cabrillo was the first hotel built in La Jolla since the 1896 burning of the La Jolla Park Hotel. It is now the west wing of La Valencia.) The architect for this four-story (plus basement), plain, square structure was Irving Gill. "Squire" Wilson opened the Cabrillo with its 46 guest rooms, baths, parlors, dining room and kitchen to the public in 1909.

With the arrival of the McKean gas cars in 1908, the tracks were extended north along Ivanhoe to Prospect Street, then down Prospect to Fay Avenue forming a loop around the village. The red McKean car, with its similarity to a submarine was soon dubbed "Red Devil" both for its looks and its inefficiency. The gas cars ran the loop and returned to San Diego

La Jolla Trolley Train, 1924. The location is just south of Nautilus near the La Jolla Jr.-Sr. High School. La Jolla Hermosa is in the background.
Courtesy of San Diego Historical Society Photograph Collection

without having to reverse direction.

The engines for these commuter trains came from the elevated railroad of New York City. However, when the tracks of old La Jolla Railroad were picked up in 1918, La Jolla was left without any public transportation to San Diego. La Jollans petitioned the San Diego City Council to provide them with a streetcar line. The Council negotiated a franchise with John D. Spreckles to extend his Mission Beach line to La Jolla. The expansion used a portion of the abandoned railroad right of way. The streetcar left Horton Plaza in San Diego, ran across the base of Point Loma to Ocean Beach, skirted Mission Bay across the mouth of the San Diego River (south end of Mission

Beach at the jetties), and proceeded up Mission Boulevard. From Mission Blvd to the present day bicycle path at Via del Norte and the Fay Ave. extension, the trolley right of way used the old train bed by paralleling La Jolla Blvd. on Electric

Avenue (now La Jolla Hermosa Avenue), and paused at the lovely San Carlos substation.

At a cost of $50,000, San Carlos substation was constructed simultaneously with the La Jolla streetcar terminal in October, 1924, and was the first of many substations constructed in San Diego patterned after California Missions. The San Carlos substation housed electrical transformers that boosted power line voltage so cars could reach the end of the line. Unlike the La Jolla terminal, San Carlos survived the Depression, war, and time. It was located near a development in the southern end of La

The San Carlos Trolley Substation.
Courtesy of San Diego Historical Society Photograph Collection

Jolla called the Hermosa Tract, "San Diego's socially correct spot to live" (according to one advertisement in 1926). Certainly, having the station there gave incentive to potential customers to consider building their future homes in this exclusive location.

Going back to the late 1920s, Balfour Realtors of Prospect Street announced their intention to develop Hermosa Terrace. Advertisements claimed Hermosa Terrace would be the finest sub-division in California. To develop this sub-division, a new Belfour office would be built on the site east of La Jolla Boulevard at Mira Monte Avenue. In addition to the planned home sites, a large billboard on the Boulevard proclaimed that lots for commercial ventures were also available. The office was built next to and north of the San Carlos streetcar substation.

Soon advertising ceased and Belfour Realtor listings in the San Diego Directories stopped with the 1929 edition. Apparently, the company and its grandiose plans fell victim to the Great Depression as did subdivisions throughout San Diego and La Jolla. Lot prices dropped from $1500 to $300. The main architects associated with this development, Thomas Shepherd and Edgar V. Ullrich, found little work. Ullrich pursued his artistic talent and sold drawings and sketches on a custom basis. It was another ten years before Upper Hermosa was developed.

During W.W.II, two defense industries used the San Carlos Administration Building as a school for aviators and a place to train workers. After the war, it was an art school. Some time later, Mr. Locke opened La Plaza, a Mexican restaurant, and El Toro Bar.

Meanwhile, the terminal itself fell to disuse following the 1940 electric railway closure. In 1953, a former military chaplain, Reverend Tom Denman, came to La Jolla and inherited a congregation of Methodists consisting of twenty-four members. With the assistance of his parishioners, Rev. Denman searched for a new permanent church. "I was looking for a Safeway place," he said. A Safeway? "Yes, I wanted a place that was accessible, had a road nearby and was easy to find. Just like any Safeway has to be." Rev. Denman located the abandoned railroad station in Hermosa and acquired it for his church. Within less than a year, his congregation grew to over two hundred. The church initially used the waiting room as its chapel, seating 125 members.

The El Toro Bar lease ran for three more years and placed the church in the precarious position of owning an establishment that dispensed alcohol. The Methodist Church maintained the lease agreement but, according to Assistant to the Pastor, Mrs. Jessie Brubaker, the income funded no church related activities. Eventually, membership growth necessitated the purchase of the restaurant and bar.

Remodeled by church members and architect, Thomas Shepherd, La Plaza housed the Methodist congregation for the next ten years.

Completed in 1970, the current chapel stands south of the old San Carlos Station, now used as a storage room. The terminal platform has been enclosed and is a meeting hall. The original Fine Arts and Administration Building is a reception hall.

Rev. Tom Denman was also responsible for the lovely oval rose garden in front of the building. Now retired, Rev. Denman is just as proud of his garden as he is of the church he procured so many years ago. The mission style railroad depot survived and is all the more beautiful as today's La Jolla United Methodist Church, an architectural gem.

Returning to the early days, the days of old streetcar number sixteen. After its brief stop at the San Carlos Station, the commuter street car continued north on Fay, past Nautilus Street, passing east of La Jolla Jr.-Sr. High School, and continued to Prospect where the La Jolla terminal was located. The tracks circled the depot so that the trolley car was prepared for the return trip. (Students could buy a monthly pass for a dollar; otherwise, round trip tickets to San Diego and back cost fifty

La Jolla Trolley Station on the southeast corner of Prospect
Street and Fay Avevenue, 1925
Courtesy of San Diego Historical Society Photograph Collection

Interior of the La Jolla Trolley Station
Courtesy of San Diego Historical Society Photograph Collection

cents.)

Located at the corner of Fay and Prospect, the La Jolla terminal was an elliptical-shaped building. At a cost of $100,000, it was called "one of the finest interurban terminals in America" by the Traffic Manager of the San Diego Electric Company, Fay R. Smalley. Passengers could board the cars directly from the lobby on the south side of the building. Only one photograph was ever made of the interior. Fortunately, a professional photographer took it and the good quality of the picture shows details quite clearly. Not all La Jolla residents, in fact very few, admired the building. Norma Newman Hacker, a La Jollan at the time, described the building as "pseudo-Spanish Renaissance style." However, a news item, which appeared in 1940 (when it was announced that the terminal was about to be demolished) was more complementary. "No expense was spared in its construction. This is readily seen on entering the spacious circular lobby or waiting room with glass dome in the center directly over the fountain. Tiled floors, plate glass on all sides, and also the doors. The finest of gum brush and copper glass bead. Hardly a flaw is to be found after almost 16 years of service."

Another rider/historian wrote: "At Prospect and Fay was an elaborate doughnut shaped building…. Inside the terminal were spaces for a number of small boutique type shops, usually vacant. The terminal did furnish shelter on rainy days but always seemed a dank, cold, gloomy place. Cars left only twice an hour, and no one waited at the terminal longer than could be helped. It was too deserted and spooky. In the last years of No. 16, cars no longer turned around the circle. Motormen reversed the trolley instead. Parts of the circular tracks were removed even before the line was abandoned in 1940." When it was demolished, the rubble from that Prospect Street station was dumped over the bluff onto the beach in an undeveloped area between Pearl and Marine Streets (now the White Sands Retirement Community).

Not all La Jollans were enchanted with the arrival of a rapid transit system that would place them only 45 minutes from that metropolis to the south. Nor were they happy to be connected so closely with the "Hoi Polloi" of Mission Beach. Many would have preferred to keep their privacy, enjoying their isolation rather than putting up with the expected invasion of outsiders.

When the streetcars made their inaugural runs down Fay on July 4, 1924, residents were said to have shuttered their windows. The invasion came in flood proportions, particularly on summer weekends when the line ran four-car trains to handle the large numbers of day-trippers from San Diego. Heavy demands were made on limited resources and entertainment facilities by the thousands of fun seekers who overran the streets and beaches. La Jolla's quiet bucolic atmosphere was shattered forever. Later, the streetcars not only brought holiday visitors but also regular commuters who worked in La Jolla and lived elsewhere. As a consequence, home building began in earnest and new subdivisions were added. Streets and sidewalks were paved throughout the area. (In the teens, when the first sidewalks were laid, many La Jollans had protested saying that the sidewalks would "make your feet sore and besides, they would ruin the town!")

Paying for sidewalks was the property owner's responsibility. Mrs. Gaines, who lived on Eads, used gold coins to pay for her 50 feet. The gold standard was $25/ounce in 1925. Seven years later, FDR put into effect the "Gold Act of '32" making gold coins no longer legal tender. However, law abiding and trusting citizens of 1932 dutifully turned in their gold, unaware of the last word, "tender." Nor did they know that the true value had become $35/ounce. In the year 2000, the gold standard was $288/ounce. Using today's calculations, 7320 Eads would be the most expensive sidewalk in La Jolla.

Back to the old railroad story: On the southbound run from La Jolla, the usual nickel fare increased to a dime at the San Carlos station. To avoid paying the extra fare, high school students who lived a few blocks farther south in Bird Rock would exit the trolley at the station. On occasion, when approaching from the north, if no one was seen on the platform, the conductor would accelerate the car and pass the station at a high speed. Then he would cut the power and coast down the tracks to a stop closer to the students' homes. Apparently, the logic of his altruistic action was that if no power was used beyond the station, it didn't cost the company anything. In the morning, students, who always seemed to be late, raced along the tracks up to the trolley station and the five-cent fare. For the students' sake, the conductor would reduce speed and stop at the station although no passengers were waiting.

Japanese truck farms occupied the area north of Turquoise Street where Bird Rock Elementary School is today. Commuters called this area the Japanese strawberry patch. During the strawberry season, growers would set up tables with baskets of strawberries and a coffee can marked with the price. The conductor would stop the car and those who wished, got off to buy baskets of strawberries. Of course, it was understood, as a courtesy for this service, that the conductor could choose the biggest and juiciest strawberry from each basket.

The last streetcar to La Jolla left San Diego at 1:15 am on Sept. 16, 1940. Seventeen people took "old #16" on its last run. "Our Gang," a close group of five friends who had made the daily streetcar rides from Bird Rock during their high school

Mr. Greeley and his ice cream wagon on Girard Street, 1885.
Courtesy of San Diego Historical Society Photograph Collection

days, was there. This night, the 16th for #16, Bentley Buck ("one of our favorite motormen") was at the controls. He gave the gang permission to do what they had always wanted to do: blow the whistle and ring the bell. "We whistled and jangled all the way through Mission Beach, Pacific Beach, and down Fay Avenue, arriving at the La Jolla terminal about 2 a.m." They intentionally hoped to wake everyone up because, as "gang" member Norma Newman Hacker aptly states: "It wasn't just a streetcar going by. It was the passing of an era."

Other modes of transportation before gasoline automobiles included the Tally Ho, a covered carriage for eight people drawn by four horses. Mr. Horace Greeley had a carriage with a sign reading: "ICE CREAM, wholesale and retail, CORNUCOPIAS and PEANUTS, COLD SOFT DRINKS." Two donkeys pulled his wagon. La Jolla Transfer had a topless wagon drawn by two horses (see cover). Another small two-wheel carriage was popular. It was pulled by one horse (or pony) and could carry two people.

All the roads were dirt to accommodate the horses. By 1923, a water wagon was being used to sprinkle down the streets and cut down the dust. Occasionally, the children would chase the wagon and get soaked when the driver turned on the water and showered them.

With the advent of automobiles, priorities changed. The trains were gone and the streets needed to be paved. Repair garages sprang up along with gas stations and automobile agencies. In 1918, the train tracks were sent to Japan. No one knew that Japan was going to use the steel for the fabrication of armaments. Over the years, a section at a time, the streetcar tracks were also removed. Truly, the end of an era.

Torrey Pines State Reserve

Preserving the Past for the Future

The pine trees…(are)…making their last stand among the rugged canyons and clinging to the colorful sandstone cliffs of this monument at San Diego's gateway. Dwarfed, gnarled and twisted, they send their roots far down over the cliffs seeking a stronger foothold and nourishment. They stand as a wonderful example of tenacity….

(Guy L. Fleming, botanist, naturalist and custodian from 1921-1933)

On October 9, 1999, Torrey Pines State Reserve celebrated its 100th Anniversary of being a park. Parts of Pueblo Lots number 1332, 1333, 1336, and all of 1337, "containing and consisting of about three hundred and sixty-nine (369) acres of land more or less, said Pueblo Lots being a part of the Pueblo Lands of the City of San Diego" were set aside "now and forever as a public park, and…the same shall be hereafter used for no other purpose." (Ordinance No. 648, was passed and adopted by the Board of Aldermen of the City of San Diego, California, 24th of July, 1899.) The park was known as "Torrey Pines Park" and was probably the first area within an urban setting in the nation to be designated as a natural preserve. However, the history of this area began well before this date.

As early as 1769, the Portola-Serra Sacred Expedition set out to establish missions from San Diego, through Sorrento Valley and up to Monterey. The trail they used was called El Camino Real. The region north of San Diego was called *Soledad* (lonely or solitary) and the unique pines that grew here, Soledad pines, a name that survived until 1850. In the early years of exploration and colonization, the pines played an important role. European seamen used this distinctive tree as a charting tool for the California coast. "As this is the only pine-covered hillock for miles along the coastline it is an important landmark to vessels that are running close along shore in foggy weather." (*Coast Pilot,* 1889)

Guy L. Fleming in front of a Torrey pine tree.
Courtesy of Dorothy Shelton

In 1850, California became a State of the Union. That same year, Charles Christopher Parry, a medical doctor with a strong interest in botany who had been appointed botanist for the US-Mexican Boundary Survey, "officially" discovered the unusual and unique pine. The survey was commissioned to map and document the newly revised border between the US and Mexico following the Mexican-American War (1846-1848). After completing his assignment, Parry returned to San Diego and met entomologist John Le Conte. Dr. John Le Conte was visiting the area and had observed "some peculiar pines growing above the mouth of Soledad Valley" (Peñasquitos Lagoon). He asked Parry to visit the site. Parry obliged approaching the area from the beach. Ascending the bluffs, he reported "it was necessary to follow up some of the sharp ravines that here debouch on the ocean beach, and here (possibly to the neglect of strict geological duties) my attention was taken up by this singular and unique maritime pine…." Parry believed that this pine was indeed unique, but to be sure, he sent a sample to his mentor, one of the leading botanist of his time, John Torrey, asking for verification and requesting, "I wish it with your permission to bear the name *Pinus torreyana*." The pine proved to be the only specimen of its kind. Since 1850, these unique trees have come to be known as Torrey pines. Since the year coincided with California's entry into statehood, the Torrey pine is known as California's birthday tree.

The beauty and wonder of this tree and the terrain it calls home truly capture the imagination. The Torrey Pines Cliffs that rise an impressive 300 feet above the ocean consist of buff and green sandstones and siltstones that date back to a tertiary sea 40 to 60 million years ago. At the base of these cliffs, on the southern end, is Flat Rock. Made of resistant sandstone, this rock has a rectangular hole on its top. The hole has given rise to many legends, but it is believed that years ago, a Welch miner attempted to sink a shaft for a coal mine on the top. (It is interesting to note that years before, Dr. Parry was sent down to research the possibility of coal deposits in the same area.) Just north of Flat Rock, a line of fresh-appearing shells and loose beach sand appear. These are indicative of a much "younger" terrace. This line is said to be associated with the La Jolla terrace to the south and "probably represents an interglacial sea level over 40 thousand years ago." At sunset, the cliffs appear to be illuminated in reds and yellows, tan and gold.. However, not everyone respected the trees or their habitat.

In 1883, Dr. Parry returned and was dismayed at the deteriorating condition of his beloved pines. He wrote a historical and scientific account of the pine emphasizing the need to protect the tree from extermination and presented it to the San Diego Society of Natural History. However, it wasn't until 1899, at the behest of botanist Belle Angier and the influence of Mr. George W. Marston that the City Council was pressured to "set aside 369 acres of Pueblo lands" as a "free and public park." Nothing, however, specifically provided for the protection of the pines. It was a first step, but civilization was advancing and encroaching upon the adjacent lands. Miss Ellen Browning Scripps came to the rescue. She purchased the adjacent lots (which also contained Torrey pines) and had them held in trust for the people of San Diego. To insure protection of the trees, in 1921, Miss Scripps and the City Park Commission appointed Botanist and Park Custodian Guy L. Fleming as custodian of her and the city's properties. In 1922, she also retained a landscape architect, Ralph D. Cornell, to develop and manage the Park. "In a small way," he wrote, "such a place as Torrey Pines ranks among the natural phenomena and should hold its small, proud place among our national monuments to nature's ability as a temperamental artist who now and then exceeds even her own hopes in the creation of something unusually attractive."

In 1924, the Torrey Pines Reserve was enlarged by the addition of approximately 1000 acres and in 1927 an on-site residence for Guy Fleming was also constructed. Mr. Fleming continued to manage the Park even after Miss Scripps' death in 1932.

In 1915, the Torrey Pines grade and Coast Highway (future US-101) were completed. At the time, this was the only coastal route available. Early travelers would stop at the edge of the cliffs and picnic before continuing on their voyage. To accommodate visitors as well as weary travelers who had driven down the narrow road (State Highway 1) from Los Angeles on their way to San Diego, Miss Scripps financed the construction of a simple Southwestern style adobe lodge. The Torrey

Pines Lodge officially opened in 1923. Mr. Fleming's father built all the furniture some of which can still be seen there. The Lodge served as a popular roadside restaurant for years. Today it is a visitors' center and houses the rangers' offices as well. Miss Scripps also authorized an on-site residence for the park manager, Mr. Guy Fleming and his family. Completed in 1927, the Fleming family remained at that location until 1958 when they moved to La Jolla.

However, the San Diego area continued to grow and the small ocean-side road built around 1915 with funds contributed by Miss Scripps to connect Scripps Institution for Biological Research (the future Scripps Institution of Oceanography) to La Jolla and Del Mar was insufficient for the increase in traffic. This was a challenge and a possible nightmare for the Torrey Pines Park. The League to Save Torrey Pines Park was formed in response in the hopes of preventing further defilement of the reserve. "Is the danger to the Park very pressing?" they asked. And, in response, they answered their own question: "So pressing that only an immediate and emphatic expression of public disapprobation can save this heritage of the people from a defilement which will bring upon its perpetuators the condemnation of generations yet unborn." However, the city cut down trees in 1924 when they constructed the present Coast Highway (US-101) and again in 1930-2 when the highway along the east side of the Reserve was expanded. The road and bridge along Torrey Pines beach were specifically designed to prevent natural flushing of the lagoon. It was reasoned, by preventing flushing, the railway right of way would be protected from erosion and the lagoon would fill in allowing for more usable land. Interstate 5 was eventually built on the very route initially recommended by the League.

Two pictures of Torrey Pines and the Coast Highway. Above are two autos negotiating the switchbacks from the Lodge down to the marshland of Peñasquitos Lagoon. The Guy Fleming trail begins to the right of the road. Below Torrey Pines Lodge which housed the restaurant as a stop for weary travelers from Los Angeles to San Diego. The road is the Coast Highway and the only road which connected La Jolla to Del Mar.
Courtesy of Judy Schulman

74

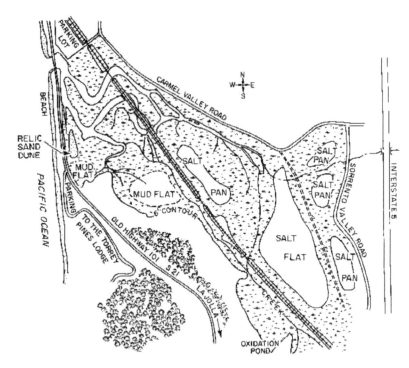

Map of Peñasquitos Lagoon just north of the more widely known part of Torrey Pines State Reserve. A portion of the hillside north of the Lagoon was also incorporated into the addition to the Park in 1970. *Courtesy of the Torrey Pines Association*

During World War II, 710 acres were leased to the United States Army and Camp Callan was constructed. This area has now become a World Class Championship Golf Course. The Craftsman-style Lodge at Torrey Pines is magnificent and the landscaping is beautiful; however, there are few Torrey pines on the property.

Some 8000 years ago, according to San Diego Zoo Arborist Daniel Simpson, a group of nomadic people (referred to as La Jollans) were thought to have lived on the cliffs just north of present La Jolla, under the shelter of the Torrey pine trees. Later, some 1500 years ago, the Kumeyaay tribe had a settlement in Sorrento Valley which was called *Istagua* ("there are trees there") and made this habitat part of their home. Surface soil throughout much of the Reserve contains shells, many of which are not fossils, but rather deposits of these and other ancient Indian tribes. But it wasn't the peaceful lifestyle of the Indians that caused damage to this unique and rarest of trees. Instead, it was the population of the twentieth century that threatened the area. Thanks to the vision of Miss Ellen Browning Scripps, the Torrey pine and its habitat have been preserved.

"The time will come when not only the scenic beauty but also the educational and recreational values of the Torrey Pines Reserve will be appreciated." (Ellen Browning Scripps)

After Miss Scripps' death, the property she owned at Torrey Pines was transferred, as per her instructions, to the city. The codicil to her will also contained the following admonition: "Permanent preservation of those rare trees and securing in perpetuity the scenic beauty of that region is vital." Guy Fleming, whom she had appointed to manage the Park, continued in that capacity but now he worked under the direction of San Diego City, Division of Parks. However, despoliation of the Park continued. People hiked off trails causing erosion and the exposure of vulnerable pine roots. Visitors also littered, but the worst crime of all was committed by people who actually cut trees down for firewood.

In 1942, Guy Fleming published an article about Torrey Pines in which he deplored the conditions existing at the Park. His plan in writing this article was to "stimulate a more aggressive guardianship of these unique trees." When confronted with this reality, the Fellows of the San Diego Society of Natural History threw the ball into the lap of the newly formed Ellen Browning Scripps Foundation and the Trustees of this Foundation responded. "The Park has been neglected since the city received this remarkable gift of Torrey Pines Point from Miss Scripps, and no provision has been made for guarding and preserving this precious heritage." In 1948, Guy Fleming retired from his position with the California State Park. It was clear that financial support as well as recognition was necessary for the Park to remain intact. This was where he would now focus his energy.

In 1950, the Foundation, upon the advice of landscape architect Ralph Cornell created the Torrey Pines Association.

Guy Fleming was named President. One of its first goals was to transfer the Torrey Pines Park from the City of San Diego to the California Division of Beaches and Parks (now called the Department of Parks and Recreation). This transfer was finalized in 1959 and the official designation became Torrey Pines State Reserve. Designation as a "Reserve" is one of the highest levels of protection available in the California State Park System.

In 1966, the widow of Guy Fleming, Margaret Eddy Fleming, was approached with the idea of acquiring 260 acres of private land just north of the Torrey Pines Reserve. This property contained an additional 3,000 Torrey pine trees. The idea appealed to Mrs. Fleming, as well as to Dr. John Comstock, then president of the Torrey Pines Association, and the council. A successful bond issue had previously passed in 1964 and finalized in 1966 to acquire more state parks and, in 1967, the State Park Commission was empowered to allocate funds. Mrs. Fleming and a committee from the Torrey Pines Association went to the commission to plead their cause. Old Town was accorded an outright $1 million dollar allocation; at the same time Torrey Pines would receive $900,000 if matching funds could be raised by June 1970. Supporting the extension besides the Torrey Pines Association were many private citizens, the Sierra Club, Torrey Pines Wildlife Association, San Diego Society of Natural History, California Academy of Science, Citizens Coordinate, Daughters of the American Revolution, and, of course, the ever generous Ellen Browning Scripps Foundation.

In 1970, because of a huge grass roots effort, the Torrey Pines Reserve Extension, on the other side of Los Peñasquitos Lagoon, was annexed to the Reserve. In 1975, the Torrey Pines Docent Society was formed. This group of volunteers assists in education, leading nature trail walks, staffing the Visitor Center, maintaining trails, as well as working on special projects. They also issue a monthly newsletter, *The Torreyana*. In 1978, Torrey Pines State Reserve was dedicated as a National Natural Landmark by the Department of the Interior.

The Torrey pine has been victorious. "It has become a source of civic pride and a symbol of hope for those working to preserve other rare and endangered species," according to Bill Evarts, author of *Torrey Pines, Landscape and Legacy*, a beautiful, detailed, photographic excursion into this scenic reserve along with prosaic "sense of place." In this book, "This very special and private place has found its interpreter," according to Robert Wohl, Supervising Ranger, Torrey Pines State Reserve.

Today, there are almost 2,000 acres of reserve plus a rare salt marsh. In addition to the trees, there are over 400 plant species that thrive on its sandy soil. Many land mammals also enjoy this rugged terrain. (The docents and rangers are always present to explain the fascinating histories of these plants and animals.) What was once an ancient dune forest—its bluffs ravaged by salty gusts and ocean surf, its Torrey pines stunted, jagged, gnarled, and twisted—is now limited to this small precarious area, the tree's last stronghold. Moreover, it is right in our own back yard, which surely obliges us all to participate in its survival.

According to the Oct. 1999 issue of *ZOONOOZ*, the Torrey pine is "not only a flagship species for this coastal sage habitat but also a foundation species. The tree canopies provide more than shelter. Fog and moist marine air condense on the needles, and the water is shed to irrigate the ground. Fallen needles insulate the ground, which reduces evaporation of precious moisture. Decaying needles form an organic layer that enriches the poor sandstone soil and provides a site for fallen seeds to germinate. Dead and fallen trees release soil nutrients and provide food and shelter for insects. This creates intricate ecosystem bonds between plants, pollinators, predators, and their prey." The writer of this article, Daniel Simpson (Arborist, Horticulture/San Diego Zoo) says that the entire "circle of life" in this area may well revolve around the tree itself.

Today fewer than 10,000 pines remain. Most are located within the confines of the Reserve, but some are being saved in La Jolla. (There are some 18 or more Torrey pine trees at the intersection of Ardath Road, Torrey Pines Road and La Jolla Shores Drive.) The only other groves are on Santa Rosa Island, one of the California Channel Islands. In addition, there are some trees on Point Loma. It is a mystery how these trees came to be located only in these two places on the globe.

"Fat Man's Misery," one of the more interesting trails within the Park. It has been closed and is no longer listed in the brochures.
Courtesy of Catriona Tudor Erler

It is also a mystery how this species survived. There is no genetic diversity among these trees. The Torrey pine "is an orphan species for which evolution has stopped." Disease, bark beetle infestation, drought and other elements of nature have killed many of these vulnerable trees.

Torrey Pines State Reserve is one of the rarest areas in the world. It is a place where the imagination of the visitor is captivated and the curiosity of the scientist is enticed. As the narrator of the park slide show says: "It is a place where we leave having rediscovered ourselves."

Greg Hackett, one of the long time park rangers, sums it up. "The way it used to be is the way it still is."

Margaret Eddy Fleming (1888-1977)

In 1924, Henry Wood and Dorothy Shelton of La Jolla invited Henry's cousin, Margaret ("Peggy") Doubleday Eddy, to come visit. Born in New York City, she had spent most of her adult life in nearby New Jersey. This would be her first trip west.

Mr. Shelton had a good friend named Guy Fleming. Often Guy would invite his pal to join him in a hike and occasional overnights. Henry reported "freezing to the bone" in a sleeping bag near the summit of the Ridge Route, but could not help admiring his friend, the naturalist and it was only natural that his cousin, Peg, would meet Guy. Although it had not been his objective, Henry Shelton was delighted when the couple fell in love. They were married in 1926.

Guy Fleming was born in 1884 in Nebraska, but when he was twelve, his family moved to Oregon and then, in 1909, down to San Diego. He and his father worked as gardeners for the Little Land Colony, a confederation of farmers in San Ysidro. "Fleming laid out and planted the village park," a project that brought him to the attention of County Horticultural Commissioner, George P. Hall. Mr. Hall inspired Guy to study botany.

In 1911, work was begun to create a world-class Exposition in honor of the pending opening of the Panama Canal. Beginning with a job in the nursery, Guy was soon promoted to foreman of the landscaping crew. When the Exposition opened in 1915, Guy became the main tour guide, giving talks on landscaping and plants.

In June, 1916, he and Mr. Ralph Sumner, representing the San Diego Society of Natural History and the San Diego Floral Association, made a two-day visit to the Torrey Pines Park to conduct botanical studies. It was their report that led to public support for the preservation of the area. The rest is history.

So now, with Guy Fleming, life for the young lady from New Jersey and New York City, would change dramatically. Peggy and Guy spent their early married life in a house at the George Scripps Biological Station (Scripps Institution of Oceanography). Employed by Miss Ellen Browning Scripps at the time, Mr. Fleming collaborated on the landscaping of the campus grounds, Scripps Hospital and Scripps College in Claremont. In 1933, he became Superintendent of the Southern District of California Beaches and Parks with his district ranging from San Simeon to Mexico and across to Arizona.

In 1929, the Flemings and their two children, John and Margaret (from Guy's first marriage), moved up to the Torrey pines land and temporarily lived in a tent while their custodian house in the preserve was being constructed, much of it by Guy's own labor and Peggy's design. Some of the wood, especially the beams, came from San Diego's first Natural History

Museum that had burned down. They lived there until 1958 when the area became a State Reserve. It was from this house that the protection of the Torrey pines was managed. To maintain the park during Depression years was a struggle, but it was made an adventure by the Flemings. They loved the isolation and the magnificence of the scene. During this time, when there was no opportunity to have a secretary, Peggy performed the task for her husband. "We worked extremely well together," she said. "I never wanted to change him; he never wanted to change me."

The isolation of the setting set her artist's hand to work. As a young girl in New York, she had studied with George Bellows (American Realist painter of the Ashcan School) at the Art Student's League on West 57th Street. She had worked in all media but preferred oils to water colors and, above all, etching. Since she liked to draw and paint landscapes best, living in such a unique setting was exhilarating. As for the trees themselves, Peggy felt they could best be depicted in etchings. She carried her sketchbooks and pencils with her constantly; any free moment was never wasted.

"My parents were largely responsible for my creativity," she said. The only child of Cynthia and William Abner Eddy, Peggy was proud of her father's accomplishments. Mr. Eddy was the inventor of the Eddy Kite, the first tailless kite used in meteorological and scientific experiments. The Eddy Kite and other material are exhibited in the Smithsonian Museum in Washington, D. C. Reminiscing she said, "My parents had the feeling a child should be allowed to sit up and listen to what was going on, with a result that this child mopped up like a blotter all she heard."

Peggy's botanical interest arose from her husband's knowledge as a naturalist. "He always wanted me to make the most of my mind and so encouraged me to continue my art work." She added, "We both had the theory that anyone interested in creativity yet in bringing up a family must set aside certain parts of every day to retain the creative urge outside the family." Pointing to a framed etching on the wall on her living room she said, "This is what you can do as a housewife." The picture was of the Torrey pine. It is one of the 80 to 100 etchings she has done; 28 to 30 of them are of the pines.

Her etchings were exhibited by the La Jolla Museum of Art May 23-June 1, 1969, as part of La Jolla's celebration of San Diego's 200th anniversary and depicted "the reflection of the trees, as studied by Mrs. Fleming during her 32-year residency among them." She also exhibited in shows at the National Society of Etchers and Printmakers, the Art Students' League (Life Member Show) in New York, the Seattle Art Museum, and the Crocker Art Museum, Sacramento. Previous one-man shows of her etchings had been held at the Fine Arts Museum in San Diego and at the La Jolla Museum of Art, of which she was an honorary trustee.

The etching used by the Torrey Pines Association was one done on the hill above the Guy Fleming Trail, so named after Mr. Fleming's death in 1960. The trail, a loop six-tenths of a mile long, was created by her husband. "He took thousands of people over that trail," she said, "and he told stories of plants and trees as though they were old friends. I brought up the rear and realized he told those stories hundreds of times, but each time he'd come up with something new and interesting to me."

Margaret & Guy Fleming, c. 1930
Courtesy of Dorothy Shelton

One of the etchings of Margaret Eddy Fleming looking south-westerly with the tip of La Jolla in the background and a hill sometimes called Lion Head around which the Guy Fleming Trail circles.
Courtesy of Judy Schulman

In 1949, the Ellen Browning Scripps Foundation published a booklet to awaken public interest and support in perpetually preserving and protecting the Torrey pines. The cover of the booklet contained the etching done by Mrs. Fleming, (now copyrighted and used exclusively by the Torrey Pines Association.)

Guy Fleming retired from State Parks in 1948, but he continued working to preserve the precious trees. Although they were allowed to stay in the house on the grounds of the Reserve, Guy and Peggy decided to build their "dream house" in La Jolla. Guy Fleming died in 1960. He was seventy-five.

In 1966, Mr. Robert Bates of Del Mar, an employee of the Naval Electronics Laboratory in Point Loma in Public Relations approached Mrs. Fleming with the idea of trying to acquire for future generations about 260 acres of private land just North of the Reserve containing some 3000 native Torrey pines. As the drive gained momentum, Mrs. Fleming spoke with interested groups, appeared on television, and gave radio talks. She was particularly touched by the generosity of the younger people. "I had grade school children hand me pennies and nickels," she said. "One group gave $12.60. Thousands of dollars were raised by the young who caught and sold fish, made fudge and sold it in the neighborhood, gathered papers, and washed cars. Everybody helped. There was even a Torrey Pines Walk that raised money."

On the occasion of Mrs. Fleming's 82nd birthday, January 11, 1970, $6700 was raised. By July 1970, the deadline for the drive, more than $800,000 of the necessary $900,000 had been raised. According to Mr. Edward L. Butler, campaign chairman, "It is safe to say the trees are safe." State officials had assured him the $900,000 state share would be released even though the local campaign fell just short of the goal. In addition, a federal grant for which the state had applied came through in October 1970, in the amount of $459,510, for acquiring the property.

At the Torrey Pines victory celebration, November 1, 1970, Dr. Thomas W. Whitaker, well-known naturalist and President of the Torrey Pines Association, said: "In my opinion, the key to this operation has been the sustained faith and determination of Margaret Eddy Fleming. Without her courage and foresight it is doubtful whether we would be here to celebrate the successful termination of one aspect of this campaign."

And so the goal was reached. But Mrs. Fleming shakes her head and says, "Anyone with a goal knows that it is never reached—there is always a new project on the horizon. In the case of the Torrey pines, there is still much to be done to save this priceless heritage for future generations."

Cornelious "Neil" Bohannon

Come to La Jolla and forget it. Maybe it wouldn't have happened anyhow.
Neil Bohannon

We know that he was born in Northern California to a large pioneer family, but it's not clear just when Cornelious Bohannon arrived in La Jolla. We do know, however, that he was the first paid lifeguard for the La Jolla Cove. Emblazoned on his swimsuit tank top was the word "instructor." He gave swimming lessons to La Jolla children for which he may have been paid by grateful parents. However, it's doubtful that he charged a certain young lady for lessons. Miss McNamara was vacationing from Pasadena with her parents. In 1913, she entered the bathing beauty contest along with other young aspirants. The judging committee selected her and she was crowned Miss La Jolla of 1913. In a group photo of the contestants, she appears center stage wearing Neil Bohannon's tank top with the word "instructor" plainly visible. If Bohannon had any influence with the judges in their choosing the girl from Pasadena, it hasn't been recorded.

What does a lifeguard do with a beauty queen on his hands? In this case, he married her. So the girl with the lilting name, Kathleen McNamara, became Mrs. Cornelious Bohannon.

One can't very well support a wife and raise a family on a lifeguard's salary. His dynamic and sociable personality propelled Cornelious to undertake numerous people oriented projects. One such enterprise was a sight seeing tour coach company he organized to show tourists the sights of the San Diego area.

A 1919 San Diego directory entry has the Bohannons located at

Bohannon's La Jolla Cove Sightseeing Bus c. 1916. Neil Bohannon is in middle with megaphone and bowler. This was one of the many occupations that Neil was to pursue over the years.
Courtesy of San Diego Historical Society Photograph Collection

The Bohannon Family in front of the Inn: Neil, Jack, Kathleen, Charles, Betty and Lynn, 1930.
Courtesy of San Diego Historical Society Photograph

"Prospect N. E. corner Girard, La Jolla." An ad placed in the Journal read as follows, "White Rabbit Roof Garden now open, regular hot meals afternoon teas, baked special ham, salads, pies, cakes, cookies etc. Special fine cook engaged." That special fine cook was the 1913 beauty queen who learned to cook in a hurry under the tutelage of her husband. On the roof of the restaurant was a pergola built over picnic like tables and benches for rooftop dining. A white rabbit was kept in a cage on the sidewalk near the restaurant entrance. This was the first of three restaurants the Bohannons were to operate in La Jolla. The 1920 San Diego directory places the family at 894 Prospect Street across Jenner Street from the Colonial Hotel. This restaurant was called the Dining Porch. It looked very much like the thousands of diners that followed in later years. One early observer wrote: "Bohannon's cafe at Prospect and Jenner has a sign 'Don't go somewhere else to get cheated come in here.' A goat was tied up to the front door." Bohannon's older daughter explained that her father didn't think the quality of commercially produced milk was good enough for his children, so the goat supplied milk for her and the other siblings.

From 1922 to 1929, various entries in the directories have the family at 5720 and 5740 Dolphin Place in Bird Rock.

Bird Rock Inn, 1963, after conversion to private home.
Courtesy of Jane Sandford.

Here on the ocean bluff over looking Bird Rock, with very little help, Bohannon built the Bird Rock Inn. The Inn was constructed with thousands of beach cobbles and old telephone poles were utilized for roof beams. It had a rustic appearance. Landscaping consisted of patios, lookouts, and pathways leading down to the beach from the Inn, which allowed diners access to the beach for after dinner strolls. A rock-lined holding pond was built at the foot of the cliff to keep seafood alive until needed. Some of the rockwork is still in place. Bohannon's handiwork has withstood time, tide and storm almost as well as the natural bluff. The Inn advertised "Fine dining on seafood, squab, and steak. The seafood was gathered off-shore, squab was raised across the street, but the steak was bought from commercial suppliers.

In 1927 Charles Lindbergh arrived in San Diego to oversee the construction of an aircraft capable of flying nonstop from New York to Paris. He had joined the race with others to be the first to make this hazardous flight. He selected Ryan Flying Company to build this plane later to be christened the *Spirit of St. Louis*. During construction, the engineers and mechanics who were building the plane would catch fish in the bay and cook them over welding torches in the shop. Lindbergh never turned down a tasty morsel when offered. When Messers. Claude Ryan and Franklin Mahoney became aware of Lindbergh's fondness for seafood, they introduced him to the Bird Rock Inn. The three men dined at the Inn on Lindbergh's last night in San Diego, the eve of his

Ryan, the Aviator

To Lynn Hurt
With best wishes
and pleasant memories of
the evenings at Bird Rock Inn,
with your father, Franklin
Mahoney and Charles Lindbergh
Claude T Ryan

Note from T. Claude Ryan after dinner at Bird Rock Inn. Franklin Mahoney had purchased the Ryan Flying Company, the builder of the *Spirit of St. Louis*, from Claude Ryan. *Courtesy of San Diego Historical Society Photograph Collection*

odyssey that was to take him to Paris via New York. Neil Bohannon was captivated with the young aviator. Mrs. Bohannon was expecting her fourth child, so he declared that he would name the baby after Lindbergh. Mrs. Bohannon delivered when Lindbergh was over the Atlantic. Charles "Lindy" Bohannon has the honor of being the first of thousands of babies named after the now famous aviator hero. It's prophetic that Lindy Bohannon made a career in aviation by way of the U. S. Army Air Corps from which he retired as a Colonel after some thirty years of service.

Neil Bohannon died in 1929. The Inn passed out of the Bohannon family hands and was eventually converted into a private residence.

An unusual early La Jollan with a genial good-natured manner complemented by what must have been a great sense of humor, in 1913 Bohannon and a partner named Brown published the *Journal*, La Jolla's first newspaper. Bohannon wrote the following editorial introducing the newspaper.

"OUR BOW

"Well, gentle Reader, here we are! Standing, hat in hand, awaiting your approval. How do you like our style, our dress, our name and our general makeup? We have tried to be as conventional as possible so as not to shock even the most delicately arranged organism. What we are aiming at is to give La Jolla the kind of paper she is entitled to and ought to have.

"The *La Jolla Journal* is, or will be a home product, gotten out by home people. Needless to say, the climate and beauties of nature have had a great deal to do with our coming here, as has been the case, no doubt, with most of you. But we have also been influenced largely by what seems to be a glorious opportunity to make an honest living...."

From a Reading Circle to the
Library Association of La Jolla

Libraries are not made; they grow.
Augustine Birrell (1850-1933)

"Every 'boom' suburb has to have its hotel, and of course it must be large and have some pretensions for splendor." (Howard S. F. Randolph) The year was 1888, and the large and elegant La Jolla Park Hotel was completed. It was located on the north side of Prospect at the head of what is now Girard Avenue with a view of the Pacific and easy walking distance to the shore. Problems plagued its opening and it wasn't until 1893 that it officially opened for business.

In 1894, the railway extended from San Diego to La Jolla. To draw visitors to the area, the railroad built the La Jolla Dancing Pavilion in a park next to what is now Coast Boulevard, just west of Girard. That same year, the La Jolla Post Office was established across from the Cove. It was later moved into the Pavilion. Notices would be posted on the bulletin board outside the Post Office announcing parties and get-togethers. In those days, everyone was naturally invited. The first store in La Jolla was opened in 1894. The village of La Jolla was coming into her own and the Park Hotel was in full swing.

On March 24, 1894, seven

La Jolla Park Hotel, 1888, at the end of today's Girard Avenue was destroyed by arson in 1896. The Patterson family is in front of the cottage on the right which is located on Prospect Street on the same parcel of land the La Valencia now occupies. Girard Avenue extension descends through the canyon before the hotel.
Courtesy of San Diego Historical Society Photograph Collection

The Reading Room at the corner of Wall and Grand (Girard), 1898. (l to r) Mr. & Mrs. Pease of Burlington, Vermont, Mrs. Catherine Spear (wheel chair) Miss Florence Sawyer (later Mrs. John R. Bransby) who gave the site and building to La Jolla, and seated on the steps is Mrs. Mudgett. The building is now located on The Bishop's School property on Draper at the west end of Silver Street.
Courtesy of The Athenaeum Music & Arts Library

The interior of the original La Jolla Reading Room
Courtesy of Barbara Dawson

women met at the La Jolla Park Hotel and created what would be known as the Reading Club. The meetings had to relocate, however, when, in 1896, the glamorous hotel burned to the ground.

A year earlier, on August 14, 1895, Mrs. Spear of Burlington, Vermont, and Miss Florence Sawyer of Oakland, California, registered as guests at the Park Hotel. Miss Sawyer was charmed by the town and wasted no time purchasing property within a month of her arrival. Girard, Prospect, Herschel, and Wall bound Block 54 (as her purchase was named). Three years later, she had Thorpe and Kennedy, the first carpenters and builders in La Jolla, construct a Reading Room on the 60 x 60 foot corner lot on Girard and Wall.

The Reading Room officially opened on July 22, 1898. It contained more than a thousand dollars worth of books, a piano, and furniture, all provided by Miss Sawyer.

"'The Reading Room'…was to La Jolla what a town hall is to other small communities…. The building…was equipped with a stove, utensils, dishes, and even an upright piano. Many club meetings and social events were held there. The Book Room was open three times a week with a volunteer librarian in attendance. Magazines were lacking, so families met to chose the periodicals, which they thought to be the most in demand. Each family agreed to subscribe for one, read it as rapidly as possible, and then give it to the library." (Marie Breder, *The La Jolla Journal*, Nov. 11, 1962)

Inside the front door, there was a room

to the left and a room to the right. The right room was the children's library where volunteers offered to read to the children. Twelve families, one for each month of the year, volunteered to maintain the facility. It was clearly a cherished place and an honor to work there.

Mrs. Spear died March 20, 1899. In her honor, Miss Sawyer renamed the reading room the Spear Memorial Library. In May, Miss Sawyer married John Ransome Bransby in Los Angeles. On May 30, 1899, Mrs. Bransby's letter promising to give the Library to the newly incorporated Library Association was received and reviewed. That same evening, Miss Ellen Browning Scripps was "voted in by acclimation" as President along with Mrs. Olivia Mudgett, Miss Francis A. Brown, Mr. C. S. Dearborn, and Mr. A. P. Mills all of whom were voted by ballot as trustees. On August 31,

The La Jolla Reading Room being moved from Girard and Wall to Silver and Draper Streets in the 1920s.
Courtesy of Barbara Dawson

1899, Florence Sawyer Bransby gave the deed for the Reading Room to the new Library Association.

La Jolla continued to grow. The Trustees realized that their little library building was too small. As early as 1907, the Board was hoping to expand. Perl Acton built a 16' X 16' addition in 1907, for $265, but it was a stopgap measure. Lack of funds during W.W.I and the influenza epidemic kept the board from expanding any further, despite the need.

April 14, 1919, the Board adopted a plan. "...to utilize the present site, the main building to be moved toward Girard St., a permanent book room to be built on the space occupied by the present book room, the new building to be planned as a unit of a complete library to be built when necessary funds should be available."

Thanks to an anonymous donor (Miss Ellen Scripps) and a matching fund plus Miss Scripps' purchase and donation of an additional twenty-two feet on Wall Street, the present building site and library building became a reality. Miss Scripps donated an additional $10,000 to the library as an endowment fund. Defining the purpose and character of the new library building, Miss Scripps stipulated that it be "first, as a memorial, and second, to serve community purposes in the best possible way, and incidentally to make it a beautiful and dignified building." As per her wishes, the La Jolla Memorial Library, as it was originally called, commemorated the heroism of those who died in the U. S. wars, including Miss Scripps' brother, John. A bronze plaque, which remains today, was placed on the loggia wall.

In 1920, the Trustees of the Library Association sold the original Reading Room. The building was moved to its present location on Draper Avenue. In 1921, the new building was completed at a cost of $33,804.31. William Templeton Johnson was the architect. His design for the new library blended Spanish Colonial Revival Style — characterized by the low-pitched roof and thirteen-inch thick walls covered in white stucco — and Italian Renaissance style — evidenced by the hip roof, classical columns at the entrance, and tall narrow casement windows. Templeton Johnson believed these styles were appropriate for the warm, sunny climate of Southern California. The modified Corinthian capitals of the columns just inside the loggia are decorated with the St. James shell motif. According to legend, St. James, the patron saint of the arts, was transported to Spain on a shell.

Originally, two ornamental wood screens separated the reading room on the right from the librarian's area and the stacks on the left. After hours, the screens were closed and locked, but La Jollans could still enter the reading room through a separate entrance located outside on the loggia. A letter written in 1921 soon after the new facility opened reflects much about the moral climate of this town in the early years. A representative of the New York office of the Library Bureau wrote:

Architect William Templeton Johnson's building for the Library Association of La Jolla—now the Athenaeum Music and Arts Library. The building was dedicated in 1921. *Courtesy of The Athenaeum Music & Arts Library.*

"It is rather interesting to see that the reading rooms and reference room will be accessible to the adults when the rest of the library is closed. I am glad to see this spirit and hope to die in a community where it permeates the atmosphere as surely Heaven must be nearer such a locality.... It is refreshing and inspiring to see the public can be trusted with its own."

Behind the librarian's desk was a patio or "reading court" as it was called. Kate Sessions, world-renowned horticulturist, spent a total of $497 planning and planting the grounds of the new library building including this rear garden using indigenous trees and shrubs. Miss Sessions felt using native material would be not only appropriate and hardy but also "would seem most appropriate in landscaping so popular a place as a public library." It must have been lovely.

In the new building, Templeton Johnson designed a room just for children. Thanks again to the generosity of Miss Scripps, an "artist's club" room was also added. A separate entrance was created for this room on Girard Avenue with twin staircases leading to an arched entrance. "…the gallery was laid out with an emphasis on fixtures and other structural details, including wood-faced walls that permitted the hanging of pictures, recessed heating appliances and special lighting fixtures. The walls were painted in neutral gray tones."

On September 24, 1939, the 40th anniversary of the Library Association of La Jolla, the library accepted the most significant donation since the original collection of books. Donated by Frances Sawyer, a complete collection of the works of Johann Sebastian Bach and hundreds of scores from other composers was presented to the library. The Bach Gesellschaft is a rare, 47-volume collection published in Germany and sold only to subscribers. At the time of this donation, only two other copies existed west of the Mississippi. It is particularly valuable because the scores are prints of originals. This significant and rare collection was a gift from the children of Eda Hurd Lord. Mrs. Lord had moved to La Jolla in 1920. A pianist and an artist herself, she gained a reputation as a patron of young musicians. After her death in La Jolla in 1938, family members from all over the country joined her children in making this donation as a memorial to her.

In 1949, the Building Committee reported to the Board that "the present building is inadequate to furnish the services which are desirable." Instead of moving or building, it was decided that the cheapest and easiest thing to do was to enclose the patio. Templeton Johnson was hired again (this time with his partners, George C. Hatch and Victor Wulff). Construction was completed on November 30, 1950. Five new rooms were added at the back of the lot: a music or fine arts room, a work room, a librarian's office, a business office, and a staff room.

All this time, the La Jolla Library had been a private facility paying for a public service. It was not a public library funded by public taxes. Because of its public function, the Board of Trustees was reluctant to charge high membership dues, at least, not enough to cover the cost of running the institution. The economics did not work.

In 1952, after doing some research, it was realized that all other communities in San Diego County had branch libraries built, staffed, and funded by the City of San Diego. La Jolla was the only community with a private library serving the public. (It was also "the only community in which San Diego rented bathrooms for library patrons." The "comfort stations" were located in the adjacent park, built in 1921.)

The Board came to realize that it was necessary for "a reexamination of the relationship now existing between the Library Association of La Jolla and the City of San Diego." For two years, nothing happened. Then, in November 1954, Brig. Gen. James H. N. Hudnall (Ret.), the Board's new assistant secretary, submitted a crisp, militarily efficient report and strongly recommended that the Board get tough with the city. Consequently, the San Diego City Council and the La Jolla Town Council were "enlisted in the Association's Cause." The San Diego Library Commission finally took formal action on the association's request. On July, 1955, San Diego took over.

The takeover, however, did not invalidate the Library Association of La Jolla. The Association still existed and its members still paid their dues.

At the 1955 Annual Meeting, Mrs. L. B. Dixon, the public relations committee chair, formally proposed building an addition to the library. The building would be built on the land that housed a small public restroom and a park. In 1956, the Board selected William B. Lumpkins to design the addition with the "same white stucco walls and tile roof as the Templeton Johnson building and doorways that echo the shape of the original building's casement windows." Dewhurst & Associates serving as contractors completed this addition in the spring of 1957.

Just before the Board selected William Lumpkins as the architect for the addition, Mrs. Marjorie Hutchinson "recommended that a name be selected for the new addition at this time so that it can be used on book plates to distinguish our books from those in the general library." The name "Athenaeum Music & Arts Library" was chosen, and this marked the beginning of the Athenaeum's history as a private membership library dedicated to art and music.

The Wilson Cousins

The spinning-jenny and the railroad, Cunard's liners and the electric telegraph are to me...signs that we are, on some points at least, in harmony with the universe.

Charles Kingsley (1819-1875)

Mr. and Mrs. Harry Wilson were Irish. Mr. Wilson's genealogy on his mother's side of the family extended back to Cromwell. In the last decade of the nineteenth century, the Harry Wilsons immigrated to the United States and settled in Randsburg in the Mojave Desert. Mr. Wilson earned his living as a telegraph operator. He used his right hand for Morse Code and his left hand for Continental Code. In 1903, a son, Bob, was born. The boy spent his first 12 years in this rural mining town.

Harry Wilson's brother was a sea captain in Ireland. After two of his ships sank, he decided to come with his wife and join his brother Harry in Randsburg. Before long, the captain and his wife had a son whom they named Spencer. Years later the two cousins, Bob and Spencer, settled in La Jolla.

Bob Wilson was a very bright and observant youngster. He remembered with pleasure the people and the primitive buildings of Randsburg comparing the town to a chapter out of the old "wild west." He also recalled seeing the local constable dragging a drunkard by his feet along the ground to the jailhouse.

When Bob's father was offered a job as manager of the Western Union Office in La Jolla, he accepted and moved his family in 1917. They rented one of the six shingled bungalows that were part of the Plaza Court on Wall Street for $20 a month. (In

Bob Wilson and his parents in Randsburg, Calif.
Courtesy of Barbara Dawson

Bob Wilson on his bicycle in front of the Western Union office in 1920. His father is standing in front of the office door.
Courtesy of Barbara Dawson

1931, these houses were moved so that a new Post Office building could be constructed on that site.) The Western Union was located in a little square wooden building at the ocean end of Girard between Wall St. and Prospect. (Later, it moved to Jenner Street, just down the hill from Prospect near the Colonial Hotel.)

After Bob finished school, he went to work as a messenger boy at his father's Western Union office. He learned other jobs as well and, for a while, served as a draftsman for Edgar V. Ullrich, a famous local architect who in 1923-24 ("designing while constructing") built a mission style hotel and cottages on a property that "cornered on the pool, looking both ways along the coast and out on the horizon." It was called the Casa de Mañana (the house of tomorrow). Facing the ocean and the Children's Pool (a gift to the children of La Jolla by Miss Ellen Browning Scripps), for years the Casa was a popular hotel with tourists; it later became a retirement community.

Bob also enjoyed preparing models of historical homes in La Jolla.

A member of St. James Episcopal Church Bob was inspired by his rector William Bedford-Jones (a fellow Irishman) who supervised his education and encouraged his study of Episcopal churches. In his adult years, he would spend his vacation taking trips to famous churches and cathedrals throughout the United States.

When Bob's father retired, wishing to keep the management of the Western Union in the family, he appointed his son as manager, a job Bob retained until he too retired.

Highly regarded for his accurate and courteous service, Bob was always willing to help anyone above and beyond taking and delivering telegrams. If he know a lady was going to be absent from home for a few days, he would drop by and leave a dish of milk for her cat. In another case, a lady who lived on Hillside Drive was scheduled to be out of town, so she sent a message to the La Jolla Western Union asking that her neighbor meet her train at Del Mar. When Bob went to deliver the telegram, the recipient was away. So Bob met the train and drove the lady home himself!

Bob always tried to help senders with their messages by finding ways to shorten them. During W.W.II, there were restrictions on unnecessary or frivolous telegrams. In 1944, Ellen Revelle's fourth child and first son, William, was born. The Revelles were living in the Washington, D.C. area at the time. Ellen's husband, Roger, was on wartime leave from Scripps Institution of Oceanography where Dr. Harold Sverdrup was Director. With Bob Wilson's cooperation and collaboration, the Director sent a message across the country to Roger saying: "Concur in recent addition to Geology Department (stop) Highly approve change in topography." They must have had a good time composing that telegram!

Bob knew just about everyone in La Jolla. He frequented many of the stores near the Western Union office. He ate dinners at Melzer's Cafe just north of his office, visited Noah's Ark Cigar Store (which had a card room behind the store), and enjoyed sodas at Putties, the place where Bishops School girls "hung out" after school. The girls loved the sundaes and sodas topped with gobs of whipped cream. Ross Putnam had an old-gold colored scale installed on the porch. On their way out, the girls would deposit one cent in the scale to learn how much weight they had gained. Bob laughed as he viewed the girls from his office window across the street.

Southeast on Prospect and just around the corner from the Western Union was Nakamura's Cafe where locals and tourists went for a good home cooked meal. Mrs. Nakamura always greeted her guests with a bow and a smile.

Barbara Dawson (Co-Author) and Spencer (Spence) Wilson at Spence's 90th birthday party. *Courtesy of Barbara Dawson*

Bob owned a very small house near the Del Mar slough. This is where he lived after his retirement. He had a small pump organ there which he enjoyed playing. However, as the years advanced, Bob came home to La Jolla and moved back into his family's cottage on Fay Avenue. His adopted grand daughter, Lisa, helped him renovate the house and garden. Before, he had been too far away to entertain his friends, but now in the cottage he could, and Lisa was happy to do the cooking. Bob died in 1990. He was eighty-seven.

But let's not forget his cousin Spencer. Spencer became so popular in La Jolla over the years that he came to be known as "Mr. La Jolla." His first job when he arrived in 1933 was working as manager of the Granada Theater at Wall and Girard. Georgeanna Lipe tells the story of going to see *'Wells Fargo'* at the

Granada. Her husband, Dr. J T Lipe, had thought the movie would distract her from the discomfort of her advanced pregnancy. Midway through the picture, Georgeanna nudged J T, "It's time." The two left through the back door. Scripps Hospital was not far away, down Prospect Street three blocks. A couple of hours later, J T returned to the theater. Spencer couldn't understand. "Did you like it so much that you had to see the movie twice?" he asked. "No, I just had a baby, missed half the feature and wanted to see how it ended," replied the new dad. To this day, Spencer calls that "baby" (Steele Lipe) "Wells Fargo."

Spencer stayed at the Granada until it closed in 1952 then managed its replacement, The Cove Theater, further up Girard, for another forty years. Described as tough but loving, Spencer has taught generations of La Jollans about work ethic, manners, and respect for others. For over sixty-five years, this special man has been a loyal member of the Kiwanis Club, never missing a meeting. He has helped raise thousands of dollars for charity and has also established the Spencer Wilson Permanent Endowment Fund dedicated to supporting local youth programs. As of this writing, Spencer is still keeping busy. You might find him at Mangelsen's "Images of Nature" store on Girard. The photographer, Tom Mangelsen, and Spencer have become good friends since the opening of the La Jolla store. "He's the most unselfish, caring, supportive best friend I've ever had," said Mangelsen, "And that's why I call him my Pop." We should all be proud that this "Pop" came to La Jolla and adopted the town.

The Irving J. Gill House
on Draper Avenue

We must boldly throw aside every accepted structural belief and standard of beauty and get back to the source of all architectural strength — the straight line, the arch, the cube and the circle.　　　　　　　　　　**Irving J. Gill**

The Bed and Breakfast Inn at La Jolla on Draper was designed by the architect Irving J. Gill in 1913 for George Kautz. Considered second only to Frank Lloyd Wright, Gill designed buildings that incorporated the Arts and Craft movement (a group who espoused the virtues of simplicity), the so-called Prairie style with it stark horizontal lines, and California's Catholic Spanish-Mexican heritage (most prominently the Mission style). Once in San Diego, Gill became a favorite of Miss Ellen Browning Scripps. In 1912, Miss Scripps hired Gill to design the Woman's Club, which she was donating to the ladies of La Jolla. The building was completed in 1914.

In 1913, George Kautz, sensing an "obligation to build within the spirit of Gill's neighboring masterworks" hired Mr. Gill to design a home for him on Draper, just to the right of the Woman's Club. Irving J. Gill, in an era of extravagant and embellished architecture, boldly returned to the first and basic principles of architecture: the line, the square and the circle. The Kautz house is a two-story, flat-roofed, austere, handsomely simple, concrete structure. While the line and the circle embodied permanence, Gill encouraged the growth of vines and creepers to em-

The George Kautz House, now the Bed & Breakfast Inn at La Jolla.
Courtesy of The Kaltenbach family

Kautz House composite, showing arches typical of Irving Gill. Note the La Jolla Women's Club in background in right panel.
Courtesy of The Kaltenbach family

body impermanence while at the same time breaking the severity of the building design. Shadows from trees or passing clouds cast their patterns on the stark walls to add to the mood as well. Gill believed that beauty should be organic and no amount of ornament could redeem a badly designed structure. Often, as is in the case at the Draper Avenue house, the entrance is at the end of a loggia, walled on the outside but facing into a garden with vines growing along arches and plants softening a sharp corner.

"…we should build our house simple, plain and substantial as a boulder, then leave the ornamentation of it to Nature, who will tone it with lichens, chisel it with storms, make it gracious and friendly with vines and flower shadows as she does the stone in the meadow." (This was written in Gill's only major published essay, *The Craftsman*, in 1916.)

The gardens were important to Mr. Gill's overall architectural plan and at the Draper Street house, the famous San Diego horticulturist Kate Sessions did the actual planning and planting of the gardens beneath the loggia and behind the house. At the same time, ivy was planted along the base of the west and street side of the building. As the years passed, the ivy grew out of control. The house became known as the house made of ivy with windows cut into it.

The Kautz family occupied the house from 1914 to 1923. Then the Kaltenbach family bought it and retained it until Mrs. Kaltenbach died in 1982; that is, with the exception of the years 1926-1935 when the son of the famous band leader, John Philip Sousa, rented it. Sousa's grandchildren, Tommy, Nancy, Pricilla, and John III lived there. They attended the local public schools and became good friends with all of the local children. Across the street from the Draper Street house is the Children's Playground and Recreation Center which Miss Scripps had built for the people of La Jolla in 1915. Again, she had chosen Irving J. Gill as her architect. Like in the Woman's Club, Irving Gill, in partnership with his nephew, Louis Gill, applied the tilt-slab system to hoist walls that measured 60 and 120 feet long. Inside the Recreation Center are exercise rooms, showers, locker rooms and meeting rooms. High clerestory windows provide light without compromising privacy or wall space. Originally, there were no ceilings above the showers; however, after a few heavy rains, Mr. Gill's open-air plan had to be altered.

Three other nearby structures designed by Irving Gill, are the La Jolla Women's Club, The Bishop's School and the La Jolla Recreation Center. The first St. James by-the-Sea Church, Scripps Memorial Hospital, Scripps Metabolic Research Clinic and the second South Moulton Villa all also designed by Gill are nearby.
Courtesy of Barbara Dawson, The Bishop's School, and Steele Lipe

Behind the Recreation Center is The Bishop's School, also designed by Irving Gill (1910-16), and across the street from the Center, in 1915-16, Irving Gill was hired by Miss Scripps to design a second residence (South Moulton Villa II), a concrete structure, to replace the wooden house which had been demolished by arson. Like the Kautz house, Miss Scripps' home was flat-roofed and concrete. To insure privacy on the street side, the house is rather plain and relatively closed. On the ocean side, however, Gill placed porches and large windows opening out to the dramatic sight and sound of the ocean.

To the east and in front of Miss Scripps' home and across the street from the Woman's Club was the St. James Church, also an Irving Gill masterwork, completed in 1907-8. It is perhaps the closest Gill ever came to Mission Revival style architecture. A swirling neo-Baroque parapet and tower crown a plain, ornament-free exterior. The portico was framed with simple, unadorned columns. Aside from the portico, the flat façade is broken only by rectangular and arched openings, typical of Gill's later work. (This church was moved to Draper and Genter Street and a new church was designed by Louis Gill and built in 1925.) Thus this entire section of La Jolla was a showcase of Gill's architecture. In the 1920s, the English artist Maxwell Armfield remarked, "The entire group of buildings is one of the most successful efforts outside of Germany to solve the problem of modern reinforced concrete construction." *(An Artist in America, 1926)*

As an aside we might mention that one of Mr. Gill's apprentices was Lilian Rice. Ms. Rice later joined the prestigious architectural firm of Richard S. Requa and Herbert L. Jackson, which had designed several Balboa Park structures. It was she who in the early 1920s was asked to plan and design the community of Rancho Santa Fe. In the Gill tradition, Rice believed that houses should conform to their surroundings and blend with nature. "I found real joy at Rancho Santa Fe. Every environment there calls for simplicity and beauty — the gorgeous landscapes, the gentle broken topography, the nearby mountain. No one with a sense of fitness, it seems to me, could violate these natural factors." Her specialty was Spanish Colonial Revival style which was the architecture of choice of this residential development. Ms. Rice, one of the first women in California to receive a state architectural license, melded the history of the Ranch land grant and her love for Spanish architecture. It is interesting that her own home on Ludington Place in La Jolla was California Ranch style and not Spanish.

In 1983, Betty Albee bought the Draper house. After months of negotiations and a vast amount of paper work plus $1 million, Mrs. Albee received permission from the city to renovate the old house, now in a sad state of disrepair. She wanted it to be upgraded and enlarged so that instead of a single family home, it could be made into a Bed and Breakfast. However, she also wanted to retain the Irving J. Gill architecture. The opposition was vehement all through the process as she went from one commission to another. One member of the town council was the owner of an inn in La Jolla. It was felt by Mrs. Albee and her architect that this man had a conflict of interest in voting against the single-family house conversion. Nevertheless, Tony A. Ciani, the architect Mrs. Albee chose for this delicate work, said, "It was her tenacity, not mine, that made this all possible." He added, "At the reception for the grand opening (of the finished construction), everyone was invited, even the opposition. That town council member was there too. He came up to me and said, 'Tony, I know you can't see it, but there is an olive branch in my teeth.'" It had taken tenacity and courage to work with a legacy of Irving J. Gill. The addition was done tastefully and skillfully leaving only the Gill original building visible from the street.

Under the Influence of Irving J. Gill, Bailey's "Barn"

What idle or significant sentence will we write with brick and stone, wood, steel, and concrete upon the sensitive page of the earth?   **Irving J. Gill**

In 1916, it was dry, so dry that San Diego hired a rainmaker. The result was too much rain and flooding. La Jolla was isolated for three days without gas or electricity. Train service was interrupted and did not resume until the following month.

Helen North (Reynolds) was a boarder at The Bishop's School at the time. She recalled that the school had run out of many things since transportation was so difficult because of flooding. Helen's great-uncle, Wheeler J. Bailey, was a trustee of the school and Miss North's guardian. He called Headmistress Caroline Cummins to ask if she needed anything. "Butter," she replied. Mr. Bailey brought her a pound of butter. He did not realize it was for the whole school!

Born in the Ohio "Western Reserve," Wheeler J. Bailey came to this area in 1888. He was a pharmacist by training but it was not long before recognizing the tremendous growth that was taking place in San Diego. He entered into the building supply business. For over forty-eight years, the Wheeler J. Bailey Company supplied material for just about every important building in San Diego, from the Hotel Del Coronado to the original San Diego Exposition buildings of Balboa Park in 1915. (The company survived the death of Mr. Bailey and continued up to the late 1950s.) The Bailey Company also developed regionally derived cement, which they supplied for the construction of dams in San Diego County. Always interested in the welfare of his community and a member of the Highway Committee, he is often called the "father of good roads in San Diego" because of his interest in laying out roads and building fine highways. Mr. Bailey built the first road up Mt. Soledad. He did this so that he could enjoy the view without hiking, but thousands of visitors from all over the world have also been able to enjoy the view

Wheeler J. Bailey
Courtesy of Mitchell, Thomas, Reviewing The Vision, A Story of The Bishop's Schools, *published by The Bishop's Schools,* 1979.

these many years because of his gesture.

Being his own contractor, architect Irving J. Gill (1870-1936) became both a loyal client of the Bailey Company and, in time, a good friend to Mr. Wheeler J. Bailey. Although the Bailey Company Store was a free-standing building in "Little Italy" (the western downtown area of San Diego) and his home apartment was in San Diego at the Lanier Hotel (designed by Hebbard and Gill), in 1907, Mr. Bailey decided to have a weekend retreat built on the bluffs of La Jolla. He chose Irving Gill to design the house. Frank Mead (1865-1940), another architect described as a "free spirit" (born in the home town of

Irving J. Gill
Courtesy of Thomas S. Hines, Irving Gill and the Architecture of Reform, *The Monacelli Press*, 2000.

another free spirit, Walt Whitman, in Camden, New Jersey), was Mr. Gill's partner on this and a few other projects. Mr. Bailey wanted his house to resemble a barn. To produce this effect, the architects created a double height wood-paneled living room with an open second story balcony-hallway which served to connect the loft bedrooms on two sides. Huge barn-like sliding doors open onto the front terrace. At the rear, a series of windows overlook the Seven Sisters Caves and the pounding surf of the La Jolla shore line. The exterior is stucco with blue-green trim. Bailey actively participated in the construction of his La Jolla home. Initially he used it as a weekend retreat, but ultimately he made it his permanent residence. The furniture was simple craftsman style, some of it designed by Mr. Gill and Mr. Mead. "There were really no comfortable chairs. There were many window seats with just straw mats on them. They weren't comfortable to sit on," according to Mr. Bailey's great-niece. Not afraid of color, Mr. Bailey chose brightly colored Indian rugs and artifacts. At the urging of both Gill and Mead, the Steinway piano was painted red. Bailey said: "I confess I rebelled when they (Gill and Mead) suggested it…a red Steinway! It seemed a sacrilege; but at length I agreed." *(The Craftsman*, Jan. 1914) Since Mr. Bailey did not like the fancy legs, "he had them boxed, creating cleaner lines consistent with the rest of his house."

In addition to his supply company, Wheeler J. Bailey was vice-president and later president of the Summit Lime Company of Los Angeles, vice-president of the Citizens National Bank of San Diego, and on the Army and Navy Committee. Other interests included philanthropies, especially the welfare of American Indians, many of whom came to work for him. Some of the art and artifacts he collected from the Indians are now in the Museum of Man in Balboa Park.

Although he remained a bachelor, Mr. Bailey undertook the guardianship of his young great-niece when her mother died. As a small child, Helen North had lived in a mining camp in Tonopah, Nevada. Her father was a mining engineer. "All uncles in my family were mining engineers." When she was two, her father went down to research a mine in Mexico. The mine was in very bad condition. An accident occurred and Mr. Edmond North was wounded. Helen was left with a babysitter in Mexico while her mother accompanied Edmond to get medical help in the United States. He died before they arrived. Helen and her mother came to stay with Uncle Wheeler. Later, they returned to Nevada where her mother remarried. She died a few years later, when Helen was only twelve. The child came back to live with her great-uncle whom she adored. In 1922, she became a five day boarder at The Bishop's School. According to Helen, "it was at this time that my Great-uncle and his niece, who was a sister of my father, sort of inherited me. Between the two of them and from then on, I spent my summers here in this house with my Great-uncle and my Aunt." Bishop's, she said, "was a strictly run academy in those days and it was not nearly the size it is today. I think there were only about ten people in my class and they of course all became very good friends. But they were from all over the United States and we had no contact with young people in La Jolla, in the village."

Wheeler J. Bailey and niece standing outside his La Jolla Home which shows the unmistakable architectural hallmarks of Irving J. Gill. *Courtesy of Mrs. Helen Reynolds*

When she was at her Great-uncle's house and not at school, Helen did not have playmates, but she was never lonely either. "I had the whole ocean at La Jolla Shores all to myself. I swam every day all alone. There were no houses, no anything at the beach." She also spent hours playing the piano. "I was supposed to be a concert pianist someday." Helen enjoyed the many interesting and often famous guests who came to visit her Great-uncle ("I have the guest book to prove it," she said with pride). Wheeler Bailey was adored not only by all the members of his family, but by the whole community. "Uncle Wheeler" loved people and was host to many men and women of note in the scientific, artistic, and literary worlds. "He collected friends. I think that was his hobby. Every interesting artist, particularly painters and musicians that came to San Diego were entertained in this house at some time or other and it was interesting to meet these wonderful people." Ellen Terry, the Shakespearean actress, Ernestine Schumann-Heink, Campbell Cooper, Leslie Lee, Charles Wakefield Cadman, Carrie Jacobs Bond, and Maude Powell came, as well as a great many college presidents and numerous archeologists. Mr. Bailey was particularly interested in archeology as a result of having explored Indian ruins in New Mexico and Arizona and collecting Indian artifacts. Another frequent visitor was Anna Held and her husband, the Opera singer, Max Heinrich. W. J. Bailey was best man at Anna's wedding. (She and Max Heinrich met in San Diego at Los Banos Bath House, also designed by Irving Gill. They were married in 1904, but it wasn't long before Max left and Anna remained in La Jolla.)

Helen North Reynolds tells us, "Every Sunday, Anna Held, a wonderful old lady and a dear friend of my Uncle," would come for dinner. Often Anna would play the piano (she had been a pupil of the Kullak School in Berlin and was exposed to many of the greatest musicians in the world throughout her life) and "Uncle Wheeler liked to sing along." Anna Held Heinrich eventually built a little cottage near Uncle Wheeler's property down on the hill. "There was a little triangular lot on the boulevard leading northward out of La Jolla, just at the junction of the street that led down to the ocean and to Wheeler Bailey's much-talked of house. This Anna Held bought and there she erected a helter-skelter house much as she

100

The Bailey House under construction. Circa 1907 showing the cliffs and caves in the background. *Courtesy of Thomas S. Hines,* Irving Gill and the Architecture of Reform, *The Monacelli Press,* 2000.

liked and put up a tiny cabin as a guest place nearby. Into the larger structure she moved her grand piano and certain of her personal belongings and Green Dragon Junior was established." (This quote was taken from *The Joyous Child* published in limited quantities in 1939 by Havrah Hubbard.) Mr. Bailey's Great-niece added to the story. "She didn't have room for a bath tub so she put it on the back porch or rather half on the porch and half on the inside." Actually, the tub was so large that it did not fit within the existing structure. Anna extended the walls of the house around the tub, thus limiting the space on the porch. Tante Heinrich, as she was fondly called in those latter years, like Wheeler J. Bailey, loved visitors and entertained her many friends in this little helter-skelter house. Just as it had been at her first Green Dragon Colony (which consisted of about eleven mostly Gill designed buildings), there were many guests of the artistic set who came to visit. Charles Wakefield Cadman (1881-1946), famous for composing operas based on American themes, especially American Indian themes like "From the Land of Sky Blue Waters," and his mother came often as well as John Doane, the New York organist with whom Anna took many trips to Europe.

Eventually, Mr. Bailey's house received its official name. It was Hilerô, the local Indian word for "cliff." The dedication was performed by the actress Madame Helena Modjeska.

Since Wheeler Bailey was such a philanthropic patron of the arts, his guest list increased over the years, so much so that Mr. Gill was eventually commissioned to design two additions to the house.

Mr. Bailey had close ties with the school that his Great-niece came to attend. Beginning with the first building constructed at The Bishop's School in 1909 and designed by Irving Gill. According to Erik Hanson (President of Save Our Heritage Organization, SOHO), Bailey was "most probably on the selection committee (hence the selection of Irving Gill) and surely was the school's financial representative with the architectural firm." Often, he took guests and friends on tours of the campus. For twenty-four years, Wheeler Bailey continued as a trustee of The Bishop's School acting as its treasurer. He was extremely tight with the budget. Miss Cummins (headmistress) chafed under his instructions not to spend more than $5 without his approval, so the Bishop set up a special fund for her from honorariums received from weddings. The cornerstone of the school's library, which bears Mr. Bailey's name, was laid in 1934. Unfortunately, he never saw its completion. Wheeler J. Bailey died on March 6, 1935. An eccentric of sorts, Mr. Bailey was also one of the patron saints of La Jolla and another example of "so few people, but what they could do!"

William Scripps Kellogg

The Man Who Brought International Championship Tennis to La Jolla

The life story of William Scripps Kellogg began in the nineteenth century. His father Frederick William (F. W.) Kellogg married Florence May Scripps in 1890, after he had proposed to her twenty one-times. Florence M. Scripps was the niece of Edward W. and James A. Scripps, both well-known publishers and Ellen Browning Scripps. William A. Scripps, her father, operated a printing shop. William and Florence had two daughters, Elena and Dorothy, before their son, William Scripps Kellogg, was born on January 29, 1897, in Cleveland, Ohio. The family moved several times and finally settled in Kansas where F. W. Kellogg became the publisher of *The Kansas City World*.

Referring to her husband, Florence May wrote, "Kellogg's meteoric rise as a journalist began when he was made Assistant Manager of the Scripps-McRae chain of newspapers in 1894. Five years later, he resigned and organized the *"Clover Leaf Papers*," which was eventually published in Minneapolis, Des Moines, Omaha, Kansas City and several other Midwest communities." He moved to Altadena when he retired. The name of the home he built in 1907, Highlawn, was given by the naturalist John Muir. In 1915, Mr. Kellogg came out of retirement converting the *San Francisco Morning Call* into an evening paper and founding the *Oakland Daily Post*. ("They became part of the Hearst syndicate when he acquired an interest in the *Los Angeles Evening Express* four years later.") Wm. Kellogg also founded the *Pasadena Post* in 1920 as well as several other "Kellogg Papers." These were eventually sold to Colonel Ira C. Copley in 1928. In 1935, Kellogg purchased the "ailing" La Jolla Beach and Yacht Club.

Florence and F. W.'s son, William Scripps Kellogg was approximately four or five years old when a harrowing experience almost cost him his life. William's older sister, Elena, was attending Central High School. Her class had decided to go on a country hayride, and she very kindly asked little brother if he would like to go along. Of course, he

Fredrick William Kellogg and Florence Scripps Kellogg, 1890.
Courtesy of Barbara Dawson

would. So about 15 or 20 young people boarded the beautiful hay wagon drawn by two stalwart horses and proceeded into the country. Going up a steep hill, all occupants, except little William, got off to make it easier for the horses. William, while staying aboard, inspected every detail of the wagon but when he stepped on the big brake attached to the iron rimmed 5-foot high wheels, he fell to the ground in front of the right rear wheel. No one noticed, not even the drivers who encouraged the horses to surmount the rock they thought was in the road. The right wheel passed over Willie's right shoulder. He had fallen face down with hands stretched out along his body. He lost consciousness. As soon as they realized what had occurred, they took the boy to a nearby farmhouse. A telephone call brought his father rushing from his office to his son, driving his new Ford so fast that he was arrested for speeding.

Highlawn, the Kellogg's home on Mariposa Street in Altadena as named by John Muir.
Courtesy of Barbara Dawson

In 1907, when the Kellogg family moved to Altadena, young Willie was enrolled in the fourth grade at the Polytechnic Elementary School. In 1911 when he entered Pasadena High School, he developed a passion for tennis. He was the fifth member of the four-member tennis team and was only able to play when one of the regular members was ill.

After high school, William was enrolled in Stanford University. During the summers, he entered the work-a-day world with some of his friends at the suggestion of his father. This was the time when Mr. Kellogg was the publisher of the *San Francisco Call*. F. W. Kellogg felt that Willie and his friends, Creayer Clover, Ken Hawks, and Norman Jensen could solicit annual subscriptions to the *Call* from the farmers in the vineyard country, north and east of San Francisco. The following was their mode of operation.

As there were no automobiles available to the boys in those days, they took a train from San Francisco to their first destination. There they usually rented just one room to save money, went to the local post office and requested the rural routes that the postman used when delivering mail. Each of the boys took one list. Then they rented a horse and buggy and began canvassing the farms. They tied their horses to a tree near the farmhouse. Usually the lady came to the door and they were very polite and courteous as they wanted very much to make a sale, and offered her one of the premiums if she would subscribe to the *Call* for one year at the rate of $2.50. The premiums included a water pitcher with six glasses, the Holy Bible, a nice large carving set, or a dictionary. They required no money down, only a signature before giving the assurance that that the paper would start within the next week.

Many of their customers were Portuguese and many had great vineyards of which they were very proud. Before their transaction was completed, the owner would take Willie to see the large vats of their various wines and offer him a glass of wine to taste. In those days William was a total abstainer and in order not to offend him, he would put the glass to his lips, smile sweetly and then when his host turned his head away, he would empty the wine on the ground.

Each of the boys would carry a water pistol filled with a solution of water and ammonia. The reason was that the farms had vicious dogs and it was impossible to get past them. When necessary, they would squirt a small amount of the solution at the dogs' faces and that would stop the attack. On one occasion, Norman Jensen was besieged by five Spitzes (a variety of Pomeranian). He shot each one with the mild concoction and they immediately left him. He did not try to solicit that house! About a mile down the road, the outraged farmer who held a shotgun in his hand shouting, "You have blinded my dogs for life," overtook him. Norman then explained that this was a mild mixture and that within an hour the eyesight of the dogs would return. This happened and the farmer let Norman continue on his way. They certainly met some interesting people—some very nice, some very rough, but this was all part of their education.

Alice Crowe Kellogg.
Courtesy of Barbara Dawson

During Williams' first two years at Stanford, two very important events greatly effected his life. First, he met a charming and very beautiful young lady, Alice Mary Crowe from Long Beach, California who was also a Stanford student. She proved to be the best thing that happened in his life. Second, America became embroiled in WWI and William was assigned to Officers Training School at Little Silver, New Jersey and from there he was sent to the 220 Field Signal Battalion, Camp Severe, Greenville, South Carolina. His orders to go overseas were received two weeks before the Armistice was signed, and he was discharged a few months later. While he was in the service, Alice Mary Crowe went to Washington, D. C. and worked with the War Risk Insurance Agency. After the Armistice was signed, both Alice and William resumed their education at Stanford.

In the early days, before the Rose Bowl, the annual East-West football game was held on the gridiron adjoining Polytechnic School and Cal Tech. This particular year, Harvard was persuaded to come out for the first and only time to play Oregon. Of course, William's family was always interested in those annual football games. His parents invited Alice Crowe to ride with them in the Packard Twin Six (which is still in existence in La Jolla) to see the game. William was circulation manager of the *Pasadena Post* at the time and decided a very unusual and exciting stunt would be good publicity. He persuaded his friend, Al Makepiece, to take him in his monoplane to drop a football in the center of the field before the game started. They went to the Altadena Country Club and took off from one of the long fairways and headed straight for the football field. They arrived just in time and at a signal from Al, Bill dropped the ball in the center of the field and the great Eddie Casey, Harvard's football star, picked it up with some amazement before the game started. Bill was not sure it increased the circulation of the *Pasadena Post*, but he had the satisfaction of completing the job that he had set out to do.

He was a very creative person. The next time the City Fathers met, they passed an ordinance prohibiting any airplane to fly lower than 1000 feet over the city of Pasadena.

His parents were very pleased when Bill told them that he hoped to marry Alice Mary but she had not yet accepted. As a matter of fact, she had already turned him down on two occasions. However, by 1920, Bill was financially secure in the newspaper business with his father and when he again asked her to marry him, she agreed. They were married in Los Angeles on August 3, 1920. In the next seven years, they had three children: William Crowe Kellogg, Ogden Ellis Kellogg, and Jean Kellogg (Schuyler).

William Scripps Kellogg worked on the *Pasadena Post* until it was sold to *Pasadena Star News*. Then he remained with Copley Newspapers as publisher of the *Glendale News* until 1940 when his father died and he was appointed manager of his estate. This created a big change in his life. Bill moved his family to La Jolla and assumed the management of the La Jolla Beach and Tennis Club and the surrounding properties, which today now includes the Sea Lodge and various business buildings. In the second half of his life, he had become a permanent member of the La Jolla community and at the Club he was able to enjoy the sport he learned to love as a teenager.

William Scripps Kellogg
Courtesy of Wm. J. Kellogg

In 1941, he started the La Jolla Beach and Tennis Club's 1st Annual Invitational Tennis Tournament, which later became the National Hard Court Championship. In 1942, he acquired the 2nd oldest tennis tournament in California, the Pacific Coast Men's Doubles Championship. He continued to attract many prestigious tournaments. In 1947, the Club hosted the Davis Cup competition between France and the United States, won by the American team which included Jack Kramer and Ted Schroeder. Year after year more outstanding men and women players participated at LJBTC, players like Bill Tilden, Rod Laver, Jimmy Connors, Pancho Gonzales, Bobby Riggs, Bill Bond, Poncho Segura, Arthur Ash, Les Stoefen, Terry Holladay, Maureen Connolly, Pat Todd, Alice Marble, Karen Hantze Susman, Billie Jean King, and Elizabeth Ryan.

Bill's interest in the tournaments and players never stopped. He served on the Board of Directors of the Southern California Tennis Association and held many positions on the United States Lawn Tennis Association. The founding of the International Federation Cup women's championship in 1963 was largely due to his efforts. These games were held at the Queen's Club in London. He received one of the most outstanding tributes he could have hoped for, an honorary membership in the All England Lawn Tennis and Croquet Club (Wimbledon).

La Jolla Beach and Yacht Club

Predecessor to the Present La Jolla Beach and Tennis Club

In 1923, *The San Diego Union* newspaper described La Jolla as "a bit of sea coast of many moods and manners." La Jolla was sparsely populated in those days and her disposition was mirrored by the whims of the climate and the sea, but the dominant mood was "soothing and restful." In 1926, fourteen acres of land by the sea in an area called Long Beach was purchased by a group of businessmen that included Frederick William Kellogg, a newspaper publisher from Pasadena. Downhill from the village of La Jolla, the land included a large marshy pond. The idea behind the purchase was the establishment of an exclusive private yacht club. It was believed that the indentation of the coast where Long Beach was located plus the pond would be advantageous for boats.

Construction began in 1927 with an estimated cost of close to $900,000. The *La Jolla Journal* described the first building of "La Jolla Beach and Yacht Club" with the following: "The clubhouse exterior is in Spanish farmhouse style. The building is 200 feet long and runs parallel to and adjoining the promenade. It contains a lounge 100 feet long, a dining room 75 feet long, offices, parcel rooms, a kitchen, dressing rooms, and shower and locker rooms. The club is also notable as being the first institution of its kind in the United States to utilize the Mayan or Aztec style of architecture. This is the motif of the interior architecture, and will prevail as the interior decoration style in all of the club structures." The architect was Robert B. Stacy-Judd, of Hollywood, who had designed the famous Aztec Hotel in Monrovia, California.

1926 architect's rendition of the proposed La Jolla Beach & Yacht Club from the offering prospectus. *Courtesy of William Kellogg*

According to Mr. William J. Kellogg, great grandson of the founding Kellogg, "Although the original investors had very grandiose ideas about the future, they didn't quite foresee how it would ultimately turn out. Nevertheless, many of the architectural details of the club reveal the original Mayan theme that architect Robert Stacy-Judd had in mind. The current 'Walnut Lounge' was originally called the 'Mayan

Architect's artistic rendition of the Mayan Lounge that was proposed for the La Jolla Beach and Yacht Club.
Courtesy of William Kellogg

A 1931 photo of La Jolla Shores and the La Jolla Beach and Yacht Club with the excavated yacht basin. The Spindrift Inn is located next (left) to the complex.
Courtesy of William Kellogg

Lounge' and featured the tiled floors, thick wood-beam ceilings and imposing arches that can be seen in the picture. Whenever someone claims that our modern-day ideas are too wild I just chuckle because I have seen how the club started out."

The grand opening, an invitation-only event, was held July 22, 1927. Soon the second phase of construction began. 60,000 cubic feet of soil were removed as part of the reconfiguration of the "inner harbor." Unfortunately, the construction of two off-shore breakwaters "proved to be an engineering nightmare." There was also a question of the environmental impact, especially on the beaches south of the site. The yacht harbor was unfeasible and with its demise, membership in the club dwindled. In October, 1927, the Club was reincorporated. A group of San Diego residents paid $500,000, a great loss to the original investors, and took over ownership. However, by 1933, with the Depression claiming its victims, a notice of default was filed. In the spring of 1934, the George M. Hawley Company, a San Diego Investment firm, took legal possession.

August 19, 1935, F. W. Kellogg purchased the property transferring "all its assets to himself and his wife, Florence Scripps Kellogg." It was his idea to make the club an "oceanfront tennis resort" and change the name to the La Jolla Beach and Tennis Club. An Olympic sized swimming pool was built as well as apartments on the south end of the property for visitors from out of town. To protect these oceanfront apartments during construction, Mr. Kellogg built a cofferdam. This dam later became the foundation for the Marine Room.

The Marine Room has a story of its own. In 1916, a cozy, four bedroom roadside Inn named the Spindrift Inn was built next to the ocean in the area of La Jolla known as Long Beach, a quiet stretch of beach in an unpopulated area with cows and horses enjoying the surf and the sand. It is now called La Jolla Shores. The original structure was built with lumber from the ruins of the Congregational Church by R. C. Rose. In 1922, Mr. and Mrs. Peter M. Hannay bought the Inn and ran it for about twenty-two years. The Inn also included a restaurant. While the customers enjoyed good food, Mrs. Hannay provided beautiful music. Anna Held Heinrich was one of the early

The south end apartments of the La Jolla Beach and Tennis Club just after completion. *Courtesy of William Kellogg*

regular patrons and often brought her friend, Charles Wakefield Cadman who would play the piano to everyone's enjoyment. (Cadman was one of the Indianist composers of the early twentieth century, but his and his school's homage to the Native American music was mostly in their melodies.) In 1935, Mr. Frederick W. Kellogg purchased the property. It was his intention to make the Spindrift Inn into solely a restaurant since he had previously bought the adjoining property. However, because they were not able to obtain thick enough plate glass, the windows facing the ocean were smashed in by waves. Mr. Kellogg was forced to board up the exterior and leave the interior unfinished. Only one meal had been served, a luncheon for one hundred guests in honor of Jacob C. Harper, the late Ellen Browning Scripps' attorney, to celebrate Mr. Harper's 80th birthday. The date was August 17, 1938. Although Frederick William Kellogg did not live to see his dream realized, his son, William Scripps Kellogg, was able to continue the project, still using plate glass, the only kind of glass available at the time. It is the William (Bill) J. Kellogg's recollection that F. W. Kellogg built the Marine Room's dining room immediately adjacent to the Spindrift Inn. "He simply 'knocked a hole through the wall' and incorporated it into a restaurant," said Bill Kellogg. "I believe my grandfather told me that the Spindrift Inn is actually part of the Marine Room." In any case, in 1941 the new restaurant opened and was named the Marine Room. A private celebration was held the evening before the grand opening. It was an elaborate black tie dinner. Later, however, the occasion became considerably less formal. One of the biggest grunion runs in La Jolla's history was taking place just outside the windows. It was too tempting to stick to protocol. Off went the shoes, even those of the ladies, and out onto the wet sand went the guests each vying to capture the most grunion. Later. the Marine Room chef, Charlie, prepared the fish and at midnight, served French fried grunion to all the guests. The next day was more normal and the public came to enjoy the new restaurant. The opening day menu featured fresh Lobster à la Newburg in a shell for $1.35, Rainbow Mountain Trout Sauté Amandine for $1.25 and martinis for 35 cents.

Interior and exterior views of damage from the storm of 1982.
Courtesy of William Kellogg

Unfortunately, Mother Nature had the last word. A year after its opening, winter storms raised the surf and the windows overlooking the ocean had to be boarded up again. Smashing windows became a common occurrence until 1948 when the Spindrift Lounge was added (in memory of the former Inn) and the plate glass was replaced with 3/4 inch Hurculite glass. For 34 years, these windows withstood the ocean's attack. It was exciting for the guests who courageously dined in front of the windows while the waves beat upon the glass like a modern interactive art project. However, the El Niño of 1982 brought a new threat to the Marine Room. The restaurant became the focus of every major newscast when the waves won. The glass shattered and the restaurant was flooded. The most scenic restaurant in San Diego County had to close. Nine months of extensive remodeling took place before it was able to open again, but the wait was worth it. As Executive Chef Bernard Guillas says, "When I look out the windows of the Marine Room, I see my favorite Monet and Manet paintings." Chef Bernard also translates his meals into impressionistic masterpieces, truly the art of the palate!

Over the years, the Marine Room has been the favorite dining spot of Hollywood stars like Bob Hope, Gregory Peck (La Jolla's own) and Bill Cosby; tennis stars like John McEnroe and Jimmy Connors; the many Nobel Laureate recipients who reside in La Jolla, as well as local residents. When the surfs up, the dining is safe and nothing beats cascading ocean surf on the windows for atmosphere and romance.

The La Jolla Beach and Yacht Club has gone, replaced by the La Jolla Beach and Tennis Club, but yachting was not yet dead in La Jolla. In the 1950s another "Yacht Club" was formed, Captain J. G. Johanson (who was married to Grace Scripps), a master pilot in steam and sail, formed the "La Jolla Corinthian Yacht Club." As there was no location in La Jolla for moorings, this was a "paper club" with meetings at the La Jolla Country Club and La Jolla Beach and Tennis Club. Members included William S. Kellogg, Willis A. Allen (Real Estate Broker), Alfred Iller (Iller's Department Store), Dr. Walter Munk (recipient of the Prince Albert I Medal in the physical sciences), Jack Mosher (who bought the Green Dragon Colony in 1944 and was Commodore of the Corinthian Yacht Club), Philip P. Barber (who started what came to be known as the Barber Tract), John P. Scripps, Dr. William J. Doyle, and Dr. J T Lipe. The Club faded away in 1960.

Mural Painting

I have a predilection for painting that lends joyousness to a wall.
Paul Auguste Renoir

Some 19,000 years ago, from 17,000 BC to 14,000 BC, the oldest known murals were painted on the walls of caves in France and Spain. Bison, horses, and deer along with symbolism portrayed and documented our ancestors' lives and beliefs. When Picasso visited the Lascaux cave in the 1940s, he was quoted as saying, "We have invented nothing."

Over 300 years ago (1677), the Spaniards arrived in Baja California with the goal of building missions. They discovered a prior tradition depicted on the walls of caves. The native Indians could not explain the origins of these paintings other than to say that the coastal and mountain animals depicted and the stories they represented had been passed on from generation to generation. Archeological evidence estimates the age of the newest cave paintings as more than 2000 years old with many murals dating back 3500 years. Some of the figures are 40 feet off the ground. You wonder how the artists were able to negotiate such heights and still depict such graceful and accurate artistic work. One La Jollan has spent over thirty years attempting to answer this and other questions surrounding the Baja murals.

Harry Crosby, a former La Jolla High School student and teacher turned freelance photographer, has, since 1967, been a dedicated amateur archeologist. He came upon the "Great Murals" by accident and has been hooked ever since, spending weekends and holidays exploring Baja California. Some parts of the trip he trav-

Los Tres Reyes, The Three Kings depicted by three figures in red on granite.
Courtesy of Harry W. Crosby, from The Cave Paintings of Baja California (*Sunbelt Publications*).

eled by mule, some on foot. The terrain was rugged and barren. Originally published in 1975 but expanded in a new edition by Sunset Publications in 1997, *Cave Paintings of Baja California* is a documentary account of over 200 painted caves Crosby discovered himself. He has seen more of the Baja mural art than anyone alive.

Back in Europe, the Roman Empire made great use of mural paintings. Early Christian art (5th-6th century) used the technique of mural paintings but few have survived. The peak of European mural painting was reached during the Renaissance, in particular, in the biblical images painted by Michelangelo on the ceiling of the Sistine Chapel, begun in 1508 and completed in 1512. (The complete restoration of the ceiling, begun in 1980, was finally completed in 1994. Now the Chapel can be seen as it was originally intended, in all its brilliance of color and style.)

In India, murals belonging to the 5th or 6th centuries AD rank among the greatest paintings in the world.

In the United States, painters of the late 1800s or early 1900s returned to the technique of mural painting to depict revolutionary ideas. Of particular note was San Diego artist Diego Rivera (1886-1957).

During the Depression of the 1930s, murals enjoyed another resurgence in popularity, largely though government sponsorship of art on public buildings. One of the greatest of these "Depression artists" was Hugo Ballin.

Hugo Ballin (1879-1956) was born in New York. At 17, he began his studies at the Art Students League. Later, he studied in Germany, France and Italy. His work received many awards including several from the National Academy of

Interior of the La Jolla Branch, 1st National Bank (Girard & Silverado) with Hugo Ballin's mural on the back wall.
Courtesy of San Diego Historical Society Photograph Collection

Design. Ballin was a member of the National Institute of Arts and Letters, an associate member of the National Academy of Design, a member of the Architectural League of the National Arts Club of Rome, and a painter member of the Lotus Club, New York.

About 1921, Ballin moved to Los Angeles where he became involved in the movie industry as a producer and stage designer for Samuel Goldwyn at the new MGM studios. He also became an independent producer, working on or producing more than 100 feature motion pictures. Hugo Ballin authored several books as well whose setting was Southern California. When talking pictures replaced silent films, Ballin returned to painting, specializing in murals.

Ballin received commissions for the most prestigious murals ex-

The mural from the La Jolla Branch, 1st National Bank now adorning the west wall of the Recreation Center. *Courtesy of Steele Lipe*

ecuted in Los Angeles during the late 1920s and early 1930s. One example is the Griffith Observatory rotunda. Other Ballin murals appear in the Wilshire Temple, the Los Angeles Times Building, One Bunker Hill, the Title Guarantee Building and the LA City Hall Council Chambers.

Here in La Jolla, we take pride in having an original Hugo Ballin mural. Titled, "Progress of California," it was painted for the La Jolla branch of the First National Bank at the corner of Silverado and Girard Streets. Designed by Herbert J. Mann (some sources credit Requa & Jackson as the architects), the bank was dedicated on Feb. 1, 1930. The mural depicting early California scenes originally decorated the wall above the vault door. The mural wall faced Girard and was lighted at night giving La Jollans even more enjoyment of the work. The bank was so proud of its mural that it used a reproduction as its letterhead. In 1972, the bank was demolished; however, the mural was preserved and presented to the City of San Diego by the Bank and the La Jolla Historical Society. In 1975, it was installed in the Recreation Center and was rededicated on Oct. 3 that same year.

The 1929 Ballin mural needed to be restored. The initial request for restoration was made in 1990 but it was ten years before the work began. To defer conservation of this work of art would have only make any eventual conservation more expensive and difficult according to Balboa Arts Conservation Center (BACC) who, at the request of the La Jolla Town Council, were asked to make an assessment of the project. BACC had also completed the conservation of the Belle Baranceanu mural inside the La Jolla Post Office on Wall Street.

The 20' x 16' "Progress of California" mural is a semi-circular format with a pointed arch-shaped top with a Roman style insignia in the pitch. Unfortunately, some of the edges of the canvas have been cut off, presumably to fit the mural in its new location. On the left panel, representatives of the Diegueno Indian tribe, Father Junipero Serra, founder of the 21 California missions and Captain Gaspar de Portola, of the Spanish Army who later became Governor of Baja, California, gather on a La Jolla cliff, while below on the blue Pacific a square-rigged sailing vessel, its sail full from a westerly breeze is a reminder of the arrival of Cabrillo in 1542. The central section portrays Warner's Trading Post (precursor of today's Warner's Hot Springs) where a Julian miner and his wife have brought their gold to be weighed. As a native Indian and a Chinese man look on, John Warner weighs the gold. In the background, Brig-General Stephen Watts Kearney (named civil governor of the California territory by President Polk, March 1-May 31, 1847) observes, his rifle held in front of his stern stance like a cane. On the right section, a pioneer family in a Conestoga wagon has just arrived in the new land, the heads and front legs of their two driving horses having already stepped off the canvas. The Spanish architecture of the Exposition buildings of Balboa Park appear below on the right while a lone red monoplane reminiscent of the *Spirit of St. Louis* flies against a gold leaf sky. Even the little stalks of flowers, the barrel, the hanging light fixture and other incidentals are exquisitely

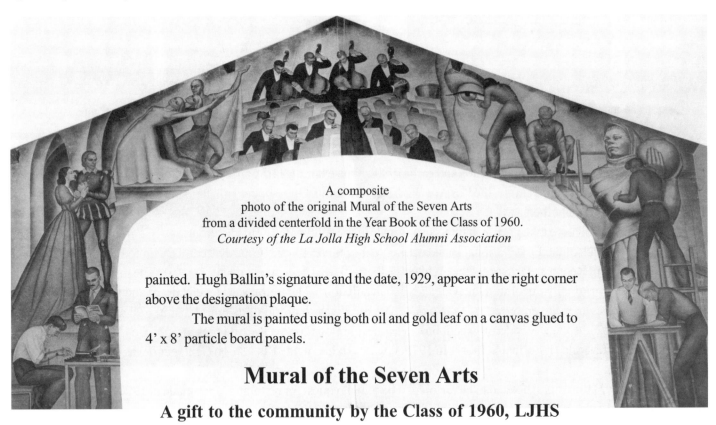

A composite
photo of the original Mural of the Seven Arts
from a divided centerfold in the Year Book of the Class of 1960.
Courtesy of the La Jolla High School Alumni Association

painted. Hugh Ballin's signature and the date, 1929, appear in the right corner above the designation plaque.

The mural is painted using both oil and gold leaf on a canvas glued to 4' x 8' particle board panels.

Mural of the Seven Arts

A gift to the community by the Class of 1960, LJHS

The earthquake that was felt in La Jolla in 1976 triggered events that resulted in sad news for the art world. San Diego building inspectors were called upon to check local buildings that might have been damaged to the point of being no longer earthquake resistant. As a result, the La Jolla High School's auditorium was condemned as unsafe. Some La Jollans were excited at the prospect of having a new modern replacement. However, the beautiful mural crowning the auditorium stage would be destroyed when the building was demolished. Its creator, Belle Baranceanu, sat in the audience when this was announced and was distressed. This was her largest and best work and it would no longer exist. She had painted it in 1940.

For years, the La Jolla Playhouse presented its plays in the then Jr.-Sr. High School auditorium. The audience was equally mesmerized by Miss Baranceanu's mural painting as they were by the plays. The artist's only other La Jolla work has been preserved and can be seen on west wall of the La Jolla Post Office lobby. Harry Crosby, who came to La Jolla in 1935, remembers seeing Miss Baranceanu painting the mural in the Post Office in October of that year. "She was on a couple of sawhorses with planks across and was wearing blue coveralls not pink like the ones she depicted herself wearing in the High School painting. She was a tiny thing," said Mr. Crosby. The mural portrays a scene in La Jolla supposedly overlooking La Jolla Shores and the coastline, "supposedly" because it depicts more a feeling of the place than the specifics. Art is not meant to be specific and certainly this mural lends itself not to historical evidence but rather to a pleasant and familiar impression of La Jolla's hilly peninsula.

For years after the High School auditorium was demolished, people continued to talk of the popular mural and wished that it could be replaced. Then in 1999, members of the class of 1960 met. They began to make plans for the 40th class reunion and entertained suggestions about replacing the mural. Art-

The mural that surrounds the stage of La Jolla Jr.-Sr. High School as painted by Belle Baranceanu in 1940, the location of the original Playhouse. This picture was taken during the demolition in 1960, Muirlands can be seen in the background. *Courtesy of La Jolla High School Alumni Association*

ists were needed who could duplicate the style of Belle Baranceanu who had since passed away. They also needed a school official to approve an area on which a mural could be painted. Finally, plans began to gel. Two women who were both La Jolla High graduates and mural artists were located.

Sandy McGuire Brabon, class of 1960, and her cousin, Ida Jessop, class of 1976, agreed to undertake the ambitious, artistic project. The mural was begun in the Parker Auditorium foyer on a horizontal 19 x 74 foot curved wall in February 2000.

The two artists studied Belle's unusual technique of blending colors using rare brushstrokes. Fortunately, they had Belle's other mural to refer to at the La Jolla Post Office.

While the artists were busy working after hours and on weekends recreating the mural of the Seven Arts, two of the class of 1960, John Campbell and Stan Smith were busy fund raising. This project took five months to complete and cost approximately $25,000. Belle Baranceanu would be pleased.

The Pacific Ocean, a Prized Part of La Jolla's Past

Pre-Surfing and the First Surfer in La Jolla:

From a taped interview with Gene McCormack (1917-1984): "I wasn't rich enough to learn to swim but there was always somebody down (at the Cove) teaching kids to swim (and) there was that rope that went from the beach out to the raft out there and if you couldn't swim, you could pull yourself up to the raft by going up that rope…. We got inner tubes out of old automobiles and we could patch them…. You get the inner tube out in the water and then you could ride it in. Nice thing about an inner tube, you never hurt your head on it. Then there was a time when they came out with Mattress covers made out of cotton like (a) bed mattress and (when) you get that wet, it would hold air. Then you and your buddy would run down the beach holding that thing out there, it would fill with air, you would tie it shut, and go out and ride the surf until the air oozed out.

"There was all kinds of things you could do in the surf. To go diving, some of the rich guys even had eyepieces they put over their eyes and do what they now call scuba diving…. They were made out of cow horns…to fit your eyes and somebody put a piece of glass in it. Then you had rubber bands around your head. But, boy, you had to have them cut to fit your own eyes. You never loaned them to anybody. Some of the guys would go down there with their tire iron or the spring leaf out of a car. You'd get abalones. Of course, us kids could get them at low tide without having to dive…. Surfing you could do without anything. You could surf that way and ride the waves. Then finally some rich kid named Hiomi Nakamira went over to Hawaii and brought back a thing called a surf board…. It was as long as Hiomi was. It was made of redwood and balsam wood. Redwood to make it strong. Balsam to make it light. And then, from then on, you weren't anything unless you had a surfboard."

Windansea and the Renaissance of Surfing

The surf was up at the County Fair and the famous boards and legends of surfing that are the archetypes of a lifestyle unique to California, and to La Jolla's Windansea Beach in particular, were on display. Allan Seymour, enthusiast Hal Sachs, J Richards, and legend

Loren Swan was 16 years old when this picture was taken at Windansea in 1962.
Courtesy of Loren Swan

Hobie Alter were there at the opening of the California Dreamin' Exhibit Del Mar Fair 2000.

A little background is needed to explain the phenomenon of Windansea. There is a break at Windansea which at first looks to the untrained eye as relatively flat and close to shore. According to experts, "your first paddle out proves this wrong." Chris Ahrens writes (*The Surfer's Journal,* Vol. 9,#3), "The peak is thick and can unload more water than most any other wave in Southern California." It is tricky and the distance out is deceptively long. "Offshore canyons, abrupt reef systems, water clarity and open-swell windows give the La Jolla reef waves a mass and energy level more Hawaiian than Californian."

Back at the Fair, the interview begins: "I'm J (known to surfers as LJ, not for La Jolla but for Little John) Richards. I live in Carlsbad. I've been surfing since 1953. I grew up in Oceanside but I surfed at WindanSea Surf Club starting in 1963 when they had the first Malibu Surfing Club contest. They asked several of us from all over the U. S. to be on the team and compete in this particular event and that's when I started with Windansea."

(The Malibu Club Challenge was the result of the area traditionally used by the Malibu Surf Club being converted into a yacht harbor. This would be the club's last challenge. The first nine clubs to send $100.00 would be accepted. In order to compete, the participants had to be members of an organized surf club. Hastily, in response, the surfers of Windansea organized the WindanSea Surf Club. Over the years, the club has recruited top surfers from around the world. "Working together as a team, we became world champions in surfing for four straight years," wrote Chuck Hasley.)

To return to the interview, we asked LJ, "Tell us about Windansea."

"Well, they were rascals. I can't elaborate too much on this!"

Tony Banzuelo (Architect and surfer from Orange, CA) broke into the interview: "I can because I'm not in the club. Those guys have always been crazy!"

"There, in La Jolla, is a famous break (known) throughout the world (considered a "hazard" until Woody, aka 'Spider' Brown rode a green-water wave there with an 8 foot long, 23" wide, 4" thick, 12 pound hand-made "plank" in 1937)…home of some of the best wave riders like Butch Van Artsdalen and Pat Curren" (father of professional surfer Tom Curren, and one of the first big wave pioneers to surf the North Shore of Oahu, Hawaii). "And they were the first ones to ride the bigger waves…. They were all notable surfers…like Bobby Patterson."

According to Guy Hansen, treasurer of WindanSea Surf Club, "Pat shaped beautiful big wave boards which today are highly prized by surf memorabilia collectors." Pat Curren began body surfing and belly boarding in Mission Beach, but it was in La Jolla in 1950 at age 18 that he began stand-up surfing. "At Windansea, Buzzy Bent, Towney Cromwell, Buddy Hall, and the Eckstrom brothers were riding 10-11 foot planks. Buzzy was the first to ride the Quigg chip, a fiberglass and balsa surfboard 9 feet long, 22 to 23 inches wide, turned down rails, trying to get rocker with a pretty flat bottom," said Pat in another interview. As for who taught him, he replied tersely, "Does anybody teach anybody? It's kind of like learning to ride a bike. Somebody gives you a push, then watches you crash into a pole."

How about the surfboard itself, did it change a bit over the years?

LJ: "The surfboards? Oh ya, they became much smaller, much lighter. I think it's because of the wetsuits. People can get down in the water…Wet suits started in the late '50s…The beaver tail didn't become popular until '63."

Was it a tougher group before the wet suits?

LJ: "It was a crazier group. The waves that the kids are riding now days I wouldn't think about riding…like in Tahiti and other places. I think some of the pioneers of big wave riding came out of Windansea."

Who was from La Jolla?

LJ: "We have David Cheney, Mike Hynson, Skip Frye (Skip's wife, Donna, is an avid environmentalist and is a member of the San Diego City Council).... Almost every other surfing club around the world has copied WindanSea. The WindanSea guys started it all."

When did the WindanSea Club get started?

LJ: "I would say in the late '50s, but I'm not really sure because I wasn't familiar with the club until they asked me to compete for them in this particular event (the Malibu Club Challenge) in 1963."

Who was the president of the club?

LJ: "Chuck Hasley was one of the guys and, I think, Thor Svenson and Bobby Burns." (According to Tiger Gomez, an avid '50s-'60s surfer, Chuck was truly the "father" of the WindanSea Club. Mike Hynson was vice-president, Loren Swan was social chairman, Rusty Miller, secretary, and Thor Svenson became executive director. Butch Cornelies designed the club logo. According to Chuck Hasley, "Most of the early members of the WindanSea Surf Club were free independent spirits and not 'joiners' of anything. But everyone wanted to be part of the WindanSea Surf Club. The Club has never been about 'I'; it has always been about 'we'.")

Paddleboard surfing, early La Jolla Shores.
Courtesy of Hans Newman

At this point, Hobie Alter was introduced to us.

Hobie: "The palm shack at Windansea has been there continuous since the '30s (it was actually replaced two years ago after a wind storm demolished the original shack. Designated by Hans Newman and Melinda Merryweather, the Palm Shack is now a historical site) and famous, famous surfers have come out of there like Buzzy Bent, Bob Simmons, Butch Van Artsdalen, and guys like Mike Diffenderfer. Windansea for San Diego County has probably the best waves!"

What can you tell us about Windansea, Hobie?

Hobie: "Well, it was a hard break. It peaked over that reef out there and with a steep break. It was really the one break you knew of (for us) in Orange county. The first thing you heard was Windansea in La Jolla. Buzzy Bent was one of the key riders and also made surfboards down there, which would be in '51, '52, or '53.

"Buzzy and Joey Cabel (who) were the founders of the Chart House Restaurant, which they did at Aspen, and Pell

Mell were other names of early guys at Windansea."

LJ: "Bob Simmons was a great innovator in the '40s of surfboards and he was actually killed at Windansea in the early '50s." (There was a photograph of John Elwell with a Bob Simmons surfboard taken in 1952 at the Fair.)

According to Rennie Yater (Santa Barbara's "most honored" surfboard manufacturer who had worked for Hobie), "If anybody was ever to get the credit of being the 'Father of the Modern Surfboard', I would say it would have to be Simmons. He changed board design in a shorter period of time than anybody has before or since." (According to Melinda Merryweather, Michael Hynson designed the first down rail surfboard in the '60s. He also helped invent the first removable fin.)

Hobie: "The first board I had was a Catalina Paddle board. They (the big boards) were around but I didn't know where to get one. You saw the heavy ones, and they were hard to ride in Laguna Beach. So a guy came around with a real surfboard. I copied it and made my own. Because they were hard to find, I think I sold it to two people. And so it really happened! So pretty soon, I made more…it's better than being a lifeguard. About three years of building in my garage…."

What year are we talking about?

Hobie: "Well, the first board I built was in 1950. And I built in the garage until 1953, which, I think, came up to about 80 boards. I got through Junior College and…I had a little money saved up and some my grandfather gave me and started a shop in Dana Point…. I couldn't make enough boards from the day I opened up…and we kept growing…and…the only other competition we had was other surfers and they're about as good in business as I was."

Guy Hansen tells us that Hobie was not only one of the first surfboard manufacturers, but an industry innovator as well. "Hobie and a friend, Gordon "Grubby" Clarke (who was working for Hobie as a glasser and who also had some training in engineering from college) are generally credited with developing surfboard 'foam' blanks (the inner surfboard core) which are still used in the surfboard industry today."

In January '58, Hobie "threw out all his balsa-wood stuff and said, 'This is the way it is going to be. Foam."

While browsing through the surfing exhibit at the Fair, we met Hal Sachs who filled us in with antidotes. Although we cannot share these stories with our readers, we will tell you that, yes! The surfing crowd, at least those of the '50s and '60s, was a wild bunch! "Some crazy guys!"

More on our local "Surf Culture"

"All over La Jolla," harmonized the Beach Boys in the early sixties. Surfing really was all over La Jolla by 1955: Black's, the Shores,

Black's
Cove
Shores
Boomer
South Boomer

La Jolla's Surfing Spots, 1950's

Hospital

Horseshoe
Dunemere
Little Point
Simmon's Reef
Windansea
Big Rock
North Bird Rock
South Bird Rock

Map of La Jolla showing many of the surfing sites.
Courtesy of Joan Oglesby

the Cove, Boomer and South Boomer, Hospital (in front of old Scripps Clinic), Horseshoe, Dunemere, Little Point, Windansea, Big Rock, North and South Bird Rock.

Black's Beach was named for the Black family who, at one time, had a horse farm overlooking the beach. The Black family sold the land, which was then subdivided into the La Jolla Farms lots. The Farms' residents retained Mr. Black's private road to the beach.

"Not many surfed Black's," according to former surfer The Ogg. "It was a long walk from Scripps pier. We all had long boards back then. They could get pretty heavy if we needed to walk very far. I was fortunate in that my Godparents lived in the Farms. They would sometimes allow me to use their gate key, so my surfing friends and I could access the private road to the beach. We would have the surf all to ourselves." That kind of privacy is rare, almost unheard of today.

Each of the surfing spots had their own unique style. Black's usually provided long walls of surf as at the Shores. Sometimes, Black's broke in peaks, that is, falling off on each side of the wave. Boomer was popular for body and board surfing. There were no "Boogie" boards back then; so you either body-surfed or used a big board. (There were some skim boards, however, which were always homemade.) Boomer broke on a north swell. The surf was shallow, making it easy to hit rocks. South Boomer broke on a south swell. The Cove broke only on a BIG north swell, producing

Two views of the Windansea surf shack; top as seen in the 1940s and bottom during a recent winter storm.
Courtesy of Hans Newman and Steele Lipe

quite a challenge. It took many surfers years to build the confidence needed to try the Cove.

(Mike Hynson, Mike Diffenderfer and Thor Svenson, by sheer strength of conviction, were able to preserve another surfing spot. Located between Bird Rock and Pacific Beach, this section of beach is called Tourmaline. Tourmaline is actually a green, or sometimes pink, gem found in the mountains around Julian. Armed with petitions, the threesome went to the powers that be in San Diego. They were not only successful in convincing the city to preserve this area, but they caused the creation of "surfers rights." The city went one step further by creating a veritable park in an area that would have been the private domain for the people who owned condos next to Tourmaline. The park and the surfers' rights marked a milestone in the relationship between serious surfers and the City of San Diego.)

The surfing culture of the fifties and early sixties was territorial. Occasional surfing safaris provided an opportunity to explore and try something different. Mostly, though, surfers stayed on their own beaches. You surfed La Jolla, or you surfed Pacific Beach, or wherever it was you and your friends were associated. Surfing out of one's territory wasn't usually welcomed by the locals. That was a part of the etiquette and honor among surfers. ("Right of Wave" means never taking off in front of another surfer.)

Hawaii surfer Ronald Patterson moved to La Jolla early on, and surfed La Jolla in the fifties. He also made surfboards. There were several people in the area who made boards; however, it was not yet an established retail business. Sales were usually generated by word of mouth and were often between fellow surfers. Those who made the boards usually used their garages for shaping and finishing; surf shops were yet to evolve in the La Jolla area. The boards were shaped from balsa wood and finished with fiberglass. The Ogg remembers, "The first used board I bought was a classic. The top was completely covered with liquor bottle labels. They were sealed with fiber glass."

Many well-known surfers also shaped boards. Boards were ordered by the name of the surfer who was shaping.

Rick Greg surfing a 20 foot wave at La Jolla Cove, 1963.
Courtesy of Hans Newman

For example, a Carl Eckstrom board could be had at the right time and place. It depended who was in town and probably who needed money. (Mike Hynson was one of the most important people who not only shaped and designed but also surfed. He won the first professional nose-riding surfing contest ever in Ventura. The contest was organized by Tom Morey. Mike not only won the contest, he designed and shaped the board that he used, according to Melinda Merryweather. She ought to know. She was married to Mike.)

A kind of pecking order had evolved by the mid fifties. The older guys who had been surfing since the early fifties were looked up to. Guys like Mike Diffenderfer, Pat Curran, Al Nelson, Butch Van Artsdalen and David Chaney.

David Chaney grew up in La Jolla and joined friends in founding South Coast Surf Boards in Encinitas in the late '50s. He shaped balsa wood boards, but his reputation was as a prankster and a risk-taker. Always in search of challenging surf, Chaney traveled from the San Diego coastline to Hawaii and to Mexico. According to his friend Elaine Vescovi, David "lived a simple life, with deep respect for the environment and a special appreciation for the natural beauty of the Baja landscape." David was not only a surfer, he was an artist and a talented flamenco guitar player. But most of all, Chaney was a "free spirit" who found the rhythm of the surf enchanting.

Butch Van Artsdalen ultimately moved to Hawaii where he became a famous lifeguard. This group from the '50s was legendary, but they paved the way for the next group, which included Mike Doyle, Mike Stewart, Mike Hynson, Jimmy Tejada, and Ronnie McCloud.

Mike Stewart caught one of those classic waves out of the Cove. His ride was published in Surfer magazine. Butch Van Artsdalen became famous for being one of the first to surf Bonsai Pipeline on Oahu north shore. Mike Hynson and Robert August made the classic film, "Endless Summer."

Bud Brown, Bruce Brown, and John Severson were also doing surfing movies. The films had names like "Slippery When Wet," "Barefoot Adventure," and "Surfing Safari." They would usually be shown in the auditorium of La Jolla Jr.-Sr. High School. La Jolla was a small town then; venues though not abundant, were easy to access. The surfer(s) who made the film would play taped music and narrate through the movie. Certain music lent itself very well to amplifying the surfing action being seen on the screen. Edited pieces from music such as, "Bull Dog," "Tokai," "Walk, Don't Run," and "Peter Gunn" seemed like surf music when accompanying these films.

Film narration, that is, a surfer standing on the stage holding a mike, incorporated esoteric terms, which at that time were used only by surfers. Accomplished surfers could "walk the nose" (long boards provided enough balance), "hang five or ten" (toes off the board) and were noted to surf "standard" (left foot forward) or "goofy foot."

Surfing terminology included nicknames. Most of the surfers had them. In fact, nicknames were indigenous to beach culture in general, whether or not one surfed. Most of the names were descriptive and some not necessarily flattering. Bill Ogelsby (called "Ogg") says he never minded his nickname, although he does not remember how it came about. The names somehow evolved, stuck, and continue to be used today.

ALL NEW 1961 SURFING ADVENTURE FILM

GRANT ROHLOFF
—— presents ——
"Too Hot To Handle"

Featuring

BEST SURF FROM CALIFORNIA
TO HAWAII

LA JOLLA - SHERWOOD HALL

Three Performances - Tues., Wed., Fri., March 14, 15, 17

ADM. $1.25 - Tickets at Door   8:00 P.M.

— THRILLS! — EXCITEMENT! — HUMOR! —

Advertising poster for "Too Hot to Handle"
Courtesy of Joan Oglesby

When smaller boards began evolving, it was a sign of a changing society. The slower, graceful long boards gave way to shorter, quick turning, faster moving boards. The beaches became busier, the waves crowded, "and La Jolla no longer has a small town intimacy," says the Ogg.

Local Diving Legends

Surfing was not the only water sport of distinction in La Jolla's early history. Mention should be made about diving. In 1939 the headline in *The San Diego Sun*, stated: "La Jolla Dentist Turns into 'Human Eel' to Catch Own Supper." Dr. Quintin Stephen-Hassard, La Jolla dentist may have been the area's first spear fisherman. The interview confirms the reporter's disbelief that any human could "stalk" fish.

Quintin Stephen-Hassard with a 22+ pound halibut obtained off La Jolla in 1939.
Courtesy of Q. D. Stephen-Hassard

"Doc had on short swimming trunks. From his sweater pocket he produced an indescribable gadget that looked something like red gums from a set of false teeth.

"'Looks like false teeth,' I suggested, hesitatingly, as I didn't want to offend him.

"'You're right,' he answered, 'and they're what do the trick. They are water-proof goggles. I made them in my office from rubber used in making false teeth. The part near the lenses is hard rubber. The edges, which fit close to my face, are soft, making them perfectly water-proof. The lenses must be exactly on a plane or I'll see double under water.'" These lenses were actually an improvement over his first "goggles." Back in 1924, Dr. Stephen-Hassard knocked the bottoms out of a couple of eye cups, cemented in glass, making himself a crude but effective pair of goggles. He said that in those days, he "had the whole sea bottom to himself." Along with the goggles, the doctor made himself a spear. The biggest fish he speared was a twenty-two pound Halibut in 1939.

Dr. Stephen-Hassard wasn't your ordinary dentist. True, he had an office in La Jolla on Wall Street where he worked on people's teeth. But he also was the dentist for the animals of the San Diego Zoo. Besides understanding the idiosyncrasies of the animals, it seems that he an equal affinity with the fish of the ocean. For example, one of his most unusual discoveries made of this underwater population was that "all fish, from the beautiful sea trout to the lowly, unsporting garibaldi perch, grunt when alarmed! These grunts are plainly and, at first, startlingly audible under water, and invariably precede the disappearance of said startled denizens." Dr. Stephen-Hassard compared the noise "in function, though not in

Then, with a chuckle, he added, "And you see the Damndest things down ther."

In 1933, San Diegans Jack Prodanovitch, Glenn Orr, and Ben Stone formed a group known as the "Bottom Scratchers." This group, which also included Max Dekking, was recognized by the Scuba America Historical Center as the first of many sport diving clubs in America. In 1939, Wally Potts became a member. The following year, the Bottom Scratchers adopted fins. Wally, however, remained a free diver. In fact, it wasn't until much later that he even used a snorkel. Most important for Wally Potts was a good set of lungs. (It was an encounter with a shark many years later that converted him to the use of a snorkel.) Wally was accurately described as "the father of free diving." He had an incredible tolerance for the cold water (remember this was the era before wet suits) as well as acute vision earning him the title "radar eyes." His mask was crude and his fishing spear (like Quintin Stephen-Hassard's), at least in the early years, was improvised. And despite his limited gear, it was Wally Potts who was the first Bottom Scratcher to land a fish weighing more than 100 pounds. In 1945, he caught a 110 pound gulf grouper.

After World War II, lots of people speared and "scratched bottom," but it was Wally Potts' design that revolutionized spear fishing. A master metal worker, Wally designed a reel and a two-part trigger mechanism that is still "defining standards of modern spear fishing equipment," according to San Diego diving enthusiast Jim Cahill. Wally worked with Jack Prodanovitch creating designs for equipment in Wally's garage. "I don't think anybody had more experience in the field than the two of us," said Prodanovitch. "We worked with companies like Swimmaster and Scuba Pro." One of the designs was a plastic reel that allowed divers to subdue large fish underwater. "When the fish was speared, it would fight the line and float." Other designs included underwater camera housings in an aluminum mold. Jack Williams of *The San Diego Union-Tribune,* writes, "A fellow Bottom Scratcher, Lanar Boren pioneered underwater cinematography and modeled his first camera housings based on the Potts design. Boren went on to film the pilot for 'Sea Hunt,' a TV series that debuted in 1958, starring Lloyd Bridges."

The clear beauty of our Pacific with its kelp and seaweed and incredible underwater sea life begs us, perhaps no longer to spear, but to snorkel and dive. This beautiful part of the Pacific has been a prized part of La Jolla's past.

The Bishop's School Motto:
Simplicity, Serenity, Sincerity

A vision can be reviewed and explained, but our response to it depends finally upon associations we bring to it from deep within ourselves. **John Canaday**

In 1909, the population in the United States was 90 million. Women's right to vote, anti-discrimination, integration, and child labor were honest concerns of the nation. Ladies wore "merry widow" hats and sheath gowns. Men sported derbies and drove around in model T's. Approximately 40,000 people lived in San Diego, a city that boasted that churches outnumbered saloons. Its schools were overcrowded, some with more than sixty students in a classroom.

Recognizing the need for college preparatory schools, The Right Reverend Joseph Horsfall Johnson, first bishop of the Los Angeles Diocese of the Episcopal Church, established The Bishop's Schools. Although The Bishop's Schools were under the auspices of the diocese, they received no budgetary support from the church, nor did they come under its control. Bishop Johnson was sixty-two when he undertook founding the schools. His appreciation for young people and talent for captivating them was remarkable. He greeted all students by name; and he did the same with parishioners in outlying parishes of the diocese even though he saw them but once a year. With the help of benefactors, Rev. Johnson designed a beautiful facility and a program that "provided the mental training needed to pursue higher education along with an understanding of the social requirements of courtesy and public usefulness."

Bishop's first La Jolla Building, Scripps Hall, 1910.
Courtesy of The Bishop's School

The Bishop's School, c. 1916 showing the main buildings and the San Diego-La Jolla Railway which crossed the property along the extension of Cuvier Ave. There was a train stop opposite Scripps Hall.
Courtesy of The Bishop's School

Ellen Browning and Virginia Scripps
Courtesy of The Bishop's School

This was a scholastic education that also included "character building."

Initially the school was called The Bishop's Schools for Girls; however, the 1910 articles of incorporation specified that education would also be provided for boys. Originally there were two campuses, a day school in San Diego that was available for boys as well and a boarding school for girls only in La Jolla. Walter Fuelscher entered as part of the inaugural class at the day school. In 1913, although a member of the first class to complete four years at the school, Walter refused to participate in the graduation. He was embarrassed to graduate from a "girls' school." He did not set a precedent however. Boys remained part of the student population until the early 1920s. Then in 1971, The Bishop's Schools merged with the San Miguel School for boys and in June, 1983, the boarding facility closed.

Ellen Browning Scripps and her half-sister Eliza Virginia Scripps, known to many as Miss Jenny, played major roles in founding Bishop's. A large sum of money and seven of the school's eleven La Jolla acres were donated by the Scripps sisters.

Miss Ellen Scripps loved living in La Jolla. She especially loved the ocean. It was her habit to spend many of her daytime hours in the sun room in the back of her house overlooking and listening to the Pacific. At night, she slept outside on a porch she had constructed on the Prospect Street side of the house. She believed sleeping outside was good for your health. The air, she said, was so fresh. Feeling closer to nature was probably also a consideration. At The Bishop's School, the students were asked to sleep outside, above the arcade of the first building, Scripps Hall (on Cuvier St). They were also, in the name of health, asked to take cold baths (to "stimulate intellectual activity.")

In contrast, her sister, Miss Jenny, was known for her flamboyance and eccentricity. A frequent visitor to the campus, for a time she was in charge of the school grounds. A fanatic when it came to neatness and order, Miss Virginia banned trees from the school grounds. She considered them "dirty." In 1914, the senior class named Miss Jenny their mascot.

There are many stories about the eccentric sister. One time a Bishop's student accidentally spilled hot tea on Miss Jenny's purple satin dress. The terrified student braced herself for the inevitable outburst. But it did not happen. Instead, Miss Jenny offered profuse assurances not too worry, the dress was old and only needed to be hung to dry. Then to the shock of all ladies present in the parlor, Miss Jenny removed her gown and proceeded to sip her tea wearing undergarments only. When asked how she accounted for the differences between herself and her dignified sister, Miss Ellen, she quipped, "Ellen's mother was a lady, mine was not."

For its first 90 years, The Bishop's Schools were led by a succession of strong headmistresses (and headmasters). They, along with the faculty, have instilled discipline and academic excellence as well as simplicity, sincerity, and serenity, the school's motto, in generations of students.

The Benthams, c. 1913
Courtesy of The Bishop's School

When The Bishop's School La Jolla campus was formally opened in 1910, the first Headmistress was Mrs. Charles E, Bentham, (whose husband became the Vicar of St. James-by-the-Sea Church in La Jolla). She was also the head of the San Diego campus which had only day students. It took an hour riding the old steam train, but occasionally the day students came to the La Jolla campus to participate in celebrations, theater, and dinner parties.

Personal beauty and dignity best described Mrs. Bentham. It must be remembered that the concept of a private girls' boarding school was new and Mrs. Bentham accepted the challenges which inevitably came up. Manners (nineteenth century manners were strict and some quite strange to today's way of thinking), dignity, punctuality, and poise were taught side by side with academic subjects. These were the days when one of the required courses was in domestic science. The course included cooking and interior decorating. Nevertheless, the basic college admission courses were also taught. The girls were accepted to Ivy League Eastern colleges as well as the University of California and Stanford (all without college admissions examinations).

Sadly, in December, 1914, just before Christmas, Mr. Bentham died. His wife was devastated and a condition that she had carefully concealed reappeared, a severe diabetic condition. Less than a month after her husband's demise, Mrs. Bentham died in her apartment on the second floor of Scripps Hall. (It was only seven years later that

Miss Margaret Gillman
Courtesy of The Bishop's School

insulin was discovered.)

For two years, Miss Margaret Gilman came to head the Bishop's School. A rigid, formal and proper Bostonian, Miss Gilman had taught at a boy's school before coming to La Jolla. She admitted that she "liked" girls but she never really "understood" them. She was also never comfortable in the "frontier" (West Coast) and was not hesitant about saying so, however, she did enjoy tennis and beat all the faculty and students regularly on the courts. Miss Gilman's choice of uniform for the girls to wear was described as "natty" and included long sleeves, stockings, a blouse with a sailor collar, and a long skirt. (It wasn't until 1930 that this basic outfit was changed.)

By 1916, the school had grown considerably. Irving J. Gill who had designed the first buildings was again asked to construct a new dormitory and two-story classroom building. Bishop Johnson designated this as Gilman Hall. In June, 1918, the graduating class consisting of twenty-six girls "fittingly dedicated" their yearbook to Ellen Browning Scripps who was then 83 years old. She in turn gave each ember of the class a fifty-dollar war bond. However, despite the admiration of the Bishop and many pleased parents, their school's head, Miss Gilman, never adjusted to the "Wild West" ("uncouth," was her descriptive term). In 1918 she returned to her beloved Boston. In her place, another Bostonian was brought to Bishop's and was the first to be called "Head Mistress."

Miss Marguerite Barton
Courtesy of The Bishop's School

Miss Margarite Barton had graduated from Radcliffe, magna cum laude in 1898. In 1915, she completed a master's degree in English literature, with honors, from Radcliffe. This was a time in our country of an extremely inflationary economy. Miss Barton agreed to a monthly salary of $165 (compared to the $250 a month her predecessors received). Charming, fair and kind, Miss Barton was, according to Bishop Johnson, "very chary of her criticisms, but immensely stimulating by insistence upon the policy and conduct that she believed should pervade a family built upon Christian principles." Remember the challenge this lady had; this was the era of the roaring twenties! Needing help, she sent a telegram to one of her fellow teachers from Boston, Miss Cummins.

Caroline Seely Cummins was born in the midst of the 'Great Blizzard of "88" (1888) in New York City. Her father was a physician and believed in the "simple life." Their family home was in a small country town called Warwick, New York. Miss Cummins graduated from nearby Vassar College in 1910 and the following year received a master's degree in classics. Her first teaching position was at the Cambridge School for Girls in Massachusetts where the headmistress hired "no one who took courses in education because she believed teachers were born, not made." When the Cambridge School was sold, Miss Cummins along with most of the faculty resigned. After two years away from teaching, Miss Cummins received the telegram requesting her to teach at The Bishop's School in La Jolla, California from her fellow teacher from the Cambridge School, Miss Marquerite Barton.

In 1920, La Jolla was still a dry, barren remote place, but the people were friendly and it didn't take long for this Easterner to adjust and even come to love the chaparral and the sage on the dry and golden hills, the craggy cliffs and the dazzling sunsets. "It didn't take many weeks and many sunsets to know the beauty of La Jolla and appreciate the nice invigorating air compared to the sultriness of the tropics." (She had spent the past two years in Hawaii.) Her first assignment at Bishop's was teaching Latin and English to the lower school and helping with administrative tasks.

"The first year I was in La Jolla, I lived outside the school in a cottage on Draper Avenue It was called Mountain View and three other teachers and I lived (there)…the cottage was where the tennis court is now built and later it was moved across the street…." Miss Cummins writes. "The school had its own cow stable on Sea Lane and Cuvier. The horse stable was also connected with the barn." However, it was not long before the zoning laws forbade having animals and the cows had to be sold. Until that happened, "we had milk brought to the school twice a day and during my first two vacations we had so much cream that it was very bad for everybody."

The first people Miss Cummins met were Trustees and faculty members. "Miss Ellen Scripps was on the Board…and Miss Scripps was particularly gracious to me although she was in her eighties and I was in my thirties, but she was a very kind trustee and impressed me very much because, although at meetings she seemed to be dozing, when the gentlemen on the Board were getting very much agitated about some weighty problem, she'd open her eyes and in a few brief sentences settle the whole dispute."

Five months after arriving on campus, Miss Cummins' friend, Miss Barton, died from a perforated gastric ulcer. She was only thirty-nine. In her memory, the student body raised money for the rose window in The Bishop's School chapel. Each petal depicts two of the Twelve Apostles. (Later, in 1923, students raised money for the first pipe organ in the chapel and gave it in tribute to Margarite Barton.)

Bishop Johnson, after an unsuccessful search for a new Headmistress in the East was encouraged to consider the young new teacher, Miss Cummins. Although only thirty-three, Miss Cummins appeared to have the qualifications necessary for the position. According to the dean of Vassar College, "she is a good executive…cool and clear in decision in times of emergency." The former head of Cambridge School wrote that she "has qualities of mind which, in this day and generation, are rare and which are not usual among women."

"I had come to help (Miss Barton), but I hadn't really come to stay because I had a contract with a school in New York City to which I was supposed to return. I was released from that." Initially, Miss Cummins agreed to stay for one year to help the Bishop until he found someone suitable. Her stay lasted thirty-three years before retiring. (She remained in La Jolla for the rest of her long life.).

Miss Caroline Cummins
Courtesy of The Bishop's School

The twenties at The Bishop's School were memorable for the "panoply of outstanding visiting professionals who interacted with the students" including John Burroughs (nature writer), Jane Addams (Nobel Prize winner), Richard Halliburton (author-adventurer), Will Durant (author of the multivolume *The Story of Civilization*), Jan Pederewski (concert pianist and short-time premier of Poland), Jascha Heifetz (violinist), and Paul Whiteman ("King of Jazz").

In 1928, Bishop Johnson died. One of his finest achievements had been the founding of The Bishop's Schools. After his death, Miss Cummins kept alive his ideals throughout her tenure as Headmistress. Being a Bishop's girl was in essence a way of life was characterized by fairness, honesty, punctuality, responsibility, loyalty, simplicity, and good manners.

When the Great Depression hit, the school was affected as much as anything else in the country. The student population dropped from over 125 to 81 students. The teachers' salaries were drastically reduced as well.

In 1941, The Bishop's Schools became a charter member of the newly created California Association of Independent Schools. With the entry of the United States in World War II, Bishop's again suffered a reduction in the student population as well as the faculty.

After the war, the school regained its students and faculty and it wasn't long before enrolment began steadily increasing. In 1947, Reverend Frederick James Stevens became chaplain of the school. For thirteen years, Father Stevens was counselor, spiritual advisor and instructor to the girls. His class on Comparative Religions was particularly memorable and enlightening.

As an administrator, Miss Cummins took full responsibility for rules, admissions, curriculum, individual student counseling, Bible lessons, moral standards and training in being a proper lady ("Civilized living characterized a lady"). She was strict, spartan, but sympathetic at the same time. After lunch, Miss Cummins designated a "quiet time." On Sunday, quiet time might last two hours, a time for "the three R's of reading 'riting and resting." For off-campus visits hats, gloves, proper attire (plain colors, no patterns) and a chaperone were required.

In 1953, Miss Cummins retired. The Board of Trustees designated this extraordinary lady, "headmistress emeritus." "She has maintained high standards of character in a day when it was easy to be cheap and she has given the girls a sense of high purpose and desire to be of real use in modern society." For three decades, Caroline Cummins "not only maintained the founder's ideals for the school, but gave substance to them that they might become no 'vain illusion' (Ezekiel 13:7)."

As the school approached its fiftieth anniversary, a new headmistress was placed at the helm of the Bishop's School.

Rosamond Larmour was born in 1911 in Berkeley, a small community that was later incorporated with Norfolk, Virginia. Her parents, though "humble and economically limited" provided their daughter with — to use her own words — "good genes plus a loving, supportive, somewhat bookish, church-going, music-loving background." She attended Hollins College in Roanoke, Virginia, where the professors "taught us well and nobly, and even more by example than by precept: character, conduct, ethical values, self-discipline, the rewards of hard work, and the inspiration to 'go forth and do well.'"

Although teaching was not her goal, in 1933, upon graduation, it was the only door open to Miss Larmour. The first 6 years after graduation, she taught at Norfolk public schools, fifth grade through high school. Then, with the help of professors at Hollins, a part-time job in Boston was found giving Rosamond the opportunity to study for a master's at Radcliffe. In only one year and one summer of hard work, Miss Rosamond Larmour gained her degree. "I told the director of admissions I only had one year to get a master's degree, but I was determined to do it. I'll never forget her reply: 'You mean you're one of those rare creatures — an energetic Southerner?'"

Miss Rosamond Larmour, 1953
Courtesy of The Bishop's School

With her master's degree, Miss Larmour pursued various jobs included teaching, counseling, assisting deans, admissions and directing college residences at several schools and colleges including Rutgers (NJ), Middlebury (VT) and her own alma mater. At Ashley Hall, a prestigious prep school in Charleston, South Carolina, Miss Barbara Pierce from Boston was one of Miss Larmour's star students. Christmas vacation her junior year, Barbara went home for the holiday parties. When she returned to the school, Barbara told her friends, that she had met the man she was going to marry. "I only kissed one man and that was George Bush," she said. The future First Lady learned her American History from Miss Larmour. "Barbara was well organized, a good athlete and very popular."

From 1948 until 1953, Miss Larmour became principal of the upper division of another well-known college preparatory school in Dallas, Texas, the Hockaday School for Girls, her mother's alma mater. This experience was a perfect stepping stone for her final position. In 1953, Miss Larmour accepted the invitation to become Head Mistress of The Bishop's School. The fact that Bishop's was located next to the Pacific and that it was affiliated with her church appealed to Rosamond. "I took an airplane from Dallas to interview with the bishop of the [Episcopal] Church of Los Angeles and then took a train south." Mr. Loomis, a member of the Board, met her at the Del Mar train station. When she arrived on campus, one of the gardeners introduced himself to her and then said, "You must be the Bishop's new mistress." This was too good not to share!

The final piece of her career's puzzle was now in place. Miss Larmour had been a teacher at all levels and in all kinds of schools. Now she would conclude her career on the best possible note for herself and for the students who were fortunate enough to be her "girls." For nine years, Bishop's School students flourished under her guidance. Some of the strict rules were lifted. Radios were allowed in student rooms and students were allowed to attend football games at La Jolla High School. A new program of American Field Service began with students coming to Bishop's from countries all over the world and Bishop's girls spending time in other countries as exchange students. Day students (for a fee) could have meals in the dining room with the boarders. A mid-morning break with milk and chocolate covered graham crackers became a tradition. Miss Larmour (described by the *San Diego Union* as a "people person") traveled extensively throughout the country in order to make contact with alumnae and to extend the influence of Bishop's at educational conferences (Miss Larmour is listed in the first edition of *Who's Who of American Women*, 1958). For the first time, male teachers were invited to the faculty and for the first time, faculty received proper contracts each year.

Academics also changed with Miss Larmour. The honor system which began (and continues) at the University of Virginia was established. Advanced Placement courses were added to the curriculum and a course in the fine arts became a requirement for graduation. Students also participated in the National Merit Scholarship competition.

In 1957, the students, in appreciation for her warmth and her guidance, presented their headmistress with a pug puppy. Tinker had the run of the school for years. Miss Larmour also started the tradition of having students come visit at her cottage and share a meal in a relaxed atmosphere. It was a special time for the girls to voice their concerns with their "second mother."

In 1963, Miss Larmour, at the age of 52, married for the first and only time. The groom was Richard Loomis, the gentleman who had met her at the Del Mar train depot nine years before. Recently widowed, "he was sixty-one years old. He said, 'Maybe we'll have ten good years.' We had thirty-one."

The Bishop's Schools have experienced many changes since the Right Reverend Joseph Johnson established them in 1909, but change "lays not her hand upon truth." This kind and principled man wanted the students to be inspired by the "influence of simple and beautiful surroundings in a setting of natural loveliness, in the belief that the silent influences of environment play a part in the deepening and development of the mind." The beauty remains, the scholastic achievements prevail as does the belief that "Our constant purpose should be to realize God's perpetual presence."

Some of the information for this article was obtained from *Reviewing the Vision* by Thomas W. Mitchell (1979)

Tennis in La Jolla

Tennis and tennis friends are not for today and tomorrow but forever!

"Tennis anyone?" is a friendly question that most probably was heard in La Jolla beginning in the second decade of the 20th century. Ellen Browning Scripps provided the playground, recreation center, and tennis courts for the people of La Jolla. The Recreation Center itself was designed by the architectural firm of Gill & Gill (Irving J. and his nephew, Louis).

The entire facility including a playground and tennis courts was dedicated in 1915 and was one of the first public playgrounds in the United States. The original three courts located between Draper and Cuvier were used for both tennis and Saturday night dances. Twenty Mule Team Borax (soap) was sprinkled on the courts before the dances making the dancing more pleasurable but it angered the tennis players on the days following the dances. The players couldn't get traction and were apt to fall if all the Borax was not removed. One Saturday, as the piano was being moved from the Recreation Center to the courts, it fell off its trolley causing some sour notes at the dance that night.

In 1919, Mr. Talboy was made Director of the Playground, a position he enjoyed for thirty-three years. Mr. and Mrs. Archie Talboy and their children lived in a house just beyond the third tennis court on Cuvier. After the Talboy's house was removed, a fourth court was added. In later years, a fifth court was built to the east of the original complex and was named number one court. Draper Avenue bordered it on the east. A few years later, another court was added to the north of number one, hence a

Number One court, 1938
Courtesy of La Jolla Tennis Club

number two court. Much later, three more courts were added across the street making a total of eight tennis courts. This provided enough playing surfaces for tennis tournaments.

But let's go back to 1917 when a loaf of bread cost 7 cents, a gallon of milk cost 16 cents, and a new Ford cost $640. The world was at war in Europe, but in peaceful La Jolla, Roy Bleifust won the men's singles championship and Marion Williams won the women's at the 1st Annual La Jolla Tennis Tournament. Marion continued to win for eight straight years then again in 1926. Thus she holds the distinction of being La Jolla's first female tennis star.

Although they were not born in La Jolla, the Williams sisters did spend most of their lives living in and contributing to La Jolla's history. The parents of Marion and Dorothy Williams were native New Yorkers. In 1910, the family migrated to California coming to live in La Jolla, a logical choice as their father enjoyed fishing and his two daughters could be enrolled in the new private school, Bishop's, which had opened the previous year. Mr. Williams bought a lot on the northwest corner of Torrey Pines and Prospect where he had his home built. Marion, in an interview, remembered that many of her parents' friends had said, "Why are you going way out there?" Most of what was La Jolla in those days hovered close to the Cove.

It wasn't until World War I that Marion said she was able to attend dances in La Jolla. "If you weren't 16, you weren't allowed to go to dances, but I always said I was older. Wonderful dances and all kinds of men from Camp Kearney…. And that man (Mr. Talboy) was still there who always sent me home too…. He said I was too young."

In 1917, a year before she graduated from Bishop's, Marion joined with Dexter Rumsey and started the La Jolla Tennis Championships, a tournament that would attract tennis players from all over the world. In 1920, Archie Talboy took over management of the tennis tournament. The entire Bundy family, four girls and a boy, were names of note in the tennis world of the '20s and '30s. In those days, men wore long white pants and women wore dresses. The rackets were wood and strings were gut, real gut not nylon or another synthetic. (May Bundy is Dodo Cheney's mother.) For three years in a row, 1928-30, Dolf Muchleisen was Champion in the Men's Division. By the 1930s and '40s, the La Jolla Invitational Tennis Tournament was attracting other well-known players such as Robert Muench (1930 NCAA Doubles Champions), Les Stoefen (1933 & '34 U. S. Doubles Champion), Norman Brooks, John Doeg (1929 & '30 U. S. Open Doubles Champion, also 1930 U. S. Singles Champion), the Bundys, Joe Hunt, Bobby Riggs, Pauline Betz (1942, '43, '44, & '46 U. S. Open Singles Champion), Mary Arnold, and Sarah Palfrey Cooke (no fewer than 13 times in the U. S. Top Ten, she was No. 1, No. 2 or No. 3 seven times and in the World Top Ten six times between 1933 and 1939 and her husband, Elwood Cooke, was a naval officer and tennis champion winning the La Jolla Summer Tournament and the 1939 Wimbledon Doubles with Bobby Riggs). Many of these players competed in the La Jolla Tournament just prior to playing at Forrest Hills in September.

For the first tournament, Marion and Dexter solicited the village shops for prizes. Later, businesses would sponsor the games and monetary

Florence Sutton, Violet Sutton Doeg, and Ethyl Sutton Bruce on the left and May Sutton Bundy on right.
Courtesy of Pat Yeomans Collection

prizes would be given to the winners. La Jolla is unique in having no admission charge for spectators.

As a young adult, Marion Williams, after starting and winning the La Jolla Tournament, went on to win many tennis titles. She was California State Women's champion in the early '20s and then Pacific Coast champion at the Pacific Southwest Tournament.

Another local tennis star, Barbara Gaines (Dawson) came to La Jolla as a three and a half year old from London, England in 1920. "In the late 1920s, a friend of my father gave me a tennis racket. Thus began my love affair with tennis," reports Barbara Dawson. Enthusiastically, Barbara joined Mr. Talboy's Saturday morning tennis lessons for kids. "I won my first tournament in 1930. This whetted my appetite for blue ribbons, trophies, and other prizes. However, the big thrill was not the gifts but the satisfaction of becoming a winner."

Barbara's first tourney was the Del Mar Annual Mixed Doubles with partner Leonard Dworkin. They won. "As I was leaving the court with my trophy, my father called to me. He wanted to introduce me to a fan. It was Theodora Warfield, the leading lady at the Savoy Theatre in San Diego and she wanted my autograph!"

During the following years, Barbara won many San Diego and La Jolla tournaments. *The San Diego Union* reported:

Maureen Connolly Brinker
Courtesy of Maureen Connolly Brinker Tennis Foundation, Inc.

"Barbara Dawson, La Jolla High School girl and for two years singles champion in San Diego County High School Tennis Tournament, further established herself as one of southland's leading juniors by winning the runner-up laurels in the 11th annual mid-winter inter-scholastic tournament concluded Saturday at Fullerton…. The La Jolla girl met Dorothy Bundy of Santa Monica high school in the finals, with Miss Bundy winning…Miss Bundy, latest net sensation of the famous Santa Monica tennis family, won the 1st set easily, but in the 2nd Miss Gaines carried the score to four games all before submitting. In the semi-final, Miss Gaines won from Jacque Virgil of Beverly Hills, 6-0, 6-0."

Helen Roach and Dodo Bundy Chaney at Windemere, 2000
Courtesy of Barbara Dawson

Mary Struthers, Betty Ravenscroft Struthers, Mr. Acrhie Talboy, Mrs. May Sutton Bundy, and Dodo Bundy (Cheney)
Courtesy of Barbara Dawson

Barbara also played as Maureen "Little Mo" Connolly's league partner in San Diego (and won) and with Hal and John Shelton, George Devine and Jack Whitehead in mixed doubles. "In women's doubles, I played with Ruth Kayser, Mignon Summers, Betty Ravenscraft Struthers and Annette Preister of Beverly Hills." In 1940, Barbara won the woman's singles and the mixed doubles with Lyn Johnson at El Centro (Imperial Valley). One year Barbara Dawson was number 2 in the nation in the National Senior Olympics

Many of the teenagers of the '20s and '30s have continued to play right into their senior years, all this with the full support of the Tennis Association. There are tournaments for the sixty somethings, players in their seventies and even players in their eighties have special tournaments. These seniors now tour the country to play in tourneys. In 2001, Dodo Bundy Cheney, 85, was a triple title national champion, winning both Women's 80 singles and doubles action. She finished the year with 8 gold balls, running her total up to 321 balls (indicating her National Titles), thus making her the greatest tournament winner of all time.

The U. S. Tennis Association 2001 women over 80 ratings listed Dodo and her partners as both one and two in doubles and Barbara and her partner were ranked number five in the country. Since the beginning of the seeding system in 1927, only one mother-daughter combination has been able to earn a seeding. That combination was May Sutton Bundy and her daughter, Dorothy Bundy (Dodo) Cheney.

In 1939, Patricia Canning was the USTA Super National Hard Court doubles champion. She married Dick Todd and moved into a house facing the ocean just below the La Jolla courts. In 1943, her daughter "Toddy" was born. Besides playing in the La Jolla tournaments, in 1947 this young mother succeeded in becoming a U.S. Open Doubles champion. That same year, she also won the French Open Singles tournament and in 1948, the French Open Doubles championship.

In 1946, a young man by the name of Bob Perry came down from Los Angeles and won the 13 and under division. It was his first time in La Jolla. In 1956, it was Bob Perry and an Australian player named Don Candy who won the French Open Men's Doubles. Bob also played mixed doubles with Maureen Connolly. "Playing with Maureen was like playing with a man," he said. "All I had to do was to take care of my side of the court. She was far and away the best woman player I have ever played with."

In 1949 and 1950, at the outbreak of the Korean War, "Little Mo" (Maureen Connolly) took the Women's event in La Jolla. Although not a La Jollan (she was born in San Diego), she was enthusiastic about and inspiring to the La Jolla's tennis community. At 16, "Little Mo" became the youngest player to win the Women's singles title at Forest Lawn. She successfully defended the U. S. title in 1952 and 1953, won the Wimbledon championship (1952, 1953, 1954), and completed a grand slam of the world's four major titles in 1953 with the French and Australian championships. Sadly, her career ended abruptly when she fell from her horse. Nevertheless, she continued to be a major influence in the world of tennis until her death from cancer in 1968 --on the eve of Wimbledon.

In the 1940s, a talented youngster by the name of Albert Hernandez, Jr. appeared on the local tennis scene. His parents, Al and Helen Hernandez, had saved enough money working at Convair during the war to buy a home in La Jolla in 1944. It was located at 7446 Draper, just two blocks from the La Jolla Recreation Center. Little Al was eight.

One day, Helen purchased a tennis racket and hung it up in the house. She did not play, but frequently went to the courts at the Recreation Center to watch players like Jean Doyle and Betty Struthers. It was little Al who first took the racket and learned to play.

George Wernham, a local young man, helped the little Al and his parents with their strokes and strategy. Before long, the whole Hernandez family began to play in tournaments—mother and son, father and son and singles for young Al who played in his age group. Little Al had a great deal of natural talent and soon came to the attention of Les Stoefen, tennis pro at the La Jolla Beach and Tennis Club and Mr. William Scripps Kellogg, owner of the club. These two sponsors encouraged young Al to enter tournaments.

By 1951, little Al and Mike Franks entered the National Tournament at Kalamazoo, Michigan, in the 16-year-olds division. They won! Positively, one day in the near future, young Al would become a tennis

William J. (Bill) Kellogg (l) at age 12 after he was soundly beaten by Randy Thomas (r). Bill was seeded 10th in Southern California but just coudn't beat "those San Diegans." *Courtesy of William J. Kellogg*

Karen Hantze (Susman) won the La Jolla Women's singles championships in 1959, before going on to win several Wimbledon titles.
Courtesy of Barbara Dawson

champion on the national tennis scene.

Little Al began to feel soreness in his right shoulder following his successful tournament in Kalamazoo. His parents immediately took him to the doctor. X-rays revealed a tumor between his fifth and sixth vertebrae. Surgery was performed, but it was too late. Little Al died June 6, 1953. He was seventeen years old.

William Kellogg was one of the first people to come to the Hernandez home to try and console the distraught parents. Later that year, Mr. Kellogg sponsored the Albert Hernandez Junior Tennis Tournament. The annual tournament lasted until 1972. The early matches took place at the Recreation Center and the finals were held at the La Jolla Beach and Tennis club. Local tennis players who helped run the tournaments included Fred Kinne, Otis Morgan, and Ralph Trembley.

By 1950 another local child star emerged on the scene, Karen Hantze (Susman). In 1959, she won the La Jolla Women's Singles Championship and then went on to capture, in 1961, the first of several Wimbledon titles. In 2002, Karen was inducted into the Southern California Tennis Association's Hall of Fame.

California has been the forefront of tennis with the top five rankings coming from, or at least "improved" in Southern California. According to William J. Kellogg, "As far back as I can remember—in fact much longer that that—San Diego has been loaded with gifted tennis players. It should be. It has great public tennis facilities…and the best weather in the country."

Bob Perry returned to La Jolla to become the pro of the Tennis Club at the La Jolla Recreation Center. He stayed for twenty-seven years.

Although the rules have remained more or less the same, the equipment has changed drastically over the years. In 1936, racket strings cost 25 cents and a racket with professional gut cost $8.80. The racket was wood. In 2001, no longer wood, rackets like the Yonex RDTI50, cost in the $150.00-$200.00 range. But through it all, the La Jolla Tennis Championship remains a "fine tradition" attracting the best players from all over the country. Started by La Jollans who loved the game, the annual tennis tournament is a sport event appreciated by everyone for "its cleanliness, its wholesomeness, and, above all, its fine appeal to sportsmanship." (From a letter written in 1930 by the Southern California Tennis Association.)

Net Losses

When I cavort on a tennis court
My scoring frequently mingles;
I'm singularly bad at doubles
And doubly bad at singles.
(Written by Ruth Boorstin, around 1928.)

Social Service League of La Jolla

Thanks to whom, Darlington and League House
combined for the benefit of the community.

Hidden in La Jolla near the sound of the sea stand two buildings side by side. One is an apartment complex for 53 seniors who need a financial helping hand. The other is a historic villa in the style of Seville called Darlington House, once the seasonal home of Mrs. Herbert Darlington and her children. Both buildings are owned by Social Service League of La Jolla. Both houses have their own story the mansion echoing a life-style of gracious living, elegant dinner parties, and delightful musical concerts — the apartment complex called League House fulfilling a dream of the League to provide a home for refined, elderly seniors of limited income. For close to forty years the two have been inextricably intertwined.

The Social Service League of La Jolla began as an outgrowth of a small group of women from St. James by-the-Sea Episcopal Church in La Jolla. Founded in 1927, with Wynn Van Schaick as President, its purpose was to teach young adolescent girls a sense of community responsibility. Their first project was making layettes for the Mexican Settlement in East San Diego. This task was so successful that the girls were asked to join some of the older members of the church and, working in close association with the Visiting Nurse Association of San Diego, help make sick room supplies, surgical gowns, and layettes for the old Scripps Hospital on Prospect Street.

When the Depression struck in 1929, the community needs were endless. In order to raise money to lighten the increased burdens, fiestas and a "Horned Toad Derby" were held on the grounds of the Casa de Mañana. The owner, Mrs. Isabel Morrison Hopkins, was a member of the League and later its president. The hotel was designed by Edgar V. Ullrich who, like Mrs. Hopkins, was from Colorado Springs. He was requested to incorporate the mission style in his plans. Incredibly, Ullrich designed the building as it was being built completing the project in 1924. Right from its opening, the Casa was an immediate success and became the social meeting place of preference. At one event, a '49er party designed to raise funds for the League, drinks were served. It was near the end of Prohibition and many eyebrows were raised. It was agreed by all that it would be best to separate the League from the Church. Thus the Social Service League of La Jolla officially came into being in 1929.

In 1930, the young ladies of St. James were asked to join with League members to help out in the "Well Baby Clinic" founded by senior League member Katharine Stickney Sneve. According to a 1930 newspaper article:

"Among the many activities of La Jolla, whose citizens are always in the forefront where the health and well-being of the community is concerned, a new sphere of usefulness has been found, and will take the form of a free baby clinic…. President Hoover, in issuing a proclamation designating May Day as Child Health Day, said: 'The responsibility for the well-being of children is a community responsibility as well as an individual duty.' The health of the children of school age in La Jolla is under the watchful care of Miss Polly Grove, the capable school nurse. With the opening of the new Clinic, the health of the children of the preschool age will be carefully guarded."

The clinic was held every second Tuesday in two rooms donated for their use by the hospital. "The clinic extends its privileges to babies and children of pre-school age and will be a center where mothers who could not otherwise secure the services of a physician may bring their children of this age for examination and advice." Examinations were made by La Jolla doctors Truman A. Parker, Samuel T. Gillispie, and W. E. Diefenbach as well as Alfred Coningsby Jackson, D.D.S., and eye, ear, nose and throat specialist Dr. William R. Eastman. Many other doctors with offices in San Diego also responded to Miss Sneve's invitation to participate or, at the very least, be consultants for the La Jolla Baby Clinic.

Well Baby Clinic at the old Scripps Memorial Hospital, on Prospect Street as sponsored by the Social Service League of La Jolla, c. 1931.
Courtesy of the Social Service League of La Jolla

On the national front, it was asserted that "many boys and girls are burdened during their school life with defects that could have been corrected or prevented during the preschool period." Immunization against diphtheria was recommended as well as "vaccination against smallpox." Another warning read: "Have (children) play out of doors in the sunshine at least three hours daily." And: "Let them sleep from 11 to 12 hours a night, with a nap during the day." According to this news article, more than 50 percent of the children entering school for the first time had some physical defect.

During the war years, meetings of the Social Service Committee were limited. In 1947, they reorganized as a non-profit organization. Ultimately, the League's dream was to find a home for refined, elderly people of limited income who had lived and worked in the community, were past their earning years, and had difficulty living on a fixed income. Many creative ideas were put to use to raise the necessary funds to purchase property where such a home could be built with apartments for these senior citizens. One fund raising event came about as a result of the talents of Sarah Sadler Woods, a dancer who had moved to La Jolla with her son Chad.

In the forties and early fifties, Mrs. Woods opened a dance studio for children. The first classes were held at the La Jolla Beach and Tennis Club. However, when a building next to the Fire Station on Herschel Avenue between Silverado and Wall Streets became available, Mrs. Woods took possession and converted what had been a Tea Room into a dance studio with a ballet bar, wood floors and a floor to ceiling mirror on the opposite wall. The children began with the most rudimentary ballet positions and dance steps, but with diligent practice, they progressed to the more sophisticated toe shoe techniques and exercises. Several times a year, the ballet group performed for the community. These were sophisticated productions replete with parasols, tutus, and tights and the music of Schubert, Liszt and Johann Strauss.

But in the interest of the League, one program in particular stands out. Produced in 1948, it was called "The Best

Years of Their Lives." There were three performances. All proceeds were to benefit the Social Service League of La Jolla. The production took place at the La Jolla Jr.-Sr. High School in the old auditorium. The music was arranged and played by John Ward and Frieda Dekking with choreography by Sarah Sadler Woods. For weeks, the children practiced while their parents helped organize the settings, lighting, and posters. Mrs. Elaine Wade made almost all of the costumes. Businesses like the Soule Piano Company and Conover Music Store contributed. It seemed as if the entire village of La Jolla was involved one way or another. Some residents acted as guides, showing people not familiar with La Jolla where to park and how to get to the auditorium. Others acted as chauffeurs driving donated busses to take guests to and from the show. Restaurants offered pre-performance specials and after performance entrees. Everything from flowers to candies came from local merchants. Some of the children who performed that year included: Judy Chittick, Patty Highleyman (aka Daly-Lipe), Jeanne Noyes, sisters Claire and Carla Tavares (whose father built Clairemont), Marilyn Wilson, Candy Sinclair, Marilyn Marsh, Jane Trevor (whose mother was part of a group that started the La Jolla Playhouse), Gretchen Raddatz, Nancy Corbin, Sally Tidmarsh, and Nea McArthur. All the children handled their dance recitals with sophistication and skill and the production was a great success. Every performance was sold out with members of the audience coming from all parts of San Diego County. But the biggest success of all was the money raised for the Social Service League.

By 1949, enough money had been collected to purchase a piece of property 100 by 140 feet on the corner of Pearl and Olivetas for $16,500. In 1950, a Policy Committee, a Men's Advisory Board and a Building Committee were appointed to study all aspects of the project keeping in mind the "Standards for Institutions for the Aged in California." Plans were approved by the State Welfare Board. At the time, State licensure was necessary (until 1956 when regulations changed) for care, giving aid, and providing sustenance for the elderly, even though no medical care was given.

The estimated cost of building Phase I of League House was $103,000. By May, 1950, through generous donations, bequests, dues, and projects the sum of $50,000 was acquired. A loan of $50,000 was secured and construction began, November, 1954. By the following May, the L-shaped building with 15 apartments was completed and ready for occupancy. Room was left on the property for additional apartments. The kitchen facili-

"The Best Years of Their Lives" dance group at La Jolla Jr.-Sr. High School for a benefit for the La Jolla Social Service League. *Courtesy of Patricia Daly-Lipe (third from right)*

Darlington House as a single story home, c. 1940s.
Courtesy Social Service League of La Jolla from a picture
donated by James R. Mills, California State Senator

ties were large enough for future expansion.

By 1958, the mortgage was paid off and in 1960, by a written vote of the League, the second phase of League House was begun. Twelve apartments and an elevator were added and completed by April, 1961.

Sybil Darlington owned an empty lot next to the second phase of League House. As early as 1949, the League had been concerned about Mrs. Darlington's reaction to the apartment complex for seniors being built next door to her lovely mansion. Many of the League members, including Isabel Hopkins were close personal friends and shared with Mrs. Darlington their plans, emphasizing that their efforts would not conflict with her property. After Mrs. Hopkins' death, Rachel Willoughby, President of the League, wrote to Mrs. Darlington (in December, 1956):

"At the recently Board meeting…a fund was created in memory of Isabel Hopkins…to be used solely for the building of a new wing for League House. It is our hope that you will be willing to relinquish the 25 feet of property adjoining ours and put a price upon it for us to purchase…."

Mrs. Darlington replied in January, 1957:

"Isabel Hopkins was an old and devoted friend, and I am in complete sympathy with the League, but your request places me in a rather difficult position. Although titled in my name, the area which you are seeking was acquired at the request of my children. Before making any decision…I must discuss it with them…."

A month later, February, 1957, another letter to Mrs. Willoughby stated:

"…I have at last heard from my children, and they are not inclined to dispose of any of the property. As I have always promised that the final decision would rest with them, I feel obliged to abide by their wishes."

After Mrs. Darlington's death in September, 1967, the mansion and lots were put up for sale. The League tried to buy only the 25 feet they wanted for Phase III of League House but were informed that Mrs. Darlington's property had to be purchased in its entirety. The Men's Advisory Committee strongly recommended they do so. The property was purchased for $201,000 with escrow closing the end of 1968.

In the meantime, while Phase III of League House was put on hold, in 1965 the League was left a large bequest from the estate of Ruth Ingersoll Baily. This money was designated for League House or a similar residence in memory of her mother. Income from the Baily bequest helped pay off the mortgage for Darlington House.

Darlington House is a fascinating blend of Sibyl Darlington's personal imagination and the masterful architectural design of three notable architects from 1925 to 1940: Herbert Palmer, Richard Requa, and Thomas Shepherd. A little background will help explain why the League is so enamored with this residence and why it has become a blessing in terms of helping the League raise funds to maintain the League House next door.

In 1925 Sibyl Hubbard Darlington, recently widowed, purchased two cottages and the empty lots between from Grace and Fred Hill for "$10.00 and other valuable considerations." In 1937, another lot was purchased (the lot that Social Service League had tried do buy). Eventually Mrs. Darlington owned seven lots on Olivetas Avenue.

In 1926, architect Herbert C. Palmer designed a one-story central structure for Mrs. Darlington to join the two small houses on the site. Mr. Palmer, an Englishman who claimed to be the natural son of Edward VII, had just completed the famous Arcade that connects Girard with Prospect Street. In one of his few public appearances at a beautification meeting on Mt. Soledad, Palmer, a small man who wore glasses and favored white suits, urged the assemblage to "recognize the beauty of the spot" and create spaces that would "delight the senses of all visitors." A year after working with Mrs. Darlington, Palmer designed La Jolla's "Taj Mahal" on Torrey Pines Road. Herbert Palmer died in Fallbrook in 1952.

In 1931, Mrs. Darlington engaged Richard Requa, an eminent architect and authority on Spanish Colonial architecture, to create the library addition to the house and a formal Spanish garden. The architect for the Civic Center Building (County Administration Building) in San Diego, Richard Requa's first commission was in 1913 when he was appointed by E. D. Libby to reconstruct the picturesque village of Ojai in Ventura County. In 1920, he was employed by the Santa Fe Railroad to design the Rancho Santa Fe Civic Center, now regarded as one of the showplaces in San Diego County. At Darlington House, Mr. Requa also designed the Andalusian and Egyptian patios. The wooden columns in the patio were hand-carved by Mr. Herbert Palmer and came from designs by Mr. Requa. It is interesting to note that the two architects worked together on this project. The tiles and the urns of the Egyptian Patio were executed in Los Angeles from photographs taken by Mrs. Darlington and Mr. Requa. From Morocco came fountains, benches, and tiles for the garden.

In the Darlington library are magnificent built-in oak bookcases and an ornamental grille work balcony railing of Moorish design interpreted by Requa. The library also features a Moroccan fireplace inscribed in Arabic with a legend that translates: "To the faithful man I will grant whatsoever he believes me capable of giving." The urns (now in the balcony library niches), tiles, benches, and a fountain were commissioned from Seville. Marble columns were

Darlington House's formal Spanish Garden
Courtesy Social Service League of La Jolla from a picture
donated by James R. Mills, California State Senator

imported from Spain, Italy, and Greece. Mosaics from an Egyptian mosque and antique tiles, including "La Pastora" near the iron gate and "St. Vincent Ferrer" were incorporated in an alcove in the rose garden. Of special note in the library's north side are double wooden doors carved in the style of the Alhambra in Granada, Spain. They are part of a two-story high entrance portal. The portal is inscribed in Latin with a quotation from the New Testament (St Matthew Ch. 10, verse 16): "Behold, I send you forth as sheep in the midst of wolves. Be ye therefore wise as serpents and harmless as doves." This entrance was used for the weekly Sunday concerts and teas, coveted social events given by Mrs. Darlington who was also President of the Musical Arts Society of La Jolla.

Architect Thomas Shepherd (1897-1979) came to La Jolla in 1926 when he associated with Herbert J. Mann. In 1933, his fine arts building on Wall Street (across from the Post Office west of the alley) was given an A.I.A. award. He was a personal friend of Mrs. Darlington and is given credit for unifying her house architecturally. In 1940, Mr. Shepherd modified the front of the house and added the second story and the curving staircase. The Shepherd influence is evident in the second floor design which maintains an architectural simplicity at the same time that it transformed the house into a sizable mansion and one of the prized edifices of La Jolla.

The Darlington House Historical Landmark plaque with bow decoration as presented during the dedicatory ceremony, Nov 8, 2000.
Courtesy of Steele Lipe

Once purchased by the League, Darlington House has been its primary asset. This elegant house is rented to groups for corporate events, wedding and other special events, all of which help support its primary goal of maintaining and subsidizing the adjoining League House.

By 1974 the total frontage of the Social Service League property was 325 feet. It included the purchase of the small cottage and lot adjoining the property south of Darlington House and used today as the residence of the Darlington House Manager. And finally, in 1975, the Baily estate's gift made possible the start of Phase III of League House with an additional 26 apartments, a remodeled kitchen, and the Anna Roon Lounge named after a generous donation by the Roon family. On January 27, 1977, residents were moved into the new structure making a total of 53 people residing in League House.

In 1995, Darlington House was designated a Historic Site #327 in the Register of Historic Landmarks of the City of San Diego. On November 8, 2000, the League placed a bronze plaque on the building to the left of the front door to acknowledge its proud status. Darlington House and League House were now a combined story.

Hotels of La Jolla

"Life, I suppose, is a case of getting used to changes, and age, I suppose, is a definite realization of being unable to do anything about it," wrote Max Miller in *The Town with the Funny Name*. Everyone who comes to La Jolla wants to claim it as home and many do just that, make La Jolla their home. However, for most visitors, this is just a place to visit, enjoy the weather and the surf, then leave. To accommodate these people, hotels were built. But the hotel business began with a rough start. In 1888, the Pacific Coast Land Bureau began construction of the La Jolla Park Hotel. Located conspicuously on the ocean side of Prospect at the end of Girard overlooking the area where many had pitched camp to enjoy the surf, sun, and sand, the Park Hotel was completed in 1889 but did not officially open until 1893. Some say it was the lack of water that kept people away, but the empty hotel ultimately burned to the ground in 1896.

La Jolla Park Hotel, open only 3 years.
Courtesy of San Diego Historical Society Photograph Collection

The Grand Colonial's Roots Run Deep in La Jolla's History

The "Relaxed Jewelbox of a Hotel"

The first building of what would become the Colonial Hotel was opened in 1913. Known as the Colonial Apartment Hotel, it was an immediate success and "the talk of the town." The white, wood framed Colonial design was conceived by Richard Requa and described as, "A perfectly appointed apartment hotel, with the finest sun parlor and lobby overlooking the ocean on the Pacific Coast." About the same time, a second building was constructed behind the first and is now called the North Annex. Together, these two buildings housed 28 apartments and 25 single rooms. Each room had a private bath (a luxury at the time) and cost $1.00 for the night. Rates for the apartments ran from $25 to $50 per month and were completely furnished. There was a small third building where guests would have registered on the corner of Prospect and Jenner.

The original owners were A. B. Harlan and George Bane. Mr. Bane became the sole owner in 1920.

Silas O. Putnam purchased the La Jolla Drug Store next door. It occupied the right side of the corrugated tin building. To its left was a tobacco shop with a continuously burning flame inside. This was for people to "light up." Behind was a barber shop. But Putty's was more

The Old Colonial Hotel in the middle (moved to the left and down Jenner Street) with the North Annex behind. On the right is La Jolla Pharmacy (Putnam's Drug Store) and the building on the left is the Colonial Hotel Office (corner of Prospect & Jenner) which was moved to the 6600 block of La Jolla Boulevard. The Palm trees just cover the first floor.
Courtesy of the Colonial Hotel

Putnam's Pharmacy next to the 1912 Colonial Hotel. Mr. Ross Putnam (middle), his son Putty (left) and George Fleet, who lived on the corner of Kline and Girard where the Bank of America is presently and whose family grew vegetables across the street (SE corner).
Courtesy of Barbara Dawson

fun for the children. There were always "lots of boxes of chocolate" according to Spencer Wilson. Putnam's became part of the Colonial hotel later in its first year taking the huge mirror from behind the counter and its wood frames and panels from the old store to its new location.

A native of Kansas, Mr. Putnam "spent one winter in Southern California's temperate climate and decided to make La Jolla his home." After he bought the drug store, Mr. Putnam added an ice cream parlor on the front sidewalk that became famous for chocolate Cokes and banana splits. Inside the drug store "where filling more than three prescriptions a day was a big day," the pharmacist was popular and loved by the community.

In 1925, Mr. Bane, working with architect Frank Stevenson, drew up plans for a new hotel building, one that "would rival anything in the West." The original building was literally picked up and moved (a La Jolla tradition) down the hill and a new, four-story concrete apartment hotel was erected in its place. This was the first fireproof hotel to be built west of the Mississippi with the first fire sprinkler system, solid, unsupported, reinforced cement stairways, and fire doors on each floor that still exist today. The fire doors are held open by a counter balance weight. When a fire approaches, the wo-

Construction of the new Colonial in 1925-26. La Jolla (S. O. Putnam) Pharmacy is on the right.
Courtesy of the Colonial Hotel

ven cord that attaches the counter balance burns. Thus, the unrestrained weight of the door forces it shut. These extreme precautions could have emanated from a series of arsons that occurred in 1915. The Crescent Café (above the Cave)was the first fire that year, followed by the Union Congregational Church, which burned to the ground. Then there was the fire in the vestry of St. James by-the-Sea Church followed by Miss Virginia Scripps' home, and finally, the home of her sister, Miss Ellen Browning Scripps, South Moulton Villa. Although the arsonist was eventually caught, it was understandable why Mr. Bane, like Miss Scripps, chose to build with cement. As Mr. Bane said, "I've always had confidence in La Jolla, and I still do. This building is the *concrete* expression of my faith." Other fires included the Girard Garage in 1921 and the Dining Car Restaurant in 1923.

The original 1912 building was also refurbished and linked to the new structure by a walled garden. There is now a protected pool surrounded by flowerbeds between the 1912 building and the north annex building.

As part of the renovation, S. O. Putnam moved his popular La Jolla Pharmacy into the corner closest to Girard Ave. For years Putnam's remained a gathering place for La Jollans of all ages. The soda fountain was a draw for local children, their parents, residents, and La Jolla visitors who sat (reminiscent of Norman Rockwell's famous painting for the *Saturday Evening Post*) at the counter to sip sodas or spoon up ice cream sundaes and chat. Bobby Barrett remembers working at Putty's as a youth. Such a popular place, it was an oasis for the whole community to come, chat, sip, slurp and have fun. Bob says one of his regulars was Bing Crosby (who had recently established a race track at Del Mar). Sometime in the fifties, Mr.

The Colonial Hotel, 1928. The clock on the building across from the Colonial Hotel is labeled the Bank of Italy, the precursor to the Bank of America. The palm trees now reach the third floor.
Courtesy of the Colonial Hotel

Putnam's son, Putty, moved the pharmacy across the street into the Bank of America building which, in the 1928 photo, still bears its original name, Bank of Italy.

Mention should be made of the tall, Washingtonian palms in front of the Colonial. Planted in 1913, perhaps as part of Mr. Walter Lieber's beautification project for La Jolla (which included the palm trees along Coast Blvd), they have seen many changes as they and La Jolla grew. They were there when Prospect Street in front of the Colonial was graded for paving in 1918. Metates (Indian corn grinding stones) were found, indicating that in even earlier times Indians had lived here. The palms were there in 1924 when the Electric Railway (San Diego Trolley) was opened to the public and the huge, elegant round Terminal building was constructed down the street at Fay and Prospect. (The "Last Car" took its final trip in 1939 and in 1940, the Terminal building was razed.) In that time, being on the west side of a dirt street was considered a plus for the Colonial. Because of the prevailing winds, "there was absolutely no dust."

After opening the new Colonial, Mr. Bane leased the entire property to a "Hollywood man" named W. S. Beard. However, in 1931, Bane reorganized the business and brought in Roscoe C. Bulger as manager.

During World War II, the Colonial became home to many "top brass" from nearby Camp Callan. Single servicemen used the sunroom on the southwest side. One service man, a long time resident of La Jolla, Bud (Luther H.) Barber, (whose pay was $21 a month at Camp Callan) tells us that he had his wedding breakfast at Putnam's, then went down the street to St. James to wed Martha Waite. Bud told us that for a time, Martha's aunt had resided at the Colonial. She came along with her own Steinway Grand piano. Daily, Aunt Wilma Waite would practice in the drawing room. Playing the music was for her own gratification, but everyone at the hotel enjoyed listening.

The Colonial was also a temporary home for Hollywood's best who were in La Jolla performing at the La Jolla Playhouse. Charlton Heston, Dorothy McGuire, Groucho Marx, Jane Wyatt, Eve Arden, Pat O'Brian, and David Niven were among the many celebrities who stayed at the Colonial well into the late '50s.

In 1963, the La Jolla Historical Society began with Barbara Dawson as President. The Society headquarters moved

149

into various locations including La Jolla Federal Savings and Loan (Herschel and Wall St.), the Athenaeum, and then a room was offered to the Society in the Colonial Hotel. When the Putnam's moved their store across the street, they were very generous in providing a window where the Society could put memorabilia of early La Jolla. This helped the organization's membership expand to over 380 members in 3 years.

However, the Colonial fell to hard times in the sixties. La Jolla Real Estate developer Don Emerson, Del Mar contractor Herbert Tuner, and La Jolla architect Robert Jones purchased the hotel in 1976 for $1 million. During the next 4 years, the Colonial underwent a $3 million restoration that brought back the mahogany trim, the leaded glass, elegant chandeliers, and crystal doorknobs. "With 75 rooms, the Colonial's interior was designed 'like an elegant European hotel' by San Diego's Robert Carlisle." According to a review written at the time of the grand opening on July 17, 1980: "The Colonial Inn…brings out the very best from La Jolla's past tastefully into the stylish present. Elegance, continental service, graceful design and décor, plus the ambiance of a small European hotel…."

The restoration project received the "People in Preservation" award from Save Our Heritage Organization. The Colonial is also a member of and bears a plaque from the "Historic Hotels of America, National Trust for Historic Preservation."

In 1980, the space that once housed Putnam's drug store became Putnam's Restaurant. The original soda fountain was replaced by a bar.

In 1998, Franklin Croft, LLC joined forces with Fargo Hotel, LLC to create Fargo Colonial, LLC to purchase the hotel. The property is now under the leadership of hotel veteran and general manager Terry Underwood.

"Just like the hotel envisioned by George Bane, The Grande Colonial, as it is now called, will be a classic European style hotel that will 'rival anything in the West,' and continue the heritage laid down by its founders more than 80 years ago."

It is good to be aware and respectful of history and it is hoped that La Jolla will retain at least some of the flavor and charm of days gone by even though civilization and modern technology will advance into places yet unknown. There is a stability that comes with knowing the past. La Jolla is like an old relative who is being relegated to photo albums as its reality gets torn down. Let us try to remember.

Casa de Mañana

It started with a dream

In 1923 construction began on the site of the La Jolla baseball field. This triangular block of land delineated on two sides by rocks descending to the surf of the Pacific (between "Sea Dreams" and the "Pool") had been purchased by Isabel Morrison Hopkins. When visiting her mother whose home was on Pros-

Mrs. Isabel Morrison Hopkins
Courtesy of the Casa de Mañana archives

Casa de Mañana showing views of the pool (Ocean) side and the entrance just after construction in 1924.
Courtesy of the Casa de Mañana archives

pect, Isabel looked down on the field and envisioned a hotel aesthetically harmonious with the environment. With the tremendous influx of visitors, it had become apparent that La Jolla was in need of another hotel. Mrs. Morrison Hopkins took the money she received as settlement from divorcing Mr. Hopkins, and hired a fellow Colorado Springs native to design a special place, a hotel that would become the social center of La Jolla.

Edgar V. Ullrich designed a low lying "mission style" structure with arches and tiled roofs. The grounds were laid out in a free and open style with space left for cottages to be added later. The Casa de Mañana (House of Tomorrow) was constructed in seven months and two weeks, much of its design taking place during the actual construction. Bob Wilson assisted Mr. Ullrich in drafting the design before taking over his father's Western Union office. On July 3, 1924, the Casa de Mañana celebrated its grand opening along with the inauguration of the new electric railroad line connecting San Diego to La Jolla, and the installation of street lights on Prospect Street and Girard Avenue. Also nearing completion of construction was the quarter million-dollar Scripps Memorial Hospital. On August 1st, as the clock struck nine, the Pacific Telephone and Telegraph officially "cut in" at their new home on Wall Street. The first call received was for La Jolla 2151, the Casa de Mañana.

In 1930, Miss Scripps gave to the children of La Jolla a special gift. Across the street from the Casa, Miss Scripps had constructed a retaining wall curving around the Casa Cove to provide a safe place for the children to swim. In his own words, Gene McCormack describes the Children's Pool.

"...that Children's Pool down by the Casa de Mañana was something! I helped build that and inspected it a lot. There's a sandy beach there but it's not supposed to be a beach because right close to where that concrete wall is connected to the mainland, there was a tunnel under there with sliding doors...and it's supposed to be so you could lift those doors and water would run through and wash all that sand out so you could have a pool where you don't get sandy before you went swimming. You went down the steps and jumped in. But this fellow who designed it was also the fellow who designed the first dam across the Nile River in Egypt but he probably never monkeyed around with the ocean…. We could watch the water, but it didn't take too long for mother nature to just fill that up and I don't think they have opened those for generations."

Meanwhile, at the Casa, since Mrs. Hopkins belonged to every social and civic association in town, the hotel became the social hub of La Jolla. At one particular festivity, a '49er party, held to raise funds for the Social Service League, a part of the Episcopal Church, drinks were served. This was the era of Prohibition. When they heard about the drinking, the Church voiced its displeasure. In 1929, the organization became its own entity: the Social Service League of La Jolla.

Parties and celebrations came to a halt, however, during several years of World War II when the hotel was used to accommodate the Red Cross and the Civilian Defense. One La Jolla lady said that she worked in San Diego during the war and since there was severe gas rationing, she was happy to be able to board the military bus to get home to La Jolla. Although the cottages were still available for rent, guests were fearful of the proximity to the coast because the Japanese might attack by submarine. Bobby Barrett was a teenager at the time. He earned pocket money diving for abalones to supply the kitchen at the Casa, but for Mrs. Hopkins it was a financial and an emotional drain. In 1944, she gave in and sold her beloved Casa to W. F. Olson, its managing Director, and Gerald White of San Diego. Mr. White died soon after the transaction and the hotel was purchased by Colonel Henry Dutton.

After the war, Dr. Doyle introduced his wife to La Jolla. While exploring the town for a potential home, they stayed at the Casa. In 1947, he described the Casa as having spacious grounds and "dripping with Bougainvilleas, Trumpet Vines, and there was an exquisite patio with bull fight posters…it was really as if you were actually in old Spain." Dr. Doyle and his wife, Dr. Figueredo's future home would be down the street, also facing the ocean, a house designed by Edgar Ullrich and built in the late '40s at a cost of $17,000.00.

On April 1, 1953, Pacific Homes Corporation, a division of the Methodist Church, purchased the hotel and converted it into the retirement community it is today.

In 1956, Isabel Morrison Hopkins died. On her last visit to the Casa, Mrs. Hopkins remarked on the "beautiful contentment" of the residents. She said she had been interested in the welfare of the elderly and thus seeing "her" Casa as a retirement community, she was pleased. Her "dream" had been fulfilled. (We thank Steve Nossan, curator of the Casa, for his contribution to the history of the Casa.)

La Valencia, "The Pink Lady"

A Hotel Known for "Congenial Immersion"

By 1924, the village of La Jolla had three hotels. The Cabrillo, built in 1909, was La Jolla's first hotel since the burning of the Park Hotel in 1896. Though not popular when it officially opened, the hotel was designed by Irving J. Gill (1870-1936) using wood from the newly demolished Dance Pavilion in the Park built in 1884 by the railroad to entice visitors to La Jolla. The Colonial and the Casa de Mañana were the other two La Jolla apartment hotels, but the call was clear—another hotel was needed. Someone living in La Jolla in the 1920s made the observation that La Jolla had become "increasingly the escape

La Valencia as it appeared in 1927 without the tower.
Courtesy of La Valencia Hotel

of prominent persons from their prominence." With one of the shortest thermostats in the country, swimming was a year 'round activity as were golf and tennis. La Jolla was Paradise, especially for people from the East and they needed a place to stay.

In 1926, architect Reginald Johnson was chosen to design an apartment-hotel on Prospect Street, above the Cove and next to the Cabrillo Hotel. Called the Valencia Hotel, it became so popular that a second phase, designed by architects Herbert J. Mann and Thomas Shepherd, was commissioned in 1928. This addition included an eight-story structure with hotel-style rooms, a lounge with an outside balcony overlooking the park and the Pacific Ocean and a new restaurant. Also added was the distinctive tower with its gold and blue dome (used during WWII as a Civil Defense observatory). Kate Sessions, the famous so-called "pioneer horticulturist" of San Diego, was asked to landscape the Valencia. One story tells about her planting a bougainvillea by a drainpipe. It was a small plant and when the hotel manager saw it, he objected. He thought she should plant something larger. Assuring him that the smaller plant would grow faster than a larger one, she made a bet with him. For the price of three plants, she bet the smaller plant would grow up to the second floor of the hotel within less than six months. It did!

Everything went well in La Valencia's early years. She enjoyed great popularity among tourists and locals alike. Many wealthy, well-known and celebrated quests enjoyed the hotel that boasted, "whether famous or not, visitors came as guests and left as friends and devotees." Then the Depression hit. MacArthur Gorton and his partner, Roy Wiltsie, lost their hotel to creditors. "We had the vision, but our timing was lousy," Gorton said. It wasn't until a group of La Jolla residents took over ownership of La Valencia in 1946, that the hotel came back into its own and more. Richard Irwin was the Chairman of the Board, General Manager, partner/shareholder and the man most responsible for its rebirth and world wide popularity.

Born in Pittsburgh, Pennsylvania, Richard realized early in his sophomore year at Cornell School of Architecture that he was in the wrong field of study. The prior summer he had worked "anywhere and everywhere" at a hotel on Lake Erie. He loved it. Realizing that was where he belonged, Richard transferred to Cornell's School of Hotel Administration graduating in 1933. Soon he began his career, working for Carter Hotels. For several years, when the company asked, Richard moved from city to city and hotel to hotel. In 1938, he married Virginia Wood in Rochester, New York.

While managing a hotel in Toledo, Ohio, Irwin met Ben Batsch, a banker from California. Obviously impressed by the young manager, Mr. Batsch suggested, "Dick, if anything happens to my hotel in La Jolla, I want you to go there." Ben regaled his friend with glowing descriptions of the little hamlet by the sea where the hotel was located. Dick Irwin was intrigued. However, it wasn't until after World War II and a three year stint in the Navy that Dick was made the offer he could not refuse. Packing up his wife and his three year old daughter, Kathy, Dick Irwin headed west. He was so convinced this was the right decision that he recorded the exact time they drove up to the entrance of La Valencia Hotel. It was 3:00 pm, March 29, 1946. Unfortunately, this new venture was not going to be easy or smooth. In 1946, La Jolla was a small town of 8500 residents whose local loyalties ran deep. Ben's bank had foreclosed on the hotel and Ben wanted to replace the manager of eighteen years with his friend. The old manager protested and had the support of the townspeople. Nine months passed before Ben sold La Valencia to a group of local investors. This left the Irwin family miles away from family and friends and Dick unemployed. Yet somehow he knew things would work out. That day came when the new ownership group called and offered Irwin the position of manager plus part interest in the hotel. It wasn't long before the town came to know and respect this man.

In the first years as manager, Mr. Irwin expanded La Valencia's grounds including several lots on Herschel as well as land extending down to Coast Blvd. (probably the most valuable land in La Jolla). Included in this land purchase was the turn of the century house that he and his family would reside in for the next thirty-five years.

One of his most controversial expansion projects was the construction of a swimming pool. Being literally adjacent

La Valencia as it appeared in 1937 after the completion of the addition, commissioned in 1928.
Courtesy of Barbara Dawson

to the ocean, why would the hotel need a pool? Mr. Irwin stated that he didn't want La Valencia to be a "yesterday hotel, but a hotel for today and tomorrow." He knew what he was talking about. The pool was constructed.

Another Irwin contribution, enjoyed by locals and tourists alike, is the Bar Whaling Bar. Wing (Wayne) Howard, an artist from Philadelphia who lived in La Jolla, was commissioned to paint a mural depicting four photographs that Mr. Irwin had donated to the bar in the '40s. Wing was described as "a very nice guy, so calm and casual. He doesn't get excited." This tranquil temperament would prove important in the years following the initial showing of the mural.

The name of the restaurant was Café La Rue, but the bar side was called the Whaling Bar because of Mr. Irwin's old pictures depicting Boston Harbor and a whaling expedition. Painted behind the bar itself, the mural was applied directly onto the wall. Soon the painting became, despite its artistic merits, the subject of great controversy. Considered "politically incorrect," (with whalers attempting to kill a whale) it was the focal point of the "Grey Whale issue." Wing was asked to do the painting the other way around. The new painting was completed on three plywood sections and on Memorial Day, 1979, was placed over the original work. This painting depicted fishermen flying off a boat that had been broken in two by a whale.

A more recent photo of the Whaling Bar with Ray Arcival on duty. Ray has been bartender since the early '60s. The mural in the background replaced the original mural and shows a more sympathetic view towards the whales. The mural has been restored to the original since the recent Whaling Bar restoration.
Courtesy of La Valencia Hotel

Moby Dick's revenge perhaps? But then, not many years later, the mood changed again. "We want the old one back!" was the cry.

When the bar was remodeled in 1998-99, the owners agreed to restore the original mural; however, this was a difficult task. Bits and pieces came off with the removal of the plywood boards and had to be carefully glued back in place. Ron Liss was hired to clean the mural. Using cotton balls immersed in alcohol, he carefully removed the smoke stains. The job took ten days. In the past, Ron had returned every year to re-clean the "cover painting," meticulously wiping away nicotine stains. Ray Arcival, who has bartended over forty four years, said that the smoke used to create a haze around the bar before the new clean air law was passed. Part of the restoration project included a shiny sealant painted over the mural. Now the cry is to take the shine out. You can't win! In the Café, two other Howard murals depict whimsical street scenes of Deauville and Paris (painted with tempera)

To add to the atmosphere, Mr. Irwin donated pewter candle holders, New Bedford harpoons and lanterns and a display case of ivory scrimshaw. Other authentic items of the days of tall ships were donated by guests who enjoyed the Whaling Bar and La Valencia as a kind of "second home."

Then there was the famed La Jolla Playhouse, launched in 1947. Originally staged in the La Jolla Jr.-Sr. High School Auditorium, the Playhouse attracted stars to La Jolla who, though they were paid but the minimum Actors Equity of $55 per week (at least in the beginning) were compensated by being in La Jolla and staying at places like La Valencia. Often Gregory Peck (native La Jollan and one of the founders of the Playhouse) would host the cast at the Whaling Bar. In the first summers of the Playhouse, a new play was presented every week for ten weeks with one play on stage another was in rehearsal. "Day by day life at the hotel was high drama." One of Irwin's favorite celebrities was Eartha Kitt. Because of racial discrimination in the 1950s, Ms. Kitt stayed in a cottage instead of the hotel. However, every evening, her white Cadillac was driven up to the entrance of La Valencia and Eartha Kitt would emerge clad in a white dress under a white sweater and accompanied by two white poodles. The entourage would enter one of the hotel's dining rooms and not one guest objected. Instead, they wordlessly gathered for her exits and entrances. Irwin described these as the "good times." He was both a gracious and a gregarious host to the actors and actresses who insisted that he call them by their first names. Irwin remembered Joseph

Cotton ("a pain in the neck"), Groucho Marx (impish and a tease), Joan Crawford ("so outspoken that she butted opinions"), Audrey Hepburn (who visited Mr. Irwins's daughter, Kathy in school), Jose Ferrer, Ida Lupino, Ginger Rogers, Clark Gable, David Niven, Vincent Price, and so many more.

But it was not the fame that the actors brought La Valencia that was Irwin's ambition. It was the desire that the hotel would "reflect the quality of life in La Jolla; would be the center of all community activity—cultural, social, business and professional; and would contribute to community projects with leadership and financial support."

While other hotels were "modernizing," Mr. Irwin kept La Valencia's traditional Mediterranean style. "You won't find any Formica in La Valencia!" Knowing that guests were "charmed" by the hotel's tiny elevator, Irwin made sure that his "most sociable employee" be the white-gloved operator. That tradition continues today with the elevator taking visitors up to the rooftop restaurant that once had been a garden.

In 1956, the Cabrillo Hotel was added to La Valencia. Initially, this structure was purchased for its real estate value, but soon it was discovered that it could be converted into deluxe suites and guest rooms. The Irving Gill building was saved and its annexation to La Valencia as its "west wing" added another forty rooms to the already existing sixty.

In the early '60s, Mr. Irwin's wife, Ginny, died. The entire village that had once given him such a hard time, now mourned for one of its leaders' loss. (Irwin had taken his civic duties seriously becoming one of the founding members of the La Jolla Town Council and its first President.)

In 1965, fate entered again. Rebecca Johnson McDonough was visiting Rancho Santa Fe friends, John and Betty Rice. They decided to take Becky to lunch on the patio of La Valencia. Dick Irwin came up to the table and was introduced to their friend. Both Dick and Becky had lost their spouses the year before and both had been married for twenty-five years. "Was it fate that this man, like her late husband, was also a hotelier?" Becky returned to Denver, Colorado but Irwin was in pursuit. A dozen meetings and partings later, including five trips to Denver and a final trip to La Jolla by Becky and "fate faded" while "the vision of a life together began."

Irwin was a manager who believed in hands-on

Richard Irwin
Courtesy of Mrs. Irwin

management. He respected and listened to his staff and they in turn felt valued and appreciated. Some of the staff worked with him for over thirty years. Ray, the bartender at the Whaling Bar confessed to his boss one day that he missed his father. A Philippino by birth, it had been years since Ray had returned to his homeland and his father. Irwin purchased a ticket and gave Ray two weeks off to go home and see his family. When Martiano, a pantry cook who had worked at the hotel for forty-two years (since the day it opened) was ready to retire, Mr. Irwin gave him a room at the hotel rent free for the rest of his life. Martiano resided there for 35 years. He died at the age of 87. Another loyal worker was Hattie Westwood who came to the hotel in 1939 as its Social Director and Vince Clark who was called "the unhaughtiest maitre d'hotel in the world."

By the mid '60s, clinics, the University, and research facilities had moved to La Jolla. Mr. Irwin responded to this increased demand. He solicited Preferred Hotels, "an exclusive organization of the finest independent hotels in the world" to include La Valencia. Changes were made for her acceptance including the addition of marble baths, mini bars, terry robes, chocolate truffles with evening turn-down and a health spa. Now one of the "Preferred Hotels," La Valencia became legendary.

Not only actors, but royalty came to the Pink Lady including the Queen of Thailand, His Royal Highness Prince Fahad Abdulaziz, and Princess Lee Radziwill who wrote to Mr. Irwin, "Your staff is so agreeable and your hotel so incomparable, I hate to leave."

On July 5, 1985, Dick Irwin officially retired. He had served the Pink Lady for thirty-nine years. Every single employee came to pay tribute and for a moment, La Valencia took time out from business as usual. When he died in 1991, lifelong friend and co-owner Willis Allen, Sr., reflected, "You know, you don't really make a lot of money in the hotel business. At La Valencia, I guess, we were in it mostly for fun. We could have made a lot more money if we could have just bottled and sold Dick Irwin's laugh."

But even without the presence of Dick Irwin, his spirit continues. In response to demand, the house at the foot of the hill behind the Pink Lady, the home for so many years of the Irwin family, was demolished to make way for the addition of sixteen Ocean Villas, five of which are suites. Butler service is offered exclusively to the villas.

However, the Pink Lady does not only cater to out of town guests. La Jollans enjoy the elegant lady as well. From her Whaling Bar & Grill to the Patio, from the Sky Room to the Mediterranean Room, local people are treated with the same quality of care and congeniality as overnight guests. She is truly a La Jolla landmark of distinction.

In 1987, the San Diego Historical Site Board designated La Valencia as a historic site.

La Jolla Playhouse

This whole creation is essentially subjective, and the dream is the theater where the dreamer is at once scene, actor, prompter, stage manager, author, audience, and critic.

Carl Jung

The dream began in 1947 when the La Jolla Playhouse made its debut in La Jolla. The three founders were Dorothy McGuire, Gregory Peck, and Mel Ferrer, giants in the motion picture industry. Their goal was "to bridge the gap between acting before the motion picture cameras and in the theatre." At the same time, they wished "to make a contribution to the entertainment life of the community that is acting as our host."

The "host" community was excited about the prospect of bringing prominent actors and actresses from Hollywood to La Jolla during the summer. However, several ingredients were necessary to insure success. For one, sponsorship had to be secured. This was achieved by the goodwill of the local Kiwanis. Their president, Frank C. Harmon, also arranged for the rental of the La Jolla Jr.-Sr. High School auditorium the eight weeks that school was not in session. The charge was $120 per week plus the janitor's salary. Since tickets were priced at only $2.50 or $3.00, it was a challenge for the sponsors to generate the necessary income.

Marian Trevor (Mrs. Walter M. Trevor, Jr.) became Chairman (a proper term for a lady in the '40s) of the La Jolla, Del Mar and Rancho Santa Fe Woman's Committee; Mrs. Robert S. Davis chaired the Coronado committee; and Mrs. Frederick C. Sherman was chairman for San Diego. In all, the women's group consisted of over one hundred volunteers. These ladies formed a very active group giving parties, arranging transportation to and from the airport and train station, making posters, gathering props and costumes, and publicizing the plays. Marian Trevor also arranged for a Sun-

The three founders of the La Jolla Playhouse, Mel Ferrer, Dorothy McGuire, and Gregory Peck.
Courtesy of La Jolla Playhouse

Gregory Peck and Marian Trevor,
Chairman of the Woman's Committee.
Courtesy of Marian Trevor

day brunch for the cast of each upcoming play.

Prior to opening night, Izetta Jewell Miller publicized the newest production on the radio by interviewing some of the stars. Eileen Jackson, society editor for the *San Diego Tribune*, frequently included items in her daily column regarding the play or the participants. Tom Dammann was the Publicity Director. Everyone connected with the La Jolla Playhouse was giving his or her "all" and every play was a sell out. (It should be noted that there were two plays at once. One was being performed while the other was being rehearsed. The plays changed every week.)

For opening night, the local society people dressed formally and hosted elegant dinner parties in their homes or at local restaurants. The tourist trade was overwhelming. All of the hotels and inns were booked solid. La Jolla became the "in" place for the summer season.

Dame May Whitty had the lead role in the first play, Emelyn Williams' "Night Must Fall," which opened on July 8, 1947. It proved to be a huge success. Ten years earlier, Dame May had played the role of Mrs. Bramson in the movie version along with Robert Montgomery and Rosalind Russell. However, it was in 1935, when Dame Whitty was seventy years old, that she scored the greatest triumph in her acting career. That was the year of the London premier production of "Night Must Fall" and the role of the "acidulous, miserly and fright-crazed hypochondriac" Mrs. Bramson was literally "created" by Dame May Whitty. Prior to that eventful performance, Dame Whitty had appeared in almost one hundred roles. Born in Liverpool in 1865, May Whitty made her acting debut at the age of sixteen and continued to enjoy success in various plays in England and on tour up to "the Great War." Because of her "ardent and successful war activities" during WWI, King George V awarded her the title of Dame Commander of the Order of the British Empire. After the war, this talented actress continued to mesmerize her audiences in both London and New York. May, 1948, Dame May Whitty died at the age of 83, just one year after her La Jolla performance. What a distinguished beginning for the Playhouse to have had the opportunity to host such a grand lady in its inaugural La Jolla Playhouse performance.

The plays were always clean-cut and well-chosen and the actors and actresses were the most sought after of the era. Besides Dame May Whitty, other performers included Eartha Kitt, James Whitmore, David Niven, Raymond Massey, Lee Marvin, Olivia de Haviland, Tony Perkins, Dorothy McGuire, Mel Ferrer, Jennifer Jones, Gregory Peck, Groucho Marx, Ida Lupino, Howard Duff, Ginger Rogers, Joanne Dru, John Ireland, Eve Arden, Tallulah Bankhead, Joan Bennett, Loraine Day, Jose Ferrer, Ann Harding, James Mason, Una Merkel, Sylvia Sydney, Pat O'Brian, Vincent Price, Eva Gabor, Charlton Heston, Louis Jordan, June Lockhart, Aldo Ray, Robert Ryan, and Zsa Zsa Gabor—it just doesn't get any better than that!

We should pause here to mention that it was not arbitrary that Gregory Peck was one of the founders of this summer stock theatre. The only child of Bernice, known as "Bunny" and Gregory, known as "Doc" Peck, Gregory (whose birth name was Eldred) was born April 5, 1916 in La Jolla. "Doc" owned and ran a pharmacy on Girard Avenue in La Jolla for many years, but in 1917, he was forced to sell. Money was tight and the family had to move. Five years later the parents were divorced and their son returned to La Jolla to live with his maternal grandmother at her home near the ocean on Pearl Street. Besides playing on the sand dunes, young Peck loved hunting rabbits in the wilderness around Mount Soledad. Peck attended La Jolla Elementary School until he was ten when his parents sent him to St. John's Military Academy in Los Angeles, a school run by nuns for children from broken homes. "I guess they decided I was too happy in my grandmother's bungalow with my bike and my dog," he said. In 1930, he returned to live with his father in San Diego and graduated from San Diego High School. He briefly attended San Diego State College before transferring to the University of California, Berkeley, with the goal (to please his father) of becoming a doctor. One day, as he was walking across the campus, he was spotted by the school's drama professor. The professor approached Gregory and asked if he would consider auditioning for a campus production of 'Moby Dick' to be presented that semester. The young Mr. Peck apologized explaining that he was not an actor. "I am a premed student." The professor replied, "That's all right. I just need someone tall." He played the role of Starbuck and the rest is history.

Typical of many actors, Gregory was ill at ease socially, but on stage and especially in a role, the actor found words and communicated clearly. "It was hard for me to communicate with people, so I tried to reach out to that audience—to try to make contact with them, to try to make friends with them and to tell them a story that I wanted to tell." Soon he was a star on Broadway and then, in 1942, when Gregory was twenty-six, Hollywood gave him a call. His first movie was *Days of Glory*. He won an Oscar nomination for his second film, *Keys of the Kingdom*. For over fifty years, Mr. Peck has continued to inspire his audience. He may not have become a doctor but he has allowed many film viewers to receive therapy just watching his calm, quiet moral determination. Off screen, this is a man who has been active in numerous charities and politics. He was a member of the National Council on the Arts, Chairman of the Board of Trustees of the American Film Institute, President of the Academy of Motion Picture Arts and Sciences, and Chairman of the American Cancer Society. His awards include the Medal of Freedom Award, the Jean Hersholt Humanitarian Award, and in 1989, Mr. Peck received the 17th Annual Life Achievement Award from the American Film Institute. "Gregory Peck reminds us that a star, ultimately, can be an idealization of ourselves, an image that not only mirrors our aspirations but fulfills them." Peck was honored "for allowing us—for so long—to see the very best in our world and ourselves."

In 1995, the French Republic awarded Mr. Peck with the Legion d'Honneur and the rank of Commander as well as the CAESAR, the French Lifetime Achievement Award. Besides France, England, West Germany, Belgium, Chile, Cuba, Italy and Finland have honored Gregory Peck with the "Best Actor" award by their respective film critics.

It is therefore a great tribute to La Jolla that this man, one who epitomizes the tall, strong, silent, totally dependable man who always makes the right decision, in the end decided to make this contribution to La Jolla.

Prior to 1947, the founders of the La Jolla Playhouse had been interested in creating a legitimate theatre in the Los Angeles area. The High School Auditorium had limited seating, only 500 seats. The manager would reserve one row for the professional actors from Hollywood who were encouraged to attend these plays in hopes of securing their support for the idea of developing a repertory theatre.

In the second year, the Playhouse season was extended to nine weeks. La Jollans were as excited and enthusiastic as they had been the first year and the tourist trade was booming during these summer months.

The summer stock theatre in La Jolla continued to flourish for 19 years, but in 1964 production was suspended by a board of trustees intent upon restructuring the playhouse. In 1983 it was revived under the artistic direction of Des McAnuff, a two-time Tony® Award winner.

Since 1982, the new and permanent residence for the Playhouse has been the Mendell Weiss Center for the Performing Arts on the campus of the University of California, San Diego, the same grounds that once housed both Camp Callan and Camp Matthews during W.W.II. No longer concerned about "bridging the gap" between theatre and cinema, the Mission Statement now proposes that the La Jolla Playhouse advance "theatre as an art form and as a vital social, moral and political platform." This is achieved, it states, "by providing unfettered creative opportunities for the leading artists of today and tomorrow."

When another La Jollan and a great actor, Cliff Robertson, was asked if he preferred live theatre over film, his response was, "I love live theatre, and I started there—live theatre and film are two completely different mediums. I love the theatre but everything depends on the word. The written word is everything." Enough said.

In 1998, Gregory Peck appeared in a one man show at Copley Symphony Hall (in San Diego) as a fund raiser for a new expanded Playhouse. According to Ellen Revelle (widow of UCSD founder, Roger Revelle) who with Peck co-chaired the capital campaign to expand the theater's facilities, "We wouldn't have the theater we have today if it weren't for his vision." Gregory Peck died June, 12, 2003. His legacy lives on, especially in La Jolla at the Playhouse.

Copy of the 1947 "THE ACTORS' COMPANY" statement of intent:

IN INAUGURATING its first season at La Jolla Playhouse, the Actors' Company's board of producers hopes that it may be taking a step of historical importance in entertainment annals.

At least, we are offering one solution to the problem of how to bridge the gap between acting before the motion picture cameras and in the theatre.

As long as the movies, with their evident enticements, have been luring actors from Broadway, motion picture stars have periodically announced their intention of returning to the theatre. With rare exceptions, however, so long as they remain stars, this is an action that is postponed from season to season.

Playbill cover of The Actors' Company first production in 1947 at the La Jolla Playhouse.

In all truth, with the centers of the motion picture and theatrical industries done three thousand miles apart, the problem of functioning in both media is not an easy one to solve. It is particularly difficult for a star whose box office value makes his motion picture commitments both demanding and binding. Yet, as most actors with theatre background will agree, no matter what value may be placed upon him as a personality, his stature as an artist can be increased through performing in the living theatre.

The La Jolla Playhouse is our solution. Close enough to Hollywood to enable us to combine our work as actors-managers at the Playhouse with our duties before the cameras, La Jolla is still sufficiently far removed to make it possible to function independent of the movie studios. With the La Jolla Playhouse, we hope to indicate that it is possible to combine work in motion pictures and in the theatre, and at the same time to make a contribution to the entertainment life of the community that is acting as our host.

However, the results of our work and of our colleagues' work is now on the stage. We hope, in all sincerity, that the community of La Jolla will find it worth the truly wonderful interest and the cooperation it has shown us.

THE ACTORS' COMPANY
Mel Ferrer   Joseph Cotton
Dorothy McGuire   Jennifer Jones
Gregory Peck

The Legend of the Del Charro

La Jolla Shores Riding Stable Turned Hotel for the Rich,
the not so Rich, and the Famous

A building was constructed in June 1931, at the junction of La Jolla Canyon (Torrey Pines Road) and Ardath Road. (Yes, Ardath Road existed as far back as 1931; it was narrow and partly just plain dirt but it served a purpose as it meandered between fields of crops including a field of tomatoes.) Herbert J. Mann was designing the building on the corner property as a riding academy. "The buildings of the new riding club will occupy the center of a four acre tract with a practice ring in front, and a 250 foot show ring of standard type in the rear. The club house, 216 feet in length, will contain, on the lower floor, 30 box stalls with all the latest and most modern equipment and an apartment for the stable master. Upstairs, there will be clubrooms, with cliff and sea view, a kitchen and locker rooms and showers for men and women riders, also a modern and attractive apartment for Miss Jean Moore, the proprietor." Miss Moore continued to run the riding academy until 1937 when Captain W. W. Beckwith bought the facility. For eight years, he operated it as the La Jolla Riding Stables.

In 1945, the stable was sold to a Texas couple, Mr. and Mrs. J. R. Marechal. They had

Early La Jolla Shores and Hidden Valley. The La Jolla Stables were built just to the right of the dark rectangle next to La Jolla Canyon Road (Torrey Pines Rd.) and Ardath Road. The present Hidden Valley Road can be seen also emanating from the same intersection and is the dirt road in the foreground.
Courtesy of Chris Marechal

La Jolla Stables and practice ring along Torrey Pines Road. Note the row crops in the lower portion of the picture. A portion of Ardath Road (1931) is seen in the very bottom left corner.
Courtesy of Chris Marechal

Rancho del Charro under the management of the Marechals.
Courtesy of Chris Marechal

been visiting the west coast by car and knew nothing of La Jolla. In Los Angeles, they met a young Marine and his wife and offered to drive them to Camp Pendleton. On the trip south, the young wife told the Marechals, "If you haven't seen La Jolla, you haven't seen the prettiest place in California." Their curiosity piqued, the Marechals dropped off the couple at the Marine base and continued their drive south to see this beautiful place. Coming down La Jolla Canyon Road, they drove past the La Jolla Riding Stable. It was love at first sight. The Marechals paid $25,000 and became the new owners of what they called a "quaint horse stable."

After the purchase, the couple returned to Texas where they owned Texas Trails, a 3200-acre ranch near Bendera. They raised, trained, and showed American Saddle bred horses.

The Marechals were a unique couple in many ways. Evelyn Fay was only 14 when she eloped with 19-year-old James Marechal. Of course, the authorities refused to issue a marriage license, so Evelyn called her parents and was able to obtain their reluctant approval. It proved to be a good match, for before too long the young couple was able to gain financial security. Their early businesses included ice and printing industries.

After falling in love with La Jolla, it was not long before the Marechals were able to cut their ties with Texas. They were eager to devote all their energies to the transformation of the newly acquired property. At the end of three years, in July 1948, the facility became Rancho del Charro, a motor hotel with riding facilities. Mr. Benson Eschenbach helped in the design of the initial project, which included 50-60 units. Some of the horse stalls with their heavy Dutch doors became entrances to guestrooms.

Many of Hollywood's elite were frequent guests at the Marechals' motel. To some extent, this was due to the proximity of the La Jolla Playhouse which brought visiting actors and theatre workers to the del Charro. The guests included John Wayne, William Powell, Dorothy McGuire, Ward Bond, Mel Ferrer, and La Jolla native, Gregory Peck. According to James Marechal, Jr., "All the movie people would stay with us because the Casa de

Mrs. Marechal's Covered Wagon with the barren hillside of La Jolla Shores behind. *Courtesy of Chris Marechal*

Mañana (formerly a hotel) was turned into a retirement home." FBI chief J. Edgar Hoover also stayed, choosing one of the secluded bungalows that were added later. "We are not a dude ranch," they said, "nor yet a stuffy family hotel; we are not as efficient as the Waldorf nor as informal as Prospector Joe's." Instead, according to their brochure, "Words like quiet, romance, atmosphere, glamour, comfort are personified at the Rancho."

In 1951, the Marechals sold the hotel to Dallas, Texas, billionaire Clint Murchison. Mr. Murchison remodeled the buildings and added a swimming pool. The pool's unique shape came from the fact that it was placed where the riding ring used to be and took up half the ring in a horse shoe shape with palm trees and lounge chairs on the inner circle. According to this new hotel's brochure, "much of the clientele is from 'Who's Who in America.'"

$30,000 single family units, each with 2 bedrooms and 2 ½ baths, a den, patio and living room with a fireplace, were added at the rear of the property. The main structure added a story and expanded on both floors. In front of the main and original structure, an L-shaped 6-unit apartment and 2-room duplex were also built. Rancho del Charro was being transformed.

However, the del Charro tradition would not last. In the early 1970s, this legendary spot came to an end. Bulldozers cleared the land and almost got away with removing all the old trees as well. Fortunately, after much pressure was placed on the Zoning Committee of the La Jolla Town Council, some of the lovely old trees were saved. Historic del Charro became the site of condominiums but the legend lives on. Just down the street is the Andrea Villa Inn. It is owned and managed by Chris Marechal, grandson of the remarkable couple from Texas.

La Jolla's Bicycle Pioneer, Dr. Clifford Graves

There are roads that make us happy
There are roads that make us blue
But the roads that we've been traveling
Are the best we ever knew.
Captain Dan Henry

Mary Fay first heard of hosteling in about 1936. The news came to her from two young friends who had just come back from a hostel trip of Europe. Mary Fay was no longer young at that time; nevertheless, she decided that San Diego must have hostels too.

The trouble was that nobody in San Diego knew anything about hostels. Besides, with the possible exception of Joe Merrill, nobody in San Diego was ready, willing, or able to lead a local hostel trip. Undaunted, Mary Fay started one anyway. She talked to her friends, applied for a charter from the national organization, and even set up a chain of hostels from Oceanside to Dulzura. These hostels were simply empty barns and sheds, made available by ranchers at Mary Fay's urging. Lacking were the hostelers.

The war wiped out everything that had been gained. When the war was over, Mary Fay started again. This time San Diego did have a small group of bicycle riders in the San Diego Bicycle Club, which Bob Zumwalt had started in 1948. However, the San Diego Bicycle Club was a racing club. Its members had little interest in hosteling. Moreover, there were no adults. Under these circumstances, the two organizations had

Bicycling in Zion National Park. Dr. Graves is in the second row on the right.
Courtesy of Bill Pratt

virtually no contact. Hosteling remained a paper concept, admirable in philosophy but devoid of followers. The most that was accomplished was an occasional ride in the park.

In 1950, Clifford Graves, who had just come back from a bicycle trip of Europe, met Mary Fay. She asked if he would take over and he said yes. However there was very little structure, if any, to build upon. Locally, AYH (American Youth Hostels) had about a dozen members many of whom did not stay with the group once the hosteling actually had begun in earnest. Nationally, AYH had about 12,000 members in 1950. The organization functioned from its offices in New York City thanks to a sizeable grant from John D. Rockefeller III who was also its president from 1948-51. None of the money, however, reached outlying clubs like San Diego. If San Diego were to have a hosteling program, it would have to be supported locally.

Dr. Graves, a La Jolla surgeon, decided to start with a weekend trip to Borrego. He put a notice in *The San Diego Union*. Of the AYH membership, only Mary Fay and the Ronald Rickeys showed up. They met on the Saturday morning following Thanksgiving at La Jolla Junction, now the campus of UCSD. Fourteen people turned up and of these, only three were adults.

"I stationed myself in the middle of the road and waved my handkerchief" a cartoon from *Bike Centennial* the magazine of The Bicycle Touring Association, February 1986, in an article titled "*Reconnoiter*" by Clifford Graves.

Joe Merrill, who was then 55, came on his extraordinary track-bike. Howard Rogers was a rebel from the racing club. Richard Taylor was a man in his 60s who had read of the outing and thought he'd try it. Mr. Taylor was a railroad man from Iowa who had come to San Diego to retire. More a hiker than a biker, he arrived on a bicycle that he had bought the day before. Completely inexperienced, he was unable to keep up and made it only as far as Poway. Nevertheless, he remained an AYH member for 20 years and always came to the Christmas parties. When he died in '72, he left a substantial part of his modest estate to AYH.

Except for Richard Taylor, there were no road casualties and the group reached Borrego just before dark and made camp. A sagwagon brought food and sleeping bags. Joe Merrill showed everyone the secrets of his homemade bicycle. Howard Rogers introduced everyone to sew-up tires and Steele Lipe (the youngest on the ride) proved that an 84-mile ride was not beyond the ability of a 12-year old boy. Altogether, the experiment could be called a success.

La Jolla's Dr. Graves began his bicycling "career" during W.W.II. Initially sent to England during the preparations for D Day, he obtained a bicycle and found stress relief riding through the English countryside while awaiting his orders. Later, he carted the bicycle in his surgical station, which was, at least for awhile, safely behind the allied lines near the border of Belgium and Germany. However, the surgical station was caught when the enemy dropped German soldiers in American uniforms behind the enemy line. (This German counterattack was known as the Battle of the Bulge.) Having no way to get back to the allied lines, Dr. Graves turned to his bicycle and rode through the German occupied area and across the lines to safety. In his own words to Steele, he was neither caught nor fired upon but was instead hailed by the Germans because "no American would have ridden a bicycle." From this inauspicious beginning, his love of the bicycle as a mode of transportation and enjoyment began. It was not uncommon for him to be seen riding his bicycle all over La Jolla, and frequently from his Prospect Avenue office up Torrey Pines to the new Scripps Hospital, with his black doctoring bag on the back.

Besides founding the International Bicycle Touring Society and the San Diego Chapter of the American Youth Hostels, Dr. Graves was instrumental in the founding of the La Jolla Symphony Association and co-founding the San Diego Society of General Surgeons. He died in La Jolla in 1985 and his book, "My Life on Two Wheels," was published the following year.

After its humble beginning with the Borrego ride in 1950, bicycle touring became quite active with weekend rides and two-day overnights around San Diego County and Southern California. By 1954, extended trips of a week or more were taken during the Spring and Summer months including tours of the California Coast, Grand Canyon, Lake Tahoe and the Feather River Canyon, the Missions of California and most of the National Parks. Even Death Valley was toured but that was during Christmas vacation.

From its small and inconspicuous beginning, thanks to Dr. Graves the San Diego AYH grew into an organization that has given hundreds, perhaps thousands, a new skill and a new appreciation. "For many, it actually meant a new life. Simply to be able to use a bicycle for travel and transportation is a priceless asset in today's over motorized society," said Dr. Graves, a man who could be called the true trailblazer of San Diego's bicycling community.

Flaw in the Jewel: Housing Discrimination against Jews in La Jolla

Condensed from an article by Mary Ellen Stratthaus, "American Jewish History,"
American Jewish Historical Society Quarterly, Sept. 1996

"The very fact that you live in La Jolla puts you in a special class." Real Estate ad for La Jolla Highlands, *La Jolla Light*, November 6, 1958

The low mountains rising from the shore of La Jolla, California, the seaside village known as "The Jewel," serve as a barrier against the heat of the coastal desert. On summer days when low clouds provide a protective shield along the coast, temperatures beyond the canyon east of the coastal range commonly run as much as ten degrees higher. Those same mountains also break up transmission from San Diego's public radio station, KPBS, making it difficult for villagers to pick up a clear signal. In the late 1950s the citizens of La Jolla learned how another barrier to the outside world, one they had constructed and maintained to preserve their exclusivity and distinction, became a potential economic obstacle when it threatened to keep out a new university. This study examines how plans to build a new University of California campus led to the elimination of La Jolla's anti-Semitic housing policy.

(Early) real estate brokers in La Jolla developed methods of thwarting home purchases by potential buyers they considered undesirable on the basis of class, race, or ethnicity. While housing prices excluded people of lower incomes, realtors also evaluated prospective buyers through a prism of racial and ethnic assumptions. (At that time) many La Jollans considered Jews among the unworthy, regardless of their appearance, income, or education.

La Jolla had an unwritten understanding, a "gentleman's agreement," regarding Jews in the 1950s. La Jollans wanted to keep Jews out of their town because of class fears as well as anti-Semitism..... Class fears hinged on economic anxiety: residents resist poorer neighbors because their presence could lower property values....

In the 1950s in America, discrimination against outsiders represented more than class or economic anxieties. During the Cold War Americans turned inward like a wagon train circling in on itself at night for protection. During the early years of the Cold War, Americans clung to their new-found prosperity while living in fear "that the Russians could destroy the United States not only by atomic attack but through internal subversion." Fear of invasion from within and without even influenced the design of the standard suburban home in the 1950s.... To some La Jollans in that decade, an "invasion of university professors and students represented an irregularity." When a UC spokesman said a new campus would involve "all kinds of people," (one La Jolla resident) protested: "This university is not going to have any radicals in it at all…we've got to keep it pure…." In the same time period, a controversy erupted when the UC president demanded that faculty members sign a loyalty oath swearing they were not communists….

La Jolla's physical aspects contributed to its charm and sense of distinction…La Jolla has almost thirteen and a half miles of coastline, some of it consisting of rugged, cave-pocked cliffs, and is set apart from the rest of San Diego by low mountains which "almost surround the place, excluding the rest of the world…."

…La Jollans prized their inaccessibility, reserving for themselves the right of deciding whom they would allow to move into their world. La Jolla's resistance to perceived threats to its seclusion sometimes took extreme forms. When gas was first piped in, "an armed mob" greeted the crews, and the town threatened an injunction to prevent the railroad's extension to the hotel. "The residents believed even then that if La Jolla lost its feeling of seclusion, it would lose its charm…." However, part of maintaining the village's singularity meant attracting only "acceptable" tourists. During World War II, La Jolla women obstructed visits from some of the 35,000 or so military personnel who came through San Diego for training or deployment by barricading Torrey Pines Road, the northern entry into the village.

La Jolla residents even used legislation to control access to their community. In 1930 the state rerouted the Pacific Coast Highway (State 101) through Rose Canyon to bypass La Jolla…. "Most agreed that it was the Rose Canyon diversion that helped the town preserve for so long its special character."

La Jollans revealed their conviction about their town's unique personality in various ways. Although part of San Diego, La Jolla consists of "a separate postal district, a distinction long protected" and formalized by its own separate zip code in 1964…. A 1959 pamphlet about La Jolla says that La Jollans "prefer to maintain La Jolla as a distinct and separate entity in its own right," even though a judge later "ruled that La Jolla was nothing more than a state of mind without official boundaries."

In the 1920s La Jolla credited its isolation for protecting it as an exclusive resort from unwelcome visitors: "If facile transportation had come early in the history of the resort," the local paper asked, "would La Jolla have developed into a resort town unique in its refinement, its atmosphere of culture and its freedom from noisy concessions?"

Creation of the La Jolla Town Council in 1950 represented a consolidation of many groups which had developed over the years to protect and preserve La Jolla's character. The Town Council, a community improvement group with no legal status, succeeded groups such as the Chamber of Commerce, the Civic League, the La Jolla Planning Council, and the Conservation Society….

By the middle of the twentieth century La Jolla's realtors had developed an effective policy to protect its unique character by excluding unwanted outsiders from purchasing property that specifically discriminated against Jews…. "In La Jolla there was an unwritten agreement amongst brokers. They would discourage Jews and people of color…. Nobody put out signs in La Jolla" to sell a house, except for individual private sellers. The real estate companies did not identify the houses for sale and prevented Jews from buying property by ascertaining exactly what kind of house they wanted to buy — price range, neighborhood, number of rooms, everything — then showing them anything but houses fitting those qualifications….

The brokers' mission, of course, was directly linked with their livelihood. If La Jolla lost its appeal as a resort, property values would decrease, sales would go down, and brokers would lose money. Ultimately, though, La Jolla's anxiety about losing its exclusive character became an obstacle to the area's economic expansion when discrimination against Jews threatened to prevent construction of another branch of the University of California.

The decision by the Regents, the University of California Governing Body, to build a new campus in San Diego resulted from a confluence of needs. Scripps Institution of Oceanography needed a larger facility to admit the increasing number of applicants to its graduate programs. San Diego needed more engineers and technicians to staff its defense industries, and California needed additional institutions of higher learning to provide for its expanding population. La Jolla had the fewest needs….

As a Berkeley graduate student who obtained his Ph.D. at SIO in 1936 and a UC faculty member since 1941, Roger Revelle had close bonds with the University of California. His links with San Diego tightened with his career as a naval officer from 1942 to 1948. SIO did war-related research during World War II, and Revelle led the UC Division of War Research in San Diego. With his connections to San Diego's defense industry and its importance in the city's economy before, during, and after World War II, Revelle's ties to the city, the Navy and the University of California had been in place for some years before the question of a new campus arose in the 1950s. His La Jolla connections went even deeper.

Dr. Revelle had lived in La Jolla since the 1930s and had married Ellen Clark, (great) niece of Ellen Browning Scripps, the town's leading benefactor…E. W. and Ellen Scripps had provided the funding for the Marine Biological Association of San Diego, which in 1912 became the Scripps Institution for Biological Research, a research branch of the UC system.

In 1950, the University of California appointed (Revelle) director of SIO. In addition to his leadership role as a scientist, he was a community activist, serving as president of the La Jolla Town Council and the third chairman of the Board of Trustees from

Groundbreaking Ceremony, 1961, for UCSD; the impetus for solving the Jewish problem in La Jolla, (l to r) Mayor Charles Dail, Chancellor Herbert York, President of UC Clark Kerr, Governor Edmund G. Brown, Roger Revelle, State Senator Hugo Fisher.
Courtesy of UCSD, Mandeville Special Collections Library

1952 to 1954. No one was better situated to lay the groundwork for the Regents' approval of a new UC campus in La Jolla.

After the Russians launched Sputnik in 1957 the nation's demand for education and research intensified …. On November 4, 1958, after nearly a year of promotion by Revelle and speakers from the SIO faculty, voters approved Proposition D by 75%, giving 450 additional acres of The City of San Diego's Pueblo lands to the University.

In a May 30, 1957, speech to a meeting of the La Jolla Real Estate Brokers Association, Revelle spoke optimistically about the industrial growth that would accompany the creation of "a science campus" similar to the California Institute of Technology. However, he warned that the new campus would "bring inevitable changes in the texture and character of La Jolla."

A far more significant concern for Revelle was housing for SIO faculty. As SIO's director, he had struggled against La Jolla's discriminatory policies against Jews. In 1951, he and a group of associates bought land on the hillside above SIO and created Scripps Estates Association (SEA). (The cottage that Ellen Clark was born in, located to the right front of Miss Scripps' home on Prospect St., was moved to become the first home in the SEA.) Among the reasons given to the public for the construction of SEA was the problem SIO employees had with housing in La Jolla....

Community support had been more generous earlier when the Regents considered merely expanding SIO to include a School of Science and Engineering. In 1957, La Jolla Town Council President H. Bailey Gallison feared that a large general campus would alter the character of La Jolla....

John Galbraith, UCSD's second chancellor, commented, "there is no greater contrast than between this University and La Jolla.... It wasn't just anti-Semitism, though anti-Semitism is emphasized a lot. It's a feeling that these people, whether they are Jews, Christians or atheists, represent a threat to the way of life, whatever that may be, of La Jolla...."

Whether credit should go to Revelle, the University...or legislation, sometime late in the 1950s La Jolla realtors ended their exclusion of Jews. Coincidentally, the Regents approved the new campus in May 1959....

As more of La Jolla's residents realized that the arrival and settlement of Jews in their neighborhood did not damage their property values or spoil their village, their feelings about Jews may have altered. However, since anti-Semitism, like hatred against any group, is deeply ingrained and difficult to overcome, it is impossible to assume that acceptance necessarily followed integration. It is enough, perhaps, to celebrate the changed atmosphere and the chance for Jews to decide for themselves whether they wish to become residents of that distinctive community.

("A new University born in San Diego in 1962 (UCSD) from an...inauspicious birthing bed, has already become, in every rating, one of the world's top 10 research universities. Scientists everywhere know about the quality of research in San Diego." Neil Morgan, *The San Diego Union Tribune*, 2002)

Dr. John S. Galbraith served as Chancellor from 1964 to 1968, then in the 1980s, returned to UCSD as a history professor. Dr. Galbraith's commitment was the planning and construction of a library which would become one of the three largest libraries in the then-nine-campus system of the University of California. Dedicated in 1971, the concrete inverted pyramid UCSD Central Library reached a capacity of one million volumes by 1973. Following an expansion of the facility in the early 1990, the library was renamed Geisel Library in honor of the late Theodore Geisel aka Dr. Seuss and his wife, Audrey. Along with Herbert York, UCSD's first chancellor, Dr. Galbraith along with Dr. Roger Revelle literally got UCSD on its way to becoming the world famous campus it is today. Dr. Galbraith died in June, 2003. "The library is the heart of the University. A University without a great library is like a deficient body." Among the books found in the library are a collection written by Dr. Galbraith depicting "the 19th century British Empire as evidenced by its trading companies," according too his son, James M. Galbraith. 2003's UCSD's Chancellor Robert Dynes described Dr. Galbraith as a leader with the "skills of a magician and the heart of a lion." He added, "You cannot walk more than a few yards on this campus without seeing John's imprint."

Memorial Cross on Mt. Soledad

To sit on rocks; to muse o'er flood and fell;...
To climb the trackless mountain all unseen...
This is not solitude: 'tis but to hold
Converse with Nature's charms, and view her stores unrolled.

Byron

On a Spring day in 1922, many La Jolla families trudged up the rugged path bordered by chaparral and wild flowers such as Indian Paintbrush, California poppies, and shooting stars. They were climbing up to the summit of Mt. Soledad to celebrate an Easter sunrise service. Occasionally, they would pause to admire the spectacular view of the Pacific Ocean to the west and the breakers rolling onto the coastline to the north. At the summit, they stopped and took time to look all around, to admire and enjoy the panorama of country sprawled out in front of them. To the north, in the distance, were the San Gabriel Mountains, north of present day Los Angeles. To the east were the Laguna Mountains with Cuyamaca Mountain and its recognizable hump. To the south was Mexico's Table Mountain with its flat top and,

The path up Mt. Soledad looking down on La Jolla. This area represents the present day area above La Jolla County Club.
Courtesy of Barbara Dawson

The present Cross, part of the War Memorial.
Courtesy of Steele Lipe

off the coast, the Coronado Islands emerging from the Pacific Ocean. Miles of open country with canyons and hills, the bay area and the sea surrounded this mountain summit.

The only houses the climbers could see were a scattering of board and batten and shingle bungalows down in the village they had just left by foot and, far off to the southeast, a cluster of houses that were the City of San Diego. Compare the view these climbers saw in 1922 to what people see today when standing on the summit gazing in all directions. The same hills, the same land but now all of it covered with houses, high rises, and condos, all except the ocean.

In 1922, the simple Easter service was conducted by a local minister at the base of a tall wooden cross located at the summit of Mt. Soledad (named after "Our Lady of Loneliness"). The sun rose in the east as the service progressed. This first cross was made of California redwood and erected in 1913. Ten years later in 1923, it was destroyed, possibly stolen. A new cross was erected in 1934, this one made of stucco over a wood base and chicken wire, but it was not very stable. On March 13, 1952, high winds blew it down. After much publicity, funds were raised under the leadership of Colonel Hugh Miller and the Reverend Dan Griffith. The cross was to be a memorial to those who died in the first and second World Wars and the Korean War. Architect Donald Campbell was hired to design a new and durable cross. Forty-three feet high with a cross arm of twelve feet, this cross is made of cement but sections are hollowed out in rectangular and square shapes. These gaping holes were placed to avoid the wind resistance, the cause of the former cross's demise. This third and final cross was dedicated on Easter Sunday, April 18, 1954. In 1989, a bronze plaque was attached to the fence with the following inscription:

The cross was built as a memorial to veterans of both World Wars and the Korean War. Recently, atheists have challenged the right of the city to allow this landmark to be located on public property. In response, the Mt. Soledad Memorial Association was formed with William J. Kellogg as its chairman. The members rallied the La Jolla community, other interested citizens, and historians to provide financial support so that the Association could take the problem through the courts. The problem was finally solved after years of litigation. When the ground the cross sits on was put up for sale by the City of San Diego, the Memorial Association was the successful bidder. The La Jolla landmark has been saved, but new lawsuits continuously crop up.

On May 29, 2001, two of six memorial walls were dedicated. The Memorial Walls project, which had been announced on Memorial Day, 2000, at a Veterans of Foreign Wars ceremony at the historic Mt. Soledad site, will even-

> **MT. SOLEDAD VETERANS MEMORIAL CROSS DEDICATED IN 1954, AS A TRIBUTE TO ALL BRANCHES OF THE ARMED FORCES OF U. S. A. SERVICEMEN AND WOMEN, THIS PLAQUE DEDICATED NOVEMBER 11, 1989 MT. SOLEDAD MEMORIAL ASSOCIATION CITY BEAUTIFUL SAN DIEGO**

tually feature six concentric walls. Each wall will bear up to 3,200 black granite plaques etched with photographs, service information and personal remembrances of individual veterans. On Dec. 6, 2000, a 30-foot flagpole was installed and dedicated. The following day it was raised then lowered to half-mast at the exact time of the Japanese bombing of Pearl Harbor on December 7, 1941.

There is another story on the top of this mountain. In 1910, Mt. Soledad was the site chosen by a veteran of World War I, Frazier Curtis, to attempt gliding. A harness was attached to his shoulders with "wings" and with help from friends, he was able to glide short distances.

On January 29, 1930, Anne Lindbergh, under the watchful eye and guidance of her husband Charles, won her glider's license at Mt. Soledad. Obviously, since her husband had made the first trans-Atlantic flight in 1927 (in a plane built right here in San Diego), this glider was quite a bit more sophisticated than the Curtis harness with wings. The following month, on February 24th, Charles Lindbergh was able to fly his glider from Mt. Soledad all the way to Del Mar. Many La Jolla youth assisted the launch only too willing to do anything just to see the glider fly. One of the youths was ten year old Gene McCormack. In his own words Gene describes the times and that special day in particular. "In between holidays…a lot of us played cowboy. We carried big ropes and tried to get hats and everything else. We'd go up the mountains, up there on Mt. Soledad, and you could play cowboy and Indians…one day when I was up there, I got around to where I was big enough to read the paper and I read that Charles A. Lindbergh was going to fly a glider, a Boles Glider, off of Mt. Soledad. So I got up early that morning. I even brushed my teeth and combed my hair, because once he flew the Atlantic, I quit being a cowboy and became a pilot. We made model gliders to fly around and so I went up there. Being ten or eleven years old, I wasn't big enough to pull that rubber shock cord that the man ran across the hill which threw Lindy up into the air, but they did let me clear all the rocks out of the way so those cords on the cable wouldn't slip and fall down. I got all that done, went up, and Charlie smiled at me. I would never be a cowboy again after that, and so lots of things happened on Mt. Soledad." Legal and supervised gliding now takes place from the high cliffs of Torrey Pines.

The mesas around San Diego and La Jolla are about 40,000 years old. It is of interest that Mt. Soledad and the La Jolla peninsula are relatively young, only 10,000 years old. The geological upsurge of Mt Soledad and La Jolla can

Two views of Mt. Soledad. The mountain rises above the flat geologic plain around La Jolla having risen as a result of earthquakes along the Rose Canyon fault line which traverses the east and north sides of the 880 foot high mountain. The top view is from the east showing the slow rise from the south (left) with a steeper dropoff on the north. The lower view is from above Scripps Institution of Oceanography and shows the western slope from the crest down to the La Jolla shore. The steep eastern slope is best viewed from along I-5 which runs along the fault line. The mountain has been smothed by erosion and much of the northern side has been sculptured by landslides. The area of the Seven Sisters caves (lower panel) is heavily cracked (the nidus for the caves) which match many of the cracksthat may be seen among the rocks on the beach at the southern junction of Coast and South Coast boulevards. Those cracks are from the uplift of the earth's surface and run under La Jolla in a south-west to north-east direction.
Courtesy of Steele Lipe

easily be seen from the east where the uplift in the Rose Canyon fault, which surrounds Mt. Soledad on the north and east sides, has produced a gradual incline from the south with a steep dropoff on the north. This could be compared to a door with the hinge to the south and the opening to the north. The same principle applies with the gradual slope to the west and a steeper slope in the east. Thus, the north-east corner of Mt. Soledad, the location of the cross, is the highest point and has the steepest slopes.

We recommend all visitors should take the drive, hike, or ride a bicycle up to the most beautiful spot in San Diego County. Go up the mountain and watch the sun rise in the east or set in the west or simply "converse with nature's charms" and relive the magic of this place we call La Jolla.

Silent Wings Over La Jolla

by Gary Fogel, author of
Wind and Wings: the History of Soaring in San Diego

An ideal combination of regular onshore winds coupled with frequent blue sky gave San Diegans a head start on gliding efforts in the United States. For instance, it is believed that John J. Montgomery became the first person in the United States to fly in a glider, in 1883 from a site near Otay Mesa near the Mexican border. Closer to La Jolla, in 1910, Frazier Curtis of La Jolla ordered a kit for a biplane glider from an advertisement in Popular Science magazine. By July of 1910, the kit arrived, was built, and was ready for flight testing. With Curtis at the "controls," several short "hops" were made by a team of friends pulling the glider into the air with a rope, letting go when Curtis and the glider were aloft, with Curtis attempting to balance the aircraft to a successful landing. La Jolla Postmaster Nathan Rannells and others (including Curtis' wife Diana), did much of the rope pulling. Flights were made from near Pepita Way on the northwest side of Mount Soledad. Both

John Montgomery with one of his gliders.
Courtesy of San Diego Historical Society Photograph Collection

Hawley Bowlus preparing to launch in his #16 sailplane, at a 1929 glider meet on the south slope of Mount Soledad.
Courtesy of Torrey Pines Gliderport Historical Society, Inc.

Anne Lindbergh in a large Bowlus sailplane during her launch from the top of Mount Soledad in 1930.
Courtesy of Torrey Pines Gliderport Historical Society, Inc.

Rannells and Curtis had flights in this glider.

By the 1920s, the Germans were investigating motorless aircraft and developed a number of "sailplanes" that were capable of both long distance and duration flights. Lifting currents in the atmosphere are used by the pilot, to soar, like a bird, distances of tens, even hundreds of miles, all without a motor. In 1928-29, the first sailplane designed and constructed in the United States was completed by William Hawley Bowlus in San Diego. Bowlus had a keen eye for aircraft design; he had previously served as the Superintendent of Construction at the Ryan Flying Company for Charles Lindbergh's *Spirit of St. Louis* in 1927. However, Bowlus' new sailplane was a masterpiece in lightweight construction, capable of using "ridge lift" to maintain or even gain altitude over the starting location. Bowlus used this first sailplane (and several other improved designs) to set several American soaring records over Point Loma in 1929 and 1930. As a result of his records and subsequent national attention, Charles Lindbergh came back to San Diego to receive a special course in glider instruction from Bowlus. After a quick tour of the sailplane, Lindbergh made a successful 20 minute soaring flight above the ridge at Point Loma to earn his first-class glider license, the 9th such license granted in the United States. Charles then convinced Anne, his wife, to try gliding as well. On February 29, 1930, Anne Lindbergh, piloting a Bowlus Albatross, was launched from the very top of Mt. Soledad to a successful landing in the fields below. With this flight, Anne Morrow Lindbergh became the first woman in the U. S. to receive a first-class glider license, the 10th granted overall.

So amazing was this accomplishment that a number of women in the local area formed the "Anne Lindbergh Glider Club" with Anne nominated as Honorary President. The "Mount Soledad Glider Club" soon sprang up in La Jolla, including a special "women's division." Ruth Alexander, a noted aviator for powered aircraft, was launched in gliders from Mt. Soledad to achieve her third and second-class glider licenses, and many others also received their glider licenses with flights from Mount Soledad in 1930. Students at La Jolla Jr.-Sr. High School started construction on their own series of gliders under the guidance of woodshop instructor, Mr. O. E. Heckleman. A number of high school boys formed the "Falcons Glider Club" including Spencer Wilson who helped with construction. Members of the local "Associated Glider Clubs of Southern California" wrote a letter to the owner of the Mt. Soledad property asking permission for the construction of a glider hangar in light of the fact that the club had plans for a glider contest. However, these plans never came to fruition as the Great Depression and a series of strict glider licensing requirements soon took their effect on local enthusiasm.

As the Great Depression waned, a number of students from San Diego High School built their own gliders and towed them into the air behind cars on the beach near the Torrey Pines cliffs. The gliders could be released following auto-tow and then soar in the updrafts created by the prevailing wind hitting the sharp coastal cliffs. It was an ideal location, except for the fact that driving a car on the beach was not favored by the local fishermen or police. Interested in aviation, Woody Brown, noted local surfing pioneer, teamed up with the youngsters flying sailplanes and decided to hunt for a better launching location along the tops of the cliffs. In 1935, Woody became the first pilot to launch and land from the top of the cliffs. The Torrey Pines Gliderport grew out of this experimentation.

At the time, soaring was still in its infancy with various tinkerers, inventors, and youngsters eager to find inexpensive means to take to the sky. These pilots would routinely build their own aircraft, serve as test pilot, and then launch and soar along the cliffs at Torrey Pines. A great deal of testing and modification resulted in increasingly efficient sailplane designs. In effect, the cliffs and Torrey Pines were considered not only a unique recreational resource, but an outdoor wind tunnel by the local enthusiasts. John Robinson, a student from San Diego High School, flew many hours along the cliffs in the 1930s with his series of homemade sailplanes and was fortunate to obtain the R. S.-1 *Zanonia* sailplane, an aircraft that was considered to be the most efficient sailplane in the United States. With the *Zanonia,* and through his training and experimentation with new forms of instrumentation at Torrey Pines, Robinson became the first pilot to win the U. S. Soaring National Championship three times in a row. He set numerous U. S. and International soaring records with the *Zanonia* eventually becoming the first soaring pilot in the world to receive the "Diamond C" award, soaring's highest pilot achievement honor. Other local pilots including Woody Brown and Alan Essery also established new United States soaring records (in 1939, Brown

The Bowlus Baby Albatross sailplane was popular with local pilots in the 1940s and 1950s and was a common sight above the cliffs at Torrey Pines.
Courtesy of Torrey Pines Gliderport Historical Society, Inc.

flew 10 hours in a soaring flight from Wichita Falls, Texas to Wichita, Kansas to set a new world record for "distance to a goal" of 280 miles).

However, World War II soon put an end to all the fun when the local glider club, the Associated Glider Clubs of Southern California, cancelled its lease for the Torrey Pines Gliderport. This was done in order that the property be returned to the City of San Diego so that the land could be transferred to the U. S. Government for the establishment of U. S. Army Camp Callan (ironically, an artillery and anti-aircraft training facility). Many of the local glider pilots volunteered during the war as military glider instructors, helping Army pilots learn how to fly troop transport gliders that would eventually be used in key roles through a wide variety of invasions in the European and Pacific theaters.

After the war, members of the glider club jumped at the chance to reclaim Torrey Pines for silent flight. A series of glider contests, the Pacific Coast Midwinter Soaring Championships, were held between 1947 and 1980 (the longest running series of annual glider contests held at one location in the U. S.). These glider meets would attract the best soaring pilots from around the country to compete in distance, duration, altitude, spot landing, bomb drop (actually a sack of flour), and aerobatic contests. During the contest weekend it was not at all uncommon for 20,000 spectators to line the cliffs watching the action. This was to local gliding as the Annual Invitational is to golf at the nearby Torrey Pines Golf Course, which was still in planning stages. San Diego was filled with aviation companies and many of the employees used gliding as a recreational activity. The cliffs at La Jolla became famous nationally, even internationally, as one of the best sites for ridge soaring in the world.

By the 1950s, electronics and radio control became increasing refined and inexpensive. Soon, radio controlled model sailplanes were being flown off the cliffs at Torrey Pines, and Bob Chase flew his model sailplane to a world endurance record of over 8 hours in 1956. By the late 1960s, the popularity of radio control was increasing rapidly and the Torrey Pines Gulls Radio Controlled Soaring Society formed, one of the earliest model glider clubs in the nation. Later, the Torrey Pines Scale Soaring Society also started flying at Torrey Pines, with the specific interest in flying scale model versions of their full size sailplane counterparts.

In 1969, Australian hang glider pilot Bill Bennett launched his Rogallo hang glider from the tops of the cliffs to a landing on the beach below, introducing the sport of hang gliding to Torrey Pines. Bob Wills soon became the first hang glider pilot to launch and land on the top of the cliff. At least four world records for hang glider endurance were established along the cliffs in the early 1970s, once again Torrey Pines was recognized as a unique resource for soaring. Members of the San Diego Hang Gliding/Paragliding Association currently fly at Torrey Pines. By the late 1980s, a fourth form of silent flight, paragliders, soon launched from Torrey Pines. Europeans had been developing paragliders for some time, but Torrey Pines quickly became one of the most popular sites in the nation for this type of flying. The Torrey Pines Paragliding Pilots Association was formed and operates at the gliderport.

Currently, all four forms of flight share the Torrey Pines Gliderport. The full size sailplanes operate only during the winter months of January through April, the windiest months of the year. In the early 1990s, the entire gliderport was recognized by the National Soaring Museum (Elmira, New York) as a National Soaring Landmark. This was soon followed by designation of the City-owned portion of the gliderport property as a City Historical Site. The entire airport is listed on the State and National Registers of Historic Places, the first gliderport in the U. S. to receive this distinction. It is a historic recognition worthy of the many significant contributions to the history of American aviation made in this silent sport, right in our own backyard.

Nothing But the Best

It Don't Mean a Thing if it Ain't Got that Swing.   **Duke Ellington**

There are three trumpets on a table by a garden window in a house on Sea Lane. Shining, twisting, curving, brass works of art which, with the lips and breath of the musical genius who owns them, will send out sounds that caress, pleasure, please, and excite to passion anyone fortunate enough to be in their presence when they and their owner perform.

The trumpets' owner, John Best, played one of these beautiful trumpets with Artie Shaw, band leader, writer, arranger, when they cut "Begin the Beguine" in 1938. This rendition made Shaw famous. John Best, too. "Begin the Beguine" sold half a million records then. Today, it has sold several million records, tapes, CDs and is still going strong.

John Best played the Bach Stradivarius trumpet when he soloed in "Stardust" with Glenn Miller later in the forties. It was first heard in 1940 by fans in the Pennsylvania Hotel in New York City. It is still one of the most memorable pieces of music in musical history.

Starting in 1945 John played with his friend, Benny Goodman. Some of the great favorites in which John soloed with Benny were "Oh Baby," "Rattle and Roll," "Talk of the Town," and "Fascinatin' Rhythm." And what personal memories does he have of these three musical giants? "They were fantastic human beings, great friends and great musicians."

"Glenn Miller was a warm person. He was nice to people. He had a tremendous talent for pleasing audiences — as well as being a natural showman."

According to Glenn Miller, "A band ought to have a sound of its own. It ought to have a personality." The second Glenn Miller Orchestra which included Johnny Best was formed in March 1938. This group soon broke attendance records up and down the East Coast. There were record-breaking recordings as well including "Tuxedo Junction" and "In the Mood."

During World War II, Glenn was a major in the Army Air Force. "Well, one time both of us were in England at the same time — it was in October, 1944. Glenn was with his band in London and I was with the Navy in Exeter, England — and my birthday was coming up — on the 20th," recounted John Best. "Well, because of Glenn's rank and fame and very persuasive personality, he got me a five-day pass so he could give me a big birthday party in London. I came up from Exeter and had one fantastic birthday party. I played in his band of course, and we really did London (as well as dodging raining German bombs)."

Glenn was made Captain after "convincing the military higher-ups that he could modernize the Army Band and ultimately improve the morale of the men." Once in England the Glenn Miller Army Air Force Band played in over 800 performances in less than a year.

"The next time I saw Glenn was again in London when our Navy band played with his Army band. I remember Glenn was in great form. The next morning (December 15th) he had to leave for France (for a six-week tour of Europe to entertain the fighting troops). On the way over, his plane disappeared. It was a terrible shock for millions of people. I personally still miss him, but I have tapes of his (our) music. It brings back memories to me and to everyone who hears them and who lived through those times"

Abe Most, clarinet; John Best, trumpet; Nick Fatosh, drums at Florintino's
Courtesy of John Best

After a moment of quiet contemplation, a smile crossed the face of Johnny Best. "In 1995, those of us left of the Glenn Miller Band rode on a float up Fifth Avenue, New York, playing Miller music. It was the 50th anniversary of the end of World War II."

Johnny continued, "You also asked about Artie and Benny. They were really kings of jazz and swing. They made it happen; that is, after the great black musicians in New Orleans — like King Oliver, who taught Louis Armstrong."

After a pause, he reminisced, "Then there were Duke Ellington and Jimmy Lunsford and Count Basie and the great pianist, Art Tatum. Tremendous talents." Art Tatum, almost totally blind from birth learned to read sheet music using the Braille method. Self taught, he was considered one of the greatest keyboard virtuosos of jazz in the '30s and '40s.

"God bless those black musicians who showed us white men how to make music swing."

Best continued, "Benny Goodman was the first Big Band leader to integrate blacks and whites. That took guts in those days. When Benny did it, it made headlines — the first time was at the Congress Hotel in Chicago. Of course, when we were on the road we had to stay in separate hotels. But, you know, where there's good music, there are good friends and you forget color. It's music that counts. Music and your common love for playing — making it all work together — like the universe."

In 1935, Benny asked his orchestra to play something called "swing." The public loved it and from then on, there was no turning back.

"Benny demanded that his band work hard, but he worked harder than anyone. I remember one time he was blowing his clarinet for so long — like several 32-bar choruses — that he became punch drunk — he almost passed out — didn't know where he was."

Benny Goodman had style, taste, timing and technical skill setting standards for himself and his musicians unequaled before or since in popular music.

In 1950, John Best's reputation for trumpet mastery and genius took him to the Bob Crosby Show. Younger brother of Bing Crosby, Bob also became a bandleader without knowing how to play an instrument. His most famous band was called the Bobcats.

In 1953 John Best spent twenty weeks on the road with the great Billy May. It was Billy May who perfected the "slurping saxophones" sound which became popular and much sought after and it was this "new sound" that he took on the road with his own "big band." They covered every state. "Billy May is a great trumpet player and has done some of the best musical arrangements in history. He arranged for Nat King Cole and Frank Sinatra."

John returned to play with Bob Crosby's band in the 1964 Tokyo Olympics. Also in the 1960s John Best started playing with Ray Coniff. "I played more solos with Ray than with any other band I ever played with. The South Americans sure liked — still like — that music. We recorded for Columbia International. One of the favorites was, 'El dia que me Quieras.'"

John's trumpets sang along with the great Mildred Bailey one of the finest jazz singers of the 1930s. John also recorded with Bing Crosby. "And yes, I worked with Johnny Mercer. He was an outstanding writer lyricist. He sang very well too."

He was asked about Billie Holiday. "Billy

Marnie Hutchinson Gurevitz, Bernie Gurevitz and John Best
Courtesy of Barbara Dawson

Holiday? For a while she sang with Artie Shaw. She not only had a great voice, she was a great lady." This amazing singer whose grandfather was one of seventeen children of a black Virginia slave and an Irish plantation owner and whose mother was only thirteen when she was born, ended up being "found" by Count Basie and Artie Shaw. It was Benny Goodman who arranged for her first studio session. Sadly, although she recorded over 200 "sides" between 1933 and 1944, she never received royalties for any of them.

Asked about the great Satchmo, a founding father of jazz, Johnny replied, "Sure, I knew Louis Armstrong. In fact I think I still have a letter from him…he thanked me for entertaining him at my house one time." In 1957, Satchmo brought his band to play for the Las Patronas Jewel Ball at the La Jolla Beach and Tennis Club.

John was born (trumpet-less) in North Carolina in 1913. He took piano lessons in elementary school in 1919. His first paying job was for $2 playing the trumpet for four straight hours. That was in 1928 during the Great Depression.

For awhile John played in dance bands. In 1937, he went to the University of North Carolina. That's when Artie Shaw first heard John play and asked John to join him. The rest is history.

In 1966, when he was visiting in La Jolla, he was invited to a jam session being given in the home of a beautiful widow. The widow, Mary Lou, had nine children, but somehow she found the time to study jazz at University of California, San Diego.

John fell in love with Mary Lou and they married in 1967. Several years later, John and Mary Lou bought an avocado orchard in Pauma Valley, at the base of Palomar Mountain. In February, 1982, when John was picking avocados — alone (Mary Lou was in La Jolla), he fell from his ladder and lay in agonizing pain, waiting for someone to find him. He was rescued only after Mary Lou, who hadn't heard from him for two days, finally reached neighbors and asked them to go looking for him. They found him buried under leaves, which he used to keep himself warm. His back was broken.

From then on the trumpets were — and are — played by John from his wheel chair — but with as much joy and energy as if he were standing. John Best still practices two hours a day. He is still the handsome, *charming* man who draws people to him for his warmth and interest in others as well as for his talent.

In September 10, 1996, Mary Lou passed away and John played her favorite piece of music at the memorial service. It was called "Mary Lou." John plays it often.

Mary Lou's eldest son, who lives nearby, often drops by to see John. He assists him in a "multitude of ways" including helping to shine up the three trumpets, which lie, when he isn't playing them, on a table by a window in his house in La Jolla by the sea.

Doctors Doyle and Figueredo

Bareth all things, believeth all things, hopeth all things, endureth all things. Charity never faileth.

Gospel according to St. John

In 1936, Bill Doyle of New York met Anita Figueredo of Costa Rica in medical school at Long Island College of Medicine. Six years later, August 1942, the two were wed at St. Patrick's Cathedral, he in the white uniform of a Naval officer and she, a young lady who had became the first woman surgical resident at Sloan-Kettering Memorial Hospital for Cancer. According to Tica Eastman, Dr. Figueredo and Dr. Doyle's daughter, "One week after the wedding, Bill sailed away as the only medical officer on the destroyer *Nicholas*, to the South Pacific and World War II. Months later, near Guadalcanal, he had his baptism by fire as a wartime physician. His sister ship, the *DeHaven*, took a bomb between the stacks and sunk within five minutes dragging more than half her crew with her to the bottom of the Coral Sea. One hundred ten men were picked out of the burning debris, and the wounded spread over the splattered deck of the *Nicholas*. Bill Doyle and his medics treated penetrating wounds, fractures, and partly severed limbs until the survivors could be put ashore behind friendly lines. Later he himself developed pneumonia, and his condition became so critical during the week he was treated by his own corpsman, that there was an entry in the ship's log that he was 'expected to die' and the captain came to pay his last respects."

Dr. Doyle was sent back to the new Balboa Naval Hospital in San Diego and recovered. Once recovered, Bill returned to New York and his wife. They had two children before Bill was sent back to sea, this time for the invasion of Japan. Dr. Doyle was the medical officer on the *Bellerophon*, a ship headed to Guam. The year was 1945. After Guam, they were to head toward Tokyo. On August 6th, their assignment changed. The atom bomb had been dropped on Hiroshima. The ship was ordered back to the United States mainland. They docked in San Diego. Dr. Doyle had little to do medically since the young men on board were in excellent physical shape. With his spare time, the doctor went to Horton Plaza and got on a bus that was marked "La Jolla."

"I rode the bus to the end of the line and got off over where our Post Office is now, where the bus line ended, and I thought it was a pretty village and was intrigued with it," said Dr. Doyle in an interview with Barbara Dawson in 1984. He spent the day walking all over the enchanting little town. He walked near the cliffs by the ocean and he walked up the side of Mt. Soledad overlooking the ocean. Up by a house belonging to Dr. Holder, Dr. Doyle looked out on a panorama that held him mesmerized. "I just sat there on the brow of the hill on Pepita Way, with no homes in front of me at all. Looking down into the center of the village, I could see the little white Mary Star of the Sea Catholic Church, and then the tower of St. James Episcopal Church. And then, of course, the ocean beyond, and I just felt 'this is such a beautiful community' and I wondered to myself at that time that this might be a nice place to live someday." He couldn't wait to call his wife, Dr. Anita Figueredo, who was back in Washington, D.C., at this time to tell her about this heavenly place.

"I went back out to La Jolla…and covered the whole place in detail. I was that interested. I walked literally miles, from a high hill in back of town for a panoramic view, down three residential districts, looking closely at houses, yards, trees, flowers, and lawns, down through the business district and then for a mile or more along the sea.

"Main facts are," he wrote, "La Jolla is a town of about 8000 people situated directly on the sea coast, 14 miles north of San Diego…. There's a modern hospital (of about 100 beds) and an adjoining Metabolic Clinic which is supposed to be nationally famous….

Coast Blvd. home just down the hill below Scripps Hospital.
Courtesy of Anita Figueredo, M. D.

"The predominating architecture is heavily Spanish in flavor (white and cream stucco, red tiles, patios, garden walls)…. Average prices seem to be $9-10,000 for a 3-bedroom house, or $950 for a lot in a good location. There's a moderate boom on, I guess.

"I noted three doctors' offices all in little one-story separate buildings. There's a nice little Catholic Church, 'Mary Star of the Sea', which appears to be brand new, and in which I lit a candle and said a prayer for us."

The young couple had been looking for a place like Costa Rica, Dr. Figueredo's homeland, but in the continental United States. When Dr. Anita Figueredo received the phone call and heard her husband so excited about this place he called La Hoya, she knew it must be very special. One day, soon after that call, as she looked down at the courtyard of the condo complex where she was living, she saw some actors from Hollywood. They had come to Washington to make a film at the behest of the Navy. Being curious about the lovely little village her husband had clearly fallen in love with, she asked the moviemakers about the area. They said that La Jolla was the most beautiful place in the world. "Then why," she asked, "don't you live there?" They replied that they would love to live in La Jolla, but they couldn't possibly. "Why?" "Because," they answered, "you can't make a living there. We could never afford such a luxury. Only professionals can live in La Jolla!" That settled it. Professional Dr. Figueredo flew out West to see for herself.

"I expected it to be green and beautiful," Dr. Figueredo said. "From the plane, I looked down and it was all brown." She met her husband at Lindbergh Field and then drove up to La Jolla. They stayed at the Casa de Mañana, just across from the ocean, a location hard to resist. (In 1947, Dr. Doyle describes the Casa as having spacious grounds, and "dripping with Bougainvillea, Trumpet vines and there was an exquisite patio with bull fight posters, and all that sort of thing; it was really as if you were actually in old Spain.") One day, as they were taking a bus tour of the area, "we passed a house where someone was putting out a sign 'For Sale.' We stopped the bus, got out, and bought it." (According to Dr. Doyle, "that brand new beautifully built little house, on a large, nice lot cost us $17,500.00.")

"By November, 1947, Anita Figueredo Doyle was thirty-one years old and Bill Doyle was thirty-two, they settled themselves down in a romantic, unrealistically small garden of a place, a continent away from their family and friends and sterling professional connections."

The Doyle Family, 1956
Courtesy of Anita Figueredo, M. D.

As it turned out, there were no specialists practicing in La Jolla, only in San Diego. An associate of Dr. Figueredo's from a hospital in New York City, learning that the couple was moving to La Jolla, sent them a letter of introduction to an old friend of his. That friend was Dr. Hal Holder. It had been the same Dr. Holder whose house Dr Doyle had stood in front of to enjoy the view on his first trip. When they met, Dr. Holder was quite candid. "Dr. Doyle," he said, "eventually you will be able to start a pediatric practice in La Jolla, but now only the elderly live there." As for Dr. Figueredo, he said, "No woman has opened a belly in San Diego County and I don't believe ever will!" They accepted the advice, but being young, they didn't pay any attention to it as "young people generally don't." Fortunately, "by the time our kids were born, younger families were in fact moving into La Jolla."

Dr. Doyle had no problem attracting patients. In fact, Bill Doyle became not only La Jolla's first full-time pediatrician, his practice stretched from Mission Beach to Oceanside Eventually, the first woman surgeon was able to practice too becoming the first (and for fifteen years, the only) female surgeon in San Diego.

The couple had three children when they arrived. After moving here, a fourth child was born in 1947. The parents began to think about a bigger home than the one they had purchased on La Jolla Blvd. West of the Boulevard, everything was empty. A builder, however, was just beginning to develop the property. The two doctors decided to work with the builder. They designed their own house on Avenida Cresta with ample rooms for everybody, but in the back of their minds was a house they had seen when they first stayed at the Casa.

"In 1947, on our first visit, while taking a walk on Prospect, we saw this gorgeous house down the hill beyond the hospital. We took a picture of it." Over the years, they would pass by, but it always looked empty. "It turned out that we had been looking at it from the front and the garages were in the back. Then a dentist we knew told us that he had made an offer on the house. He wanted to turn it into a clinic. (There were no zoning laws then.) The owner did not want her house made into a clinic and refused his offer. I heard that and took off and bought it, but not right away." It turned out that although the owner, Mrs. Mabel David, loved the house, her son thought it was ridiculous that she was occupying all that space alone. Mrs. David had a hard time reconciling herself to sell it even though she had already moved into the back guesthouse and was renting out the main house. When it came time to sign the contract with Drs. Figueredo and Doyle, Mrs. David would leave town and disappear for months, hoping they would forget about it. Finally, when they asked if she would agree to stay as long as she liked in the lodging behind the main house, she was willing to let the contract proceed. Eventually, Mrs. David moved and "this guest house we converted into an office for my wife (Dr. Figueredo)." Before long, they had two more children. Besides live-in help, Dr. Figueredo's mother came to live with them and helped care for the children. They needed the bigger house. Later, after some research, they found out that the house had been designed by architect Edgar Ullrich in 1931. "The living room ceiling beams are all hand-carved, the stair risers are beautifully carved and the bookshelves are just treated like the finest cabinet work…and being built during the Depression, why I suppose the people were eager and anxious to have work at that time…." They had moved into this house in 1956 and to the end of his life, Dr. Doyle was still admiring the sunset every night and "the added benefit that we didn't know we were going to have until we moved here. When we have a full moon, it sits in the ocean outside our house, and when that silver path comes across the water and everything shimmers, it's exquisite."

The house was perfect not only for its size and its beauty but because it was situated directly behind Scripps Memorial Hospital and Scripps Clinic. The Clinic was designed as a specialized facility to diagnose, treat, and research diabetes and other metabolic disorders. In 1926, a nurse's annex was built to serve both the Clinic and the Hospital. In 1946, in response to expansion opportunities, the Clinic and the Hospital became separate entities although they remained adjacent to one another and, in 1951, additional floors and a new wing were added to the Hospital. "I remember so well the staff meetings that we used to have at Scripps, because the combined medical staffs of Scripps Hospital and Scripps Clinic and Research Foundation would have their monthly meetings in the living room of the Nurses' Home of the hospital, which was on the corner of Cuvier and Prospect," said Dr. Doyle. The combined staffs at that time "were about twelve doctors at the most."

Dr. Doyle was the only pediatrician in the whole area, "between San Diego and as far north as you want to go; the nearest pediatrician, I think, was at Corona del Mar." In 1950, Dr. Doyle was joined by Dr. John Welsh. They practiced together for some thirty years. "John and I spent day after day in the same office and I can honestly say in that time we never had a significant argument, disagreement—we discussed many things—but I don't remember speaking or hearing an angry word with John Welsh. You know," he adds, "there are not many medical partnerships that can say that. I really know, because doctors by temperament are sort of individualistic people and they like to have their own way, and it's sort of the way we're trained, but John and I had a wonderful, peaceful kind of practice and our office was always a fun place to be." In those years, the doctor got to know his patients well and even made house calls. Dr. Doyle warns that "in spite of the marvels of the 20TH century, we have to strive to keep humanity in ALL of our professions."

In the fifties, La Jolla was still fairly small with a population (not including tourists) of about 20,000. Dr. Figueredo said that when they moved to La Jolla, there was nothing east of US-101 (Gilman Drive). In her mind, it would be ridiculous to move the hospital "way out there in the wilderness. We needed to keep the hospital in La Jolla." Nevertheless, in 1964, Scripps Memorial Hospital decided to leave "the village" and move to the "wilds," east of the new I-5. (That area had to be incorporated as part of La Jolla to adhere to the terms of Miss Scripps' bequest, the only parcel of land east of I-5 that is in the La Jolla Zip code.) Dr. Doyle was Chief of the Medical Staff at this time and presided over the move "from Prospect to the chaparral covered mesa north of town."

By 1976, the Scripps Clinic was ready to move also. At a cost of $32.5 million, its new facility was completed in what Dr. Figueredo described as "the wilderness to the west" (Torrey Pines). A portion of this new center included the 173-bed Scripps Green Hospital.

Meanwhile, all the Doyle children had to be educated. For twenty-five years, there was at least one Doyle at Stella Maris Academy. At the graduation ceremony for their eighth and last child, Teresa, the parents were handed their own diplomas. According to the certificate, Drs. Doyle and Figueredo had set a record for years of attendance at Stella Maris School! Their daughter, Tica, went on to medical school in San Francisco where she met her future husband, Dr. Brent Eastman. Dr. Eastman writes, "She (Tica) lured me down to La Jolla, where she joined her father in pediatric practice and I joined Anita in surgery. Together and separately we are proud to have practiced 140 years on the medical staff of Scripps Memorial La Jolla."

In the late '50s, Dr. Figueredo began a long correspondence with Mother Teresa. They met in person in 1960 and continued to meet over the years in different parts of the world. In 1973, Mother Teresa designated Dr. Figueredo as a Regional Link of the Co-Workers of Mother Teresa in America and, in 1988, the doctor brought Mother Teresa to San Diego to establish the Mother House for the Missionaries of Charity in Tijuana. When Mother Teresa was sick in 1990, Dr. Figueredo came every day to visit her.

Already it is clear. This La Jollan is a phenomenon. Like Mother Teresa, serving is her credo, giving her time and talent to her family, her career, her community and her church. For sixteen years, she was trustee and then President of the La Jolla Town Council, a member of the Board of Trustees for 32 years (since its inception in 1949) and Vice-Chairwoman of the Academic Affairs at the University of San Diego, and with her husband a Eucharistic minister and lector at Mary Star of the Sea Church in La Jolla. She is the recipient of "Grand Cross," the highest rank in the Order of the Holy Sepulcher and, in 1958, Dr. Figueredo was named San Diego "Woman of the Year."

Meanwhile, after his retirement, Dr. Doyle became Director of the Order of the Holy Sepulcher for all the western states. For ten years, he worked with the organization hoping "that we can develop some reasonable leaders among the Christian Arabs (in the Holy Land) so there may be some kind of bridge of peace between the Israelis and the rest of the Arabs…we hope that eventually we can make a significant effort in bringing up people of good will in that beleaguered land so that there can be some peace there."

Both doctors were not only gifted in medicine, parenting, and social giving, they were contributors to the arts as well. A civic orchestra was being formed in the village. When Peter Nicoloff moved to La Jolla, he could not believe that his new community did not have an orchestra. A professional musician himself, Mr. Nicoloff founded the La Jolla Civic Orchestra and became its Director. Initially, the orchestra was comprised of just local folk. Dr. Figueredo became the President in 1960. "During my tenure, we thought we should be working together with UCSD, which had recently opened. We also had a civic chorus. I went around to all the churches and their choirs and asked if they would cooperate. They said yes."

While Dr. Figueredo concentrated on music, Dr. Doyle was putting his energy and talent into painting. "I had a lifetime interest in art," said Dr. Doyle, "as far back as grammar school." In medical school, his physiology notebooks were always the best. Then his practice took over and there was no time. Finally, around 1960, Dr. Figueredo talked him into starting again. He joined the La Jolla Art Association, served on their Board of Directors and was with them when they moved from the library to the little gallery next to the Athenaeum (of which he was also a member of the board). "I've always liked to do portraits; I like people and I like their faces…." Three of Dr Doyle's portraits are hanging in the Vatican. They are portraits painted of Cardinal DeFurstenberg, Cardinal Caprio, and Pope John Paul II. Several portraits are hanging in board-rooms including one of Mother O'Byrne RSCJ at Manhattanville College and one of Bishop Leo T. Maher hanging at USD, and one portrait completed in 1985 of Archbishop Beltrini, the Patriarch of Jerusalem.

Dr. Figueredo retired in December, 1996, after forty-nine years of practice as a surgical oncologist (in 1975, she scaled down to just office practice).

This all proves that the doctors who moved to La Jolla in the past did far more than practice medicine. These two doctors shared many gifts with their adopted home and La Jolla has been enhanced as a result.

Las Patronas

Formed "To foster civic and cultural activities, through fund raising projects."

For fifty-three summers, on the first Saturday night in August, the quiet evening at the La Jolla Beach and Tennis Club succumbs to the quickened pulse of hundreds of party-goers at the annual Jewel Ball. It is the culmination of 12 months of industry and controlled panic by members of Las Patronas, a group of fifty La Jolla women who give endless hours to raise hundreds of thousands of dollars to help the San Diego community.

What began as a lighthearted dinner dance, a welcome reprieve from other more formal and staid charity events, has become a huge production requiring the work of many volunteers and paid professionals and a whole year to stage, more like a coronation than a pot luck social. How can one compare the creamed chicken supreme and spiced peaches served at the first Jewel Ball in 1947 to the recent fare of Tournedos Perigueux accompanied by Seafood Mousse with asparagus and morels?

The social climate has changed radically as well. The women behind the first Jewel Ball, a committee of 14 young marrieds, were eager to plan a party that was innovative, unpretentious, modern and beautiful. The young newcomers found themselves in the seacoast village of La Jolla two years after the end of World War II. Many families, largely from mid-West backgrounds, settled in La Jolla after passing through San Diego on military duty. The original Las Patronas were a well-educated, sophisticated bunch, knowledgeable through their fathers and husbands about business, and through their mothers about their personal re-

Past Jewel Ball Chairmen: (l to r) Lynn Porter '53, Judy Keelin '55, Lynn Hughes '60, Ginny Irwin '50, Midge Preston '58, Nancy Moore '59, Emily Hunte (Black) '49, Pat Morrison (Mertz) '47, and Beverly Lambert '51
Courtesy Las Patronas archives

sponsibility to contribute toward good causes.

The new democratic social environment was open to residents of intelligence and "reasonable behavior." Finding no entrenched Old Guard blocking their way, these ladies charged ahead with an idea to raise money for the China Relief Fund. (What child of the late 40s can forget being told to clean their dinner plates?—"Remember those poor starving children in China?") "It had to be on a night with a full moon, of course," remembers Claire Tavares, a founding member of Las Patronas still residing in La Jolla. The Ball attracted 200 partygoers at $15 a couple and raised $1357. By contrast, recent Jewel Balls have had as many as 850 guests raising in the neighborhood of $400,000 for San Diego beneficiaries that have been thoroughly interviewed, screened and voted on by the membership.

The dinner menu on that first Jewel Ball night was straight from the recipe books of Mrs. Walton (Jo Bobbie) McConnell and prepared by the Marine Room at the La Jolla Beach and Tennis Club. There was gambling (unpublicized, tickets were used for chips) in the La Sala and music and dancing 'til wee hours. Staging was extemporaneous in the early years. "I remember," said Mrs. Tavares, "my husband had to build the bandstand that day." Popular entertainer Frankie Carl played for an astronomical fee of $1500, but it set a precedent for future Jewel Balls that showcased the biggest and the best of the big bands of that era.

The fourth ball, in 1950, landed Freddy Martin from the Coconut Grove. Marion Trevor, President of Las Patronas in 1949 remembers: "Midge Preston (another founding member) and I went to Los Angeles and snared Freddy Martin and his Big Band. On the way home we started to worry how in the world we were going to pay him? The mother of one of the members donated a beautiful diamond bracelet and we sold tickets to raffle it off. Beverly and Jim Lambert along with my husband, Wally, and I, stood up in front of the crowd on the night of the Ball to announce the winner, but to our horror the bracelet had disappeared from the box. Bill Kellogg, the President of the Beach Club joined us in looking through the garbage at 2:30 in the morning. We never did find it. We bought a small $50 gift the next day and gave it to the winner!"

The 9th annual Jewel Ball (1955) was held at the new White Sands Hotel. Five months later, the hotel was acquired by Southern California Presbyterian Homes as a retirement home.

Working on design flats at their Sorrento Valley warehouse.
Courtesy Las Patronas archives

In 1957, Ball attendees danced to the music of Louis "Satchmo" Armstrong who left the bandstand with his orchestra and to the song, "When the Saints Go Marching In," led a snake dance of hundreds around the pool. The pre-disco fever of 1968 brought a rock band for the first time, and 1990 saw big name Rita Coolidge entertain guests. In 2000, the Wayne Foster Orchestra accompanied a staged revue.

The post war years marked sweeping changes. San Diego tripled in population and La Jolla quadrupled. Ten thousand people lived in La Jolla in 1949. The summer scene, the mild climate, the miles of beaches and the horse racing at Del Mar attracted the rich and beautiful from star-studded Hollywood to the oil fields of Texas. The Jewel Ball, and the causes it supported, were the beneficiaries of this growth. Gregory Peck, Dorothy

McGuire, Arizona's Goldwaters and Pasadena's Fleetwoods, Earls and Rowans, all attended. From San Diego came a sprinkling of its old-line establishment: the Fletchers, the Rohrs, the Gildreds and Borthwicks.

That was the era of the pre-ball cocktail parties. Fashionably late, guests arrived at 11 p.m. for a Jewel Ball affair that was scheduled to begin at nine. Dinner was served at midnight. In 1956, the Walton McConnells gave a post-ball breakfast for fifty served at 4 a.m.!

Over the years, the Jewel Ball, has gone from a fairly improvised buffet to a sit-down catered affair which requires the detailed preparation of a military campaign. Developed and refined over the years, a thirty-three page countdown keeps volunteers, professional contractors and the Beach Club staff on track during the final week before the Ball. Husbands are recruited to help: An engineer supervises a crew erecting scaffolding, a plastic surgeon directs the building of a steel girded bridge, a venture capitalist paints last minute decor, and an amateur baseball playing boyfriend hangs furnace filters. Every moment is carefully choreographed with contingency plans in place, but Murphy's Law holds true and what can go wrong will. Glitter is not glitch-proof.

Emily Hunte (Black) chaired the 1949 Jewel Ball with a seafaring theme complete with mermaids and a boat in the swimming pool. Minutes before the guests arrived, the boat capsized and sank. The mermaid went overboard. The lovely crepe paper flowers dyed the water red and green and the mermaid lost her blonde wig.

Karen Gabsch, President '95-96.
Courtesy of Las Patronas archives

This would not be the last wonderful disaster. Like when Marilyn Burchfiel chose "Penthouse Picnic" for the theme of the '73 Jewel Ball, which over the course of the year developed an embarrassing blue twist. Like the year the invitations went out suggesting guests park at nearby Kellogg Park despite a city ordinance prohibiting parking there at night, Like the nightmare of 1983, the year "Kaleidoscope" was presented by chairman Dixie Unruh. Not only did she break her leg six weeks before the Ball, but at 4 p.m. the afternoon of the event, ominous black clouds rolled in from over the Pacific Ocean. The wind knocked over wine glasses and centerpieces and caused the heavy scenery to sway dangerously. A resourceful individual took a knife and slashed the painted flats surrounding the ballroom to keep them from blowing down. Like the celebration of the 25th annual Jewel Ball when the focal point was to be suspended swags of mirror and silver balls strung bead-fashion over the ballroom. Using 5000 tennis balls, the members painted, glittered, dyed, glued and reglittered for months until each ball weighted several pounds and the miscalculations ended up rolling around on the dance floor.

Finally, it must be admitted that not all unforeseen dilemmas are officially reported. There was one chic chairwoman whose spectacular translucent one-piece wrist-to-ankle pajama/gown was modishly underpinned by a skin tight wrist-to-ankle body stocking. One pit stop and she almost missed her entire party.

The event has evolved in many ways. It's a dinner-dance, not a ball in the traditional sense of starting late, with supper at midnight and dancing till the wee hours. Decorations have gone from "homemade" (Virginia Winegardner's 1972 Ball sported donated Bill Blass sheets cut with pinking shears to make tablecloths) to elaborate sets complete with computer controlled techno-lighting. The crowd arrives earlier and leaves earlier. Pre-parties are still thrown, but Las Patronas members rarely attend. They are most likely home soaking weary feet after the intense week-long preparations. After ball

Canine Companions for Independence (CCI) enhances the lives of individuals with disabilities by providing highly trained assistance dogs. *Courtesy of Las Patronas archives*

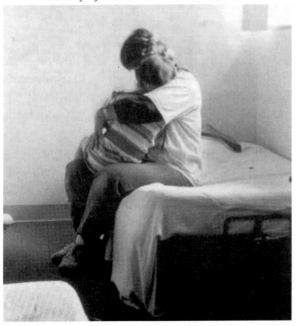

Hillcrest Receiving home, predecessor of the Polinsky Children's Center, '94 La Patronas beneficiary. *Courtesy of Las Patronas archives*

breakfasts at 4 a.m. have totally disappeared. Instead members in tennies and jeans work all night with brooms and dustpans returning the La Jolla Beach and Tennis Club to its original state by 10 a.m. so hotel guests and members can play their noontime tennis match. All decorations, plants and some tableware are moved to the Beach Club's parking lot and sold at bargain prices.

But perhaps the greatest change has been the bottom line. In 1947, $1357 was raised. By 1972, the net proceeds totaled $42,000. The banner year to date was Nicky Holland's 1998 "Quelle Soiree" which brought in $409,000. To date over $7.8 million dollars has been distributed by Las Patronas to the citizens of San Diego County.

What hasn't changed is the quality of the women needed to produce such a profitable and well-attended event. The Las Patronas founders and their successors have discovered how to impart the secret of perpetual youth. From the first, an organizational scheme was put into place to secure continual enthusiasm and a perpetual joie de vivre of the membership. Members who in the early years were housewives in their 20s and 30s are now largely professionals in their 30s and 40s who have spent years in community service and have refined their volunteer and organizational skills. They serve a seven year term working up to the larger roles as they gain experience. Las Patronas has become big business. The President and Jewel Ball Chairman oversee 24 committees and 17 administrative positions. They attend countless meetings and community functions, and keep tight budgetary controls. Underwriting by a generous base of patrons and San Diego businesses and foundations has become the backbone of fund-raising efforts.

As government funding for social, cultural, educational and health oriented endeavors has decreased, Las Patronas has helped to pick up the slack and fund organizations in all corners of San Diego County. All the while, Las Patronas has remained steadfastly noncommercial, nondiscriminatory, nonsectarian and nonpolitical. Most importantly, the women of Las Patronas have kept alive the original tenet of their founding members-enriching their own lives with the joy of giving to others.

One Thousand Made Homeless by Naval Ammunition Explosion

Praise the Lord and
pass the ammunition.
Attributed to
Rev. William A. Maguire
(1890-unknown)

It was 2:00 pm when truck driver John Ayala of the Fallbrook Naval Ammunition Depot reached Torrey Pines at the top of the Rose Canyon Grade on old Highway 101 (now Gillman Drive), and noticed his truck was on fire. He stopped the truck, loaded with 20 tons of ammunition, about 100 yards south of the junction of the highway and the La Jolla cutoff (La Jolla Junction—the present site is on Gilman Drive about the same place as the UCSD Information Booth.) It was Sunday, December 18, 1945, a beautiful warm Santa Ana day a few months after the end of the war, when the Navy was "moth-balling" destroyer type warships at the San Diego Naval Station. One of the first tasks in preparing a ship for preservation and assignment to the inactive fleet is to remove the ammunition. Ship ammunition loads consisted of 20 and 40-millimeter shells, 5" 38 shells, rocket motors, and a great amount of highly explosive bomb type ammunition in the form of

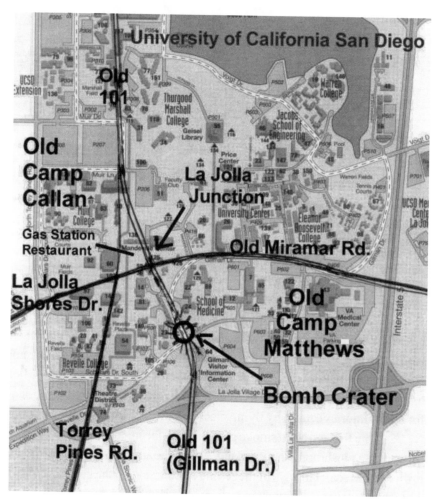

Map of the present UCSD Campus with overlay of old US 101, Old Miramar Road, Torrey Pines Road and La Jolla Shores Drive
Courtesy of Steele Lipe

Explosion site of ammunition truck on Coast Highway (US-101), December 18, 1945.
Courtesy of San Diego Historical Society Photograph Collection

depth charges. Depth charges were affectionately called "ash cans" by sailors because of the resemblance to garbage cans. This was the ammunition load mix the truck carried that day.

Surrounding the junction of the highway and the cutoff were 300 government military housing units known as Army Torrey Pines Homes on both sides of Torrey Pines Road just south of the La Jolla Junction and the Navy Libertad Housing Project. These were two-story multiple family frame buildings. Ayala leaped from his burning truck and ran to a small café near the junction, warned the proprietor, then rushed to the housing units to arouse the residents. La Jolla Fire Captain Ray Ramage arrived with his fire truck and crew and proceeded to visit every unit in the housing project shouting warnings to clear out fast. At this time of the afternoon most family members who were at home were mothers and children. The men were at sea or their various duty stations. Most women, heeding the warnings, dropped their afternoon chores and joined the slow exodus down the old Scripps Grade to La Jolla. Strollers and shopping carts were loaded with children, pets, and hastily gathered blankets, clothing, and family photo albums. A few who panicked and ran off into the woods with their children had to be rounded up and herded back to the road. The area was successfully evacuated and sealed off by the police and military authorities. The ammo truck blew up at 3:30 pm. One thousand people were made homeless in an instant by the fiery blast, but it did not claim a single casualty thanks to the prompt and heroic actions of the truck driver and the Fire and Police departments. Only thirty people sought treatment for minor injuries caused by flying glass or being knocked flat by the concussion.

The fire and acrid smoke generated by the initial blast rose like a volcanic eruption into the sky, forming a tall column capped by a mushroom-shaped cloud. When the angry roiling stopped, the cloud settled into dusty layers of smoke and slowly drifted out to sea. The rays of the setting sun shining on the gaseous cloud produced a luminescence that added color to make a spectacular sunset. There was nothing colorful on the ground at Torrey Pines unless it was the blinding inferno of burning natural gas from a ruptured gas line. The main 16 inch gas line from Manhattan Beach to San Diego ran under the highway at this point. The scene was one of destruction and misery. Many houses were twisted and damaged beyond repair. Almost all had doors and windows blown out. Refrigerator contents were spilled; furniture was tossed about into disorderly piles along with Christmas trees and gifts. Twenty and forty millimeter shells had been hurled wildly in all directions and were strewn over a large area. Long after the heavy explosives went off, scattered fires in the woods and housing area set off the small caliber shells in anticlimactic pops. Long distance telephone service out of San Diego was crippled when the blast tore off the roof of a nearby repeater station. Service to Los Angeles and points north was interrupted. The blast and secondary fires damaged numerous structures at Camps Callan and Matthews. (Camp Callan was northwest of the Junction and Camp Matthews was adjacent to the east.) The trees were stripped bare and for many years there was ample evidence of the terrific blast that had occurred there.

The intensity of the explosion played freakish tricks. It was heard 90 miles away at Mt. Palomar and felt in Santee. It knocked out a few store front windows on Broadway in downtown San Diego. Upon returning home from shopping, one La Jollan found her front door sprung and all the windows blown out, while the houses on either side remained unscathed. A few curious spectators attracted to the sight managed to penetrate police lines to collect souvenirs. The Navy issued urgent warnings to souvenir hunters who may have picked up live ammunition that could be potentially lethal. Shards of twisted metal and molten glass were soon being offered for sale on La Jolla streets. A quote from a news item describes the plight of the homeless that evening: "They sat in the mounting afternoon chill until darkness, wondering what to do and where to spend the night." The children fretted and the babies wailed with hunger. A large group of mothers had halted at Scripps Beach at the foot of the housing project in the gathering darkness. Fires could be seen on the ridges. These refugees were found shivering in scattered groups. The women had removed their coats to wrap children. One man hiked into the village and brought back as many bottles of milk that he could carry. Men folk were scarce and the women could find no firewood on the beach so they went back to the road-side and sat there by their children and pets. By darkness, a few autos appeared driven by men anxiously seeking loved ones. Mothers with young babies were taken into the autos which were parked by the road side, for there was nothing else to be done. Offers of food, clothing, and shelter poured into the La Jolla Red Cross headquarters, police and fire stations during the night. One resident took a load of comforters directly to a group of stranded refugees sitting on a downtown curb. The few who returned to their battered homes that evening were not allowed to remain because of the danger from unexploded shells. Federal housing authorities and the Red Cross found temporary shelter in the federal housing projects, Riverlawn Dormitories, and the Frontier Trailer Project in the Midway area.

Perhaps Fire Captain Ramage's name should be added to the minor injury list. He was quoted as saying: "When you tell a bunch of men to get the hell out because the place is going to blow up, they move. When some of the young mothers were told to leave in a hurry, they proceeded to collect and feed the pets and heat baby formula on the stove. I thought for sure I was going to have nervous break down right then and there."

Guns at Bird Rock

La Jolla's own Gunnery School

La Jollans carried out their patriotic duties during World War II, as did millions of other villagers throughout the country. They sent sons and daughters off to war and entertained service men from nearby military bases, men who were so far from home. However, few today know that south La Jolla had its very own military installation.

On September 3, 1942, the Navy commissioned the U. S. Naval Anti-Aircraft Gunnery Training School in the Bird Rock area. Aerial photos and city maps show gun emplacements that were installed on the bluffs in present-day Calumet mini-park and extending south along Calumet Avenue. Support structures, a galley, barracks, ready ammunition magazines, and other equipment occupied the area eastward almost reaching to La Jolla Boulevard. Bounded by the ocean to the west, La Jolla Blvd. to the east, the village of La Jolla to the north, and Pacific Beach to the south, this postage stamp size school may have been the smallest facility in the Navy wartime system.

The gun mounts were embedded on concrete slabs in front of a long, low cinderblock building which housed radar, fire control equipment, instructors, and safety observers. Gun crews loaded and manned the guns and the fire control personnel who controlled, aimed, and fired them were trained as a team, thus simulating wartime conditions found aboard ship. There were three types of guns. The smallest was a 20-millimeter gun (less than one inch in diameter). A gunner was har-

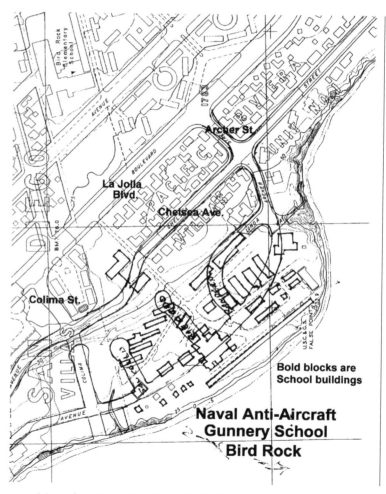

Map of southern Bird Rock Anti-Aircraft Training School superimposed on present day road map of the area. Chelsea Street and Calumet Avenue (along cliffs) did not exist south of Colima Street. The barracks and emplacements as well as the newer streets are in bold.
Courtesy of Steele Lipe

The business edge of the School right along the top of the bluff west of present day Calumet Avenue. From Calumet Park can be seen much of the concrete debris that was pushed over the bluff after the site was vacated in 1952 and developed as Pacific Riviera Village, Unit 1. *Courtesy of San Diego Historical Society Photograph Collection*

nessed to the gun and aimed it with a set of hand grips, not unlike bicycle handlebars. Next in size was the 40-millimeter which came both double and quadruple barreled. Last were the 5"/38, the largest of the Navy anti-aircraft guns. (The "38" refers to length of the barrel in inches as a multiple of the barrel diameter. A 5"/38 barrel would be 5" in diameter and 190" long. The inside of the barrel was grooved to cause the projectile to spin, which like a passed football, improves the stability of the flying projectile and increases accuracy.)

Two categories of people witnessed gunnery training practice. There were those who came down to the beaches at night and enjoyed the magnificent light and sound shows of night firing. Tracers resembling thousands of gigantic bright roman candles arched slowly up into the dark sky and ended in bright flashes followed by loud explosions. Then there were the long-suffering few who not only lived within ear-splitting sound of the gunfire, but also had to endure earth shaking vibrations. Kitchen dishes, pots, and pans rattled in resonance with the gunfire.

An airplane would tow a brightly colored sleeve target attached to the end of a long cable. The plane would tow the target at various course speeds and altitudes within range of the guns. Another type of target was a radio-controlled drone. This was a small, unmanned plane controlled by a radio from the ground. The drone would perform all kinds of maneuvers including diving directly into the guns, simulating realistic maneuvers of a hostile aircraft. If the drone was not shot down during a firing exercise or before it ran out of fuel, the controller would direct it over the land. A radio signal transmitted to the drone would cut the engine and deploy an attached parachute. The drone came down to a soft landing where it was recovered so it could be used again.

Parachute landings may have become routine to Bird Rock residents, but the keen interest of young boys never wavered. Their sights were set on the thirty or so square yards of pure white silk from which the parachutes were made. With wartime shortages, a mother would be very fortunate to have yards of silk to sew dresses and blouses for the ladies of the family. Drone recovery teams consisting of a couple of sailors, a jeep and a trailer were sent out to recover the drones and parachutes. During firing practice, boys with bicycles would station themselves at strategic spots about the area where a drone might land. When one landed, they would race to the spot, cut the parachute from the drone, stuff it into the bicycle bags and head home to mother with their treasure. One observer did not think that this was serious thievery on the part of the Bird Rock children. He noted that the parachutes were sometimes damaged on landing and that the Navy probably did not use them more than once or twice. Also, it appeared that on occasions, the recovery teams were late in arriving at the down site. They might wander off into the sagebrush or stop and have a cigarette, allowing ample time for the youthful raiders to liberate silk from the drone.

The Navy closed the Gunnery School in November 1945. More than 20 million rounds of ammunition were fired and almost 400 thousand officers and men trained in gunnery skills during the three years it operated. Most of the buildings were removed in 1952. Some of the debris was pushed over the side of the cliffs where today it rests on the pebbled beach below. Wave and tidal action are slowly eroding large pieces of concrete that remain but you can still see a few concrete blocks which have resisted the tidal pull, probably because of their sheer weight.

At night the tracers could be seen as in this photograph from Pacific Beach in 1943. *Courtesy of San Diego Historical Society Photograph Collection*

Fifty-four years have passed since the guns were silenced. The bluffs above the sea are now studded with million dollar homes where guns once roared for democracy. Few residents have any knowledge that the school ever existed. Yet on occasion, when a teenage surfer is asked where he surfs, instead of responding with a contemporary name like Colima Street, Calumet Park, or Linda Way, he might answer, "Gunnery Point."

La Jolla's Streets Turn to History for Names

When Mr. Frank Botwsworth divided La Jolla Park into lots, he named the streets after his home town, New York City. Thus we have Wall Street, Pearl, Exchange and Park Row.

As the town became more established, the town fathers decided to copy the alphabetical listing used by San Diego for its streets. Thus the street names changed, both reflecting alphabetical progression and an emphasis on famous people in the fields of science, literature, and American history. Beginning with the letter 'A', Vine Street became Agassiz Street named for Louis John Rudolph Agassiz, a Swiss-American zoologist and geologist. The name was difficult, however, and was changed again in 1913 to Olivetas Avenue. Olive Avenue became Borden Avenue (Simeon Borden was an American civil engineer), but it too changed and became La Jolla Boulevard. The next street was Palm. It was named Cuvier Street after Baron Georges Léopold Chrétien Frédéric Dagobert Cuvier, 1769-1832, a French zoologist and geologist, a founder of comparative anatomy and paleontology. Baron Cuvier rejected the thesis of continuous evolution and supported catastrophism. Next in line was Orange Street which took on the name Draper Avenue. John William Draper (1811-1882) was an American scientist, philosopher and historian. He helped organize the New York University, School of Medicine where he taught and, in 1850, became its President. His work includes Human Physiology (1856) which contains the first published microphotographics. Another book was History of the Intellectual Development of Europe published in 1863.

Continuing the alphabetical listing, Washington Street became Eads Avenue John Buchanan Eads (1820-87) was an American engineer who invented the diving bell. It was used to salvage wrecks in the Mississippi River. He also built a fleet of Civil War ironclads, a steel-arch bridge in St. Louis, and a system of jetties which made New Orleans an ocean port. New York Avenue became Fay Avenue, supposedly named after American author Theodore Sedgwick Fay (1807-98). Born in New York, Mr. Fay held numerous diplomatic posts in Europe, became an editor of the New York Mirror and a novelist. Other books he wrote include Views of Christianity, Great Outlines of Geography, History of Switzerland, and History of the Three Germanys. The main north to south street in the village of La Jolla was originally Grand Avenue. It was renamed Girard Avenue after Charles Frederic Girard, an American zoologist of the nineteenth century. To the east, Lincoln Street became Herschel Avenue. Sir William Herschel (1738-1822) was a pioneer systematizer of sky exploration. He catalogued heavenly bodies and with his own invention, a reflecting telescope, Sir Herschel discovered the planet Uranus in 1781. Herschel concluded that the solar system moves as a whole through space.

The former Garfield Avenue became Ictimus Avenue in honor of the architect of the Parthenon, but the name was too difficult and the name Ivanhoe Avenue was given instead. What was known as Franklyn Place became Jenner Street after either one of two English physicians, Edward or Sir William Jenner. Dr. Edward Jenner discovered that people working with cows developed what he called cow pox. These same people were immune to small pox. As a result, it was this Dr. Jenner

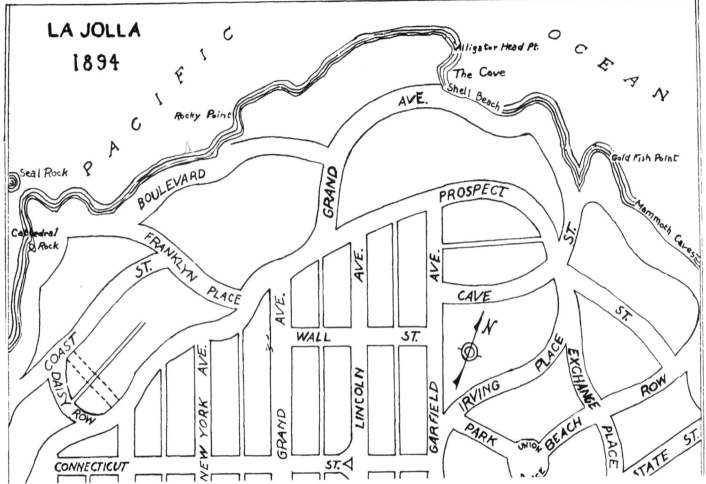

A portion of the 1894 map of La Jolla showing street names of that era. Only Wall,
Prospect, and Cave Streets, Coast Boulevard and Exchange Place remain the same.
Courtesy of Barbara Dawson as modified by Steele Lipe

who was the discoverer of vaccinations. Sir William Jenner differentiated typhoid fever from typhus and discovered the causative agent, a Salmonella bacterium transmitted by lice in the mid-nineteenth century.

Kline Street, formerly Center Street, was named after a local resident. State Street was changed to Torrey Pines Road. Connecticut Avenue became Silverado Street and College Street had already been used for a street name in San Diego, so it had to be changed. Ultimately, the name became Virginia Way in honor of the volatile but loveable Virginia Scripps. In the Barber Tract Fern Glen was originally Surfton Place. Interestingly enough, the small curved section of street named Daisy Row between Prospect Street and Coast Street Coast Boulevard) was never built, instead the street represented by dashed lines became an extension of Washington Street (Eads Ave).

Index

SUNBELT PUBLICATIONS
"Adventures in the Natural History and Cultural Heritage of the Californias"
Series Editor—Lowell Lindsay

Southern California Series:

Geology Terms in English and Spanish	Aurand
Portrait of Paloma: A Novel	Crosby
Orange County: A Photographic Collection	Hemphill
California's El Camino Real and Its Historic Bells	Kurillo
Mission Memoirs: Reflections on California's Past	Ruscin
Warbird Watcher's Guide to the Southern California Skies	Smith
Campgrounds of Santa Barbara and Ventura Counties	Tyler
Campgrounds of Los Angeles and Orange Counties	Tyler

California Desert Series:

Anza-Borrego A To Z: People, Places, and Things	D. Lindsay
The Anza-Borrego Desert Region, 4th ed (Wilderness Press)	L. and D. Lindsay
Geology of the Imperial/Mexicali Valleys (SDAG 1998)	L. Lindsay, ed.
Palm Springs Oasis: A Photographic Essay	Lawson
Desert Lore of Southern California, 2nd ed.	Pepper
Peaks, Palms, and Picnics: Journeys in Coachella Valley	Pyle
Geology of Anza-Borrego: Edge of Creation	Remeika, Lindsay
Paleontology of Anza-Borrego (SDAG 1995)	Remeika, Sturz, eds.
California Desert Miracle: Parks and Wilderness	Wheat

Baja California Series:

The Other Side: Journeys in Baja California	Botello
Cave Paintings of Baja California, rev. ed.	Crosby
Backroad Baja: The Central Region	Higginbotham
Lost Cabos: The Way it Was (Lost Cabos Press)	Jackson
Journey with a Baja Burro	Mackintosh
Houses of Los Cabos (Amaroma)	Martinez, ed.
Mexicoland: Stories from Todos Santos (Barking Dog Books)	Mercer
Baja Legends: Historic Characters, Events, Locations	Niemann
Loreto, Baja California: First Capital (Tio Press)	O'Neil
Baja Outpost: The Guestbook from Patchen's Cabin	Patchen
Sea of Cortez Review	Redmond

San Diego Series:

Rise and Fall of San Diego: 150 Million Years of History	Abbott
Only in America	Alessio
More Adventures with Kids in San Diego	Botello, Paxton
Geology of San Diego: Journeys Through Time	Clifford, Bergen, Spear
Cycling San Diego, 3rd edition	Copp, Schad
La Jolla: A Celebration of Its Past	Daly-Lipe
A Good Camp: Gold Mines of Julian and the Cuyamacas	Fetzer
A Year in the Cuyamacas	Fetzer
San Diego Mountain Bike Guide	Greenstadt
San Diego Specters: Ghosts, Poltergeists, Tales	Lamb
San Diego Padres, 1969-2002: A Complete History	Papucci
Campgrounds of San Diego County	Tyler